Foundation Drupal 7

Robert J. Townsend

with Stephanie Pakrul

friendsof

DESIGNER TO DESIGNER™

an Apress® company

Foundation Drupal 7

Copyright © 2010 by Robert J. Townsend with Stephanie Pakrul

ISBN-13 (pbk): 978-1-4302-2808-0

ISBN-13 (electronic): 978-1-4302-2809-7

Printed and bound in the United States of America 9 8 7 6 5 4 3 2 1

Distributed to the book trade worldwide by Springer Science+Business Media LLC., 233 Spring Street, 6th Floor, New York, NY 10013. Phone 1-800-SPRINGER, fax (201) 348-4505, e-mail orders-ny@springer-sbm.com, or visit www.springeronline.com.

For information on translations, please e-mail rights@apress.com or visit www.apress.com.

Apress and friends of ED books may be purchased in bulk for academic, corporate, or promotional use. eBook versions and licenses are also available for most titles. For more information, reference our Special Bulk Sales–eBook Licensing web page at http://www.apress.com/info/bulksales.

The source code for this book is freely available to readers at www.friendsofed.com in the Downloads section.

Credits

President and Publisher:
Paul Manning

Lead Editor:
Steve Anglin

Development Editor:
Douglas Pundick

Technical Reviewers:
Christian Pearce & Seth Cohn

Editorial Board:
Steve Anglin, Mark Beckner, Ewan Buckingham, Gary Cornell, Jonathan Gennick, Jonathan Hassell, Michelle Lowman, Matthew Moodie, Duncan Parkes, Jeffrey Pepper, Frank Pohlmann, Douglas Pundick, Ben Renow-Clarke, Dominic Shakeshaft, Matt Wade, Tom Welsh

Coordinating Editors:
Mary Tobin and Jennifer L. Blackwell

Copy Editor:
Kim Wimpsett

Compositor:
Bronkella Publishing, LLC

Indexer:
BIM Indexing & Proofreading Services

Artist:
April Milne

Cover Image Artist:
Corné van Dooren

Cover Designer:
Anna Ishchenko

For my family, my wife, and my son, who learned how to walk and say "cracker" while I was writing this book.

Contents at a Glance

Contents

About the Authors

R.J. Townsend became a Drupal convert in late 2006 when searching for a CMS for a project and his brother-in-law commented, "Hey, have you checked out Drupal?" He has spent the following years singing its praises to anyone who will listen. R.J. has since built more than 40 Drupal-powered web sites for clients in a number of industries, including retail, business-to-business, nonprofit, political advocacy, e-commerce, and higher education. With a passion for automating processes, research programs, and otherwise laborious tasks, Drupal has become his tool of choice.

R.J. has experience working in both the technical and business sides of application development. He has worked in a number of roles, including designer, developer, project manager, trainer, and research analyst. He currently works almost exclusively with agencies and freelance designers, providing consulting, development, training, managed hosting, and technical support services.

R.J. earned his master's degree in quantitative psychology from California State University – Fullerton and is pursuing an MBA at the University of Delaware. He is a partner with Cultivate Technologies, a technology consulting firm specializing in open source software; Cultivate's primary service, CodeMyDesigns.com, targets Drupal development services to designers and agencies. He is also active in the Philadelphia chapter of the AIGA and is currently cochair of the interactive committee.

On his off-time, R.J. loves to spend time with his family and son, visit authentic Mexican food restaurants, and play guitar. You can follow R.J. on Twitter at www.twitter.com/robertjtownsend.

Stephanie Pakrul fell in love with Drupal back in 2005 using it to create powerful websites without coding. Her background in both design and web development were nicely bridged with this emerging field of "theming" – pulling together the visual design with the underlying functionality. Her degree in I.T. Management has been a major resource when wearing the many hats of running a young, small business.

After joining CivicActions in 2007 and theming some of the highest profile Drupal sites around, Stephanie co-founded TopNotchThemes (and picked up a Masters at UC Berkeley along the way) to bring that expertise to a larger group of site owners who seek the same thing that brought her to Drupal in the first place – creating great sites without hiring a coder.

About the Technical Reviewer

 **Christian Pearce** has been working with computers since his first Atari 800. He has implemented a wide range of web and Internet technologies over the past 16 years. His skills range from deploying systems in 24/7 production environments to designing and implementing web-based software with a team of developers.

He has helped customers transition from outdated web infrastructures to Drupal, WordPress, and Ruby on Rails based on community best practices. During such transitions, he helped customers become self-sufficient at managing their new infrastructure by providing the proper training required to all levels of the organization.

Christian has been an advocate of open source software ever since he first discovered Linux in college in 1994. Over the years he has developed several web applications in Perl, PHP, and Ruby. He has worked as a system administrator configuring Apache, MySQL, Postgresql, Linux, OpenLDAP, Sendmail, and Postfix and is skilled at implementing just about any open source project that gets the job done.

Christian has a bachelor's degree in computer science from Kutztown University. Currently he is a partner with xforty technologies (www.xforty.com). He lives in Harrisburg, Pennsylvania, and most of all he enjoys spending time with his wife, Lael, and with his two children, Jazlynn and Luke.

Acknowledgments

First and foremost, to my family and friends, especially Gabs and Adam, for your support and understanding, and to Bart, for the original recommendation.

Thank you to all Drupal contributors; it's amazing to see community in action. I never really understood this until I read *The Cathedral and the Bazaar*, so thank you, ESR.

Thank you, Christian Pearce and Douglas Pundick, for invaluable feedback, and Stephanie Pakrul, for writing an awesome chapter on the Fusion theme.

Finally, to the neighbors at Benham Court. ☺

RJ

Introduction

The release of Drupal 7 is a milestone in the evolution of Drupal. The major emphasis on improving the user interface resulted in a powerful and easy-to-use system on which to build web sites. If you are considering Drupal for your web site and haven't made a decision, I encourage you to read this introduction.

This book is a guide to help you build a Drupal-powered web site from start to completion. I cover the concepts behind the Drupal system, describe modules that expand the system, and provide many step-by-step tutorials on how to build a specific piece of functionality or configure a module. I even discuss many peripheral tasks when building a Drupal site, such as setting up and configuring a server, creating test sites, and managing updates. My goal is to give you the tools you need to succeed as a Drupal site builder, regardless of how much or how little you know about creating a web site.

I have built a successful web development business specializing in Drupal. I have found that any feature you or a client requires in a web site can be accomplished through this powerful system. I don't do Joomla, WordPress, Expression Engine, or any other CMS, simply because Drupal can do it better and faster. I believe so much in Drupal that I am committing 10 percent of all profits from this book to the Drupal association to help further the goals of Drupal. I hope by the end of this book you share this same passion.

Drupal as a content management system

A **content management system** (CMS) is server-based software that allows you to manage web site content through a browser. It usually contains a number of programming languages, such as PHP, JavaScript, MySQL, HTML, and CSS, and it uses a database to save content and configuration settings. The user interface (UI) is designed for the end user, meaning little to no programming skills are required to use the system. Users can log in and easily add, edit, or delete web site pages.

Although Drupal is a CMS, it is often referred to as a content management framework. A **framework** refers to a software or application platform that allows software to run; it contains the source code upon which software is built. In this sense, Drupal has a core set of modules you can "hook" into to build and expand your web app. You can write your own modules, use modules written by others, include custom scripts, integrate with other systems, and more. As a framework, Drupal becomes the glue that holds everything together.

Why Drupal rocks

I am frequently asked why I prefer to build web sites using the Drupal framework, and my answer is simple: it's better, faster, and less expensive. Drupal is far superior to other open source content management system; it has a larger community of developers, a more flexible architecture on which to build, and a wider range of modules to spice up your site. Drupal powers many major web sites, including Fast Company, New York Observer, AOL Corporate, Yahoo! Research, MTV United Kingdom, and Warner Bros. Records.

Its full range of modules, including user permissions, security mechanisms, JavaScript menus, WYSIWYG editors, language translations, and more, helps create the foundation for a powerful web site. Combined with its templating system (and a few tips and tricks), any graphic design file can be used to easily create a Drupal web site. The drawback is the learning curve; I definitely don't recommend using Drupal for the first time when you need a site online within 24 hours.

Drupal provides you with a number of modules to speed development so you can become more efficient and productive. Once you learn Drupal, you should be able to configure and theme a simple online brochure in less than a day. There are a number of tools for every step of the process, including testing, theming, module writing, importing content, error reporting, and more. You can even write custom installation profiles that automatically configure a site exactly how you specify.

Finally, the Drupal system with its thousands of contributed modules is entirely open source, which means you don't need to pay to get full functionality. Many open source CMSs use a commercial open source business model through which the base system is free but you must pay for advanced functionality. All modules published through the Drupal web site are automatically released under the GNU General Public License (GPL) version 2, which means anyone can update the code and share it freely* with others.

* Free as in speech, not as in free beer. See `www.gnu.org/philosophy/free-sw.html`. Copyright © 1996, 1997, 1998, 1999, 2000, 2001, 2002, 2003, 2004, 2005, 2006, 2007, 2009 Free Software Foundation, Inc. Please share your code.

What's in this book

The goal of this book is to provide you with everything you need to successfully build a Drupal site. It is written for people who have little to no experience with Drupal and/or content management systems. I cover all the topics required to build a Drupal site, including configuring a web host; installing Drupal; utilizing Photoshop and Illustrator best practices; using the administrative interface; creating, organizing, and displaying content; and more. There are many step-by-step tutorials, and I also include the web site `FoundationDrupal7.com` where you can follow along and experience Drupal 7 yourself.

Chapter 1 begins with a conceptual overview of Drupal and a section-by-section examination of the administrative interface. Chapter 2 covers setting up a web host and installing Drupal using the popular cPanel server administration software. Chapters 3 and 4 take you through the process of configuring a Drupal site and include a number of topics, such as creating content, creating menu items, and setting up your front page. Chapter 5 discusses people, roles, and permissions, while Chapter 6 covers how to enable and configure core modules. Several of the most commonly used user-contributed modules are discussed in Chapter 7, including views and WYSIWYG editors. Chapter 8 describes how to take a design file and import it into Drupal using the Fusion theme, a process known as **theming**. The last four chapters focus on designing, testing, implementing, and maintaining a Drupal site. Finally, the book ends with appendixes containing code snippets, a module reference guide, site recipes, and more.

What's new in Drupal 7

The UI is perhaps the biggest improvement in Drupal 7. There has always been complaints about the cumbersome nature of the UI. The Drupal 7 UI has a number of new features, including a built-in admin toolbar with an assignable "shortcuts" feature and a core theme specifically designed for the admin section. Users of Drupal 6 will also appreciate some of the new modules that have been incorporated into core, such as vertical tabs (simply *amazing* when it comes to content creation and editing) and the jQuery overlay, which allows you to close the admin section and immediately return to your previous page.

On the back end, CCK fields are now part of core, giving you the ability to add fields to content types; note that not all the fields you would expect are part of core, so you'll still need to install modules such as Email, Link, and Phone. The Imagefield and Imagecache modules are part of core, meaning you can easily upload and resize images on the fly. Also, and most excitedly, a new Update Manager module has been added, which will allow people to upload, install, and update modules through the UI. Sweet!

What you need to know

If you can use the Internet to check e-mail, then you can use this book to understand Drupal. I really try to emphasize the point-and-click nature of Drupal throughout this book, although sometimes you will need to write a line of HTML or CSS. You may also run into situations where you ask the question, "How do I get Drupal to do XYZ?" More often than not, this is simply a case of searching Drupal.org to find out how someone else solved the problem.

To succeed as a Drupal site builder, you need to have a crystal-clear understanding of how your web site works. More specifically, you need to understand which data are collected and how they are displayed. If you understand this, then you can create some of the best web sites on the Internet using Drupal.

Layout conventions

To keep this book as clear and easy to follow as possible, the following text conventions are used throughout.

Important words or concepts are normally highlighted on the first appearance in **bold type**.

Code is presented in `fixed-width font`.

New or changed code is normally presented in **`bold fixed-width font`**.

Pseudocode and variable input are written in *`italic fixed-width font`*.

Menu commands are written in the form **Menu ➤ Submenu ➤ Submenu**.

Sometimes code won't fit on a single line in a book. Where this happens, I use an arrow like this: ➡.

```
This is a very, very long section of code that should be written all on the same ➡
line without a break.
```

Chapter 1

An Overview of Drupal

Drupal rocks! I first started using Drupal in 2006 after experimenting with a few other content management systems. I didn't know how Drupal worked, what modules to use, or even how to set up a server; all I knew was that my brother-in-law (aka professional IT guru and programmer extraordinaire) said I should give it a try. Several years later, I can honestly say 1) choosing to learn Drupal was the best decision I ever made, especially for my web development business, and 2) I still learn new things about Drupal every day. I recently took a look at the first web site I designed with Drupal and vividly remembered the frustration I felt: "How do I create a web page? Why do my menu links suddenly disappear? How do I get a text box to display in the middle of the screen?" With a "git-'er-done" attitude, I did the one thing you're not supposed to do: I rewrote code in Drupal's core modules.

In this chapter, I cover some of the more important topics to help save you from the frustration I once felt. I begin by talking about Drupal from a conceptual perspective. Using plain, non-geeked-out language, I explain how Drupal works and discuss several of the terms you need to understand when building a Drupal-powered web site. Next, I review the administrative interface and give a mile-high overview of each of the major administrative sections. Finally, I close with a step-by-step tutorial on how to create your first web page and menu link.

My goal in writing this book is to give you the knowledge and resources necessary to learn Drupal. To this end, I host a free web site at `www.FoundationDrupal7.com` for you to log in and follow along. It's a standard Drupal 7 installation configured so you can do most tasks covered in this book. I set this up because I believe you can learn best by doing; I encourage you to visit the web site, log in (you'll need to create an account), and follow along while reading this chapter.

How Drupal works

Drupal is a complex system that requires knowledge of a few key concepts to fully understand how it works. Drupal can be especially confusing if your web design experience consists of creating a new HTML file for every page (as was mine; we've all been there). This section discusses how Drupal handles data, such as web pages and users, and how templates are used to display data. Terms such as *node*, *content types*, *modules*, and *themes* are discussed. Understanding how Drupal works reduces development time, increases site functionality, and saves you from asking the question, "You mean I did it wrong and need to start from scratch again?"

Database powered

Drupal is a database-powered content management system. A **database** is a collection of data organized into rows, columns, and tables. Think of it like working with multiple spreadsheets; each spreadsheet (that is, **table**) has **columns** containing specific types of data (ID number, date, name, and so on), and each **row** is a separate record containing values for each column. Drupal stores all web site content in multiple tables throughout the database, saving information such as the web page title, web page content, time created, and more. When a web page is viewed, Drupal queries the database for the required information and displays it through HTML templates, referred to as **themes**. Themes are not saved in the database but live in a separate folder. This means there is a separation between content stored in the database and how content is displayed. This also means you do not need to create a new HTML file for every page; rather, you create templates through which Drupal presents content.

Organizing and displaying content

At the core of Drupal is the concept of the node and content type. A **node** is a single piece of content, while a **content type** is a grouping of nodes. A single blog entry, for example, is a node that belongs to the blog content type, while an informational "About Us" page is a node that belongs to the page content type. A node has several pieces of information attached to it; some pieces you provide when you create a node (such as the title and full text), and some are generated automatically (such as the date created and node ID). You can create a menu link to a node, add a custom URL path to access the node, allow web site visitors to comment on a node, or save a revision every time you edit a node. There's a lot more you can do, but I'm just talking about the basics right now.

A node belongs to only one content type, allowing you to customize the default behaviors of groups of nodes. Each content type has its own set of default settings, such as comment settings, publishing options, URL path settings, and more. You can also add fields to content types, such as drop-down lists, check boxes, and image uploads. Think of it this way: a static web page has two fields, title and body, while a blog post may have two additional fields, an image upload field and a field to tag the post with blog categories. Both of these content types have unique sets of fields, permissions, and settings, yet both live within the same web site. Furthermore, each content type can have its own template, allowing you to customize the way each content type is displayed. A Drupal site can have an unlimited number of content types (for example, blog, web page, forum, products, portfolio, and so on) with an unlimited number of nodes for each content type.

If you're logged into `www.FoundationDrupal7.com`, click the **Add content** button in the administration toolbar to see the two default content types provided by Drupal. See Figure 1-1 for details.

Figure 1-1. Click the **Add content** button to view the two default content types provided by Drupal.

Content is displayed in various **regions** of the site through **blocks**. A **region** is a section of the web site, such as a header or sidebar, containing one or more blocks. Looking at Figure 1-2, the default Drupal web site has two blocks in the left sidebar region (the search form and the management menu) and one block in the content region (the main body content). This brings up a good point: you can create a block and add content to it, or a block can display content from other sources, such as nodes, menu links, and modules. Blocks have a number of powerful mechanisms to control where and to whom the block is displayed. For example, a block can be configured so that it displays on a single page, across a number of pages, or only for a specific user group. Blocks are discussed in Chapter 3.

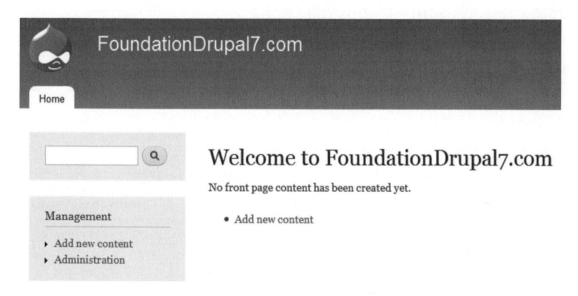

Figure 1-2. After logging in, the search form block and management menu block appear in the left sidebar region, while the main page content is displayed in the content region.

A node is special in a number of ways. Content from a node is displayed through the main page content block in the content region. But note that the outputted content will differ depending on whether you're viewing the full-page node or the teaser view (aka the summary). This can be hard to grasp if you're new to Drupal (as it was to me). Take the default front page as an example; it displays the summary view of all nodes that have been promoted to the front page, with a link (either the **read more** link or the node title) that leads to the full page view. Nodes are also special in that they can have associated comments. In a SQL sense, they have a one-to-many relationship; every one node can have an unlimited number of comments, but a single comment is associated with one node.

People, roles, and permissions

A Drupal-powered web site is a powerful social publishing tool allowing one or more people to create and add content. People have the ability to sign up for accounts, complete with e-mail verification and/or administrator approval, and you can restrict the ability to create accounts to site administrators only. People are assigned to one or more roles with a customized set of permissions for each role. This means, for example, you can give some people the permission to manage and post content to their own blog, restrict other people to only the ability to post comments, and give other people full administrative control over the site. Users have their own account settings page and can upload pictures, edit contact information, and request a new password if they forget their current one. People, roles, and permissions are discussed in Chapter 5.

Adding functionality through modules

The true power of Drupal comes from its modular framework. A module extends the Drupal system to improve current functionality or add new functionality. It "hooks" into Drupal's module system and builds upon its core features. The core Drupal package contains a number of modules, including a blog, forum, language translations, polls, and more. Using a core module is a simple process of enabling it and configuring settings so that (ideally) you do not need to write code. See Table 1-1 for a brief description of all the core modules, or read Chapter 6 for more information.

Table 1-1. Names and descriptions of all core modules

Name	Description	Enabled by Standard Installation Profile?
Aggregator	Aggregates multiple RSS, RDF, and Atom feeds into a single page or block view	No
Block	Displays content in a box that is placed into a region of a web page	Yes
Blog	Enables blogs for multiple users; the article content type should be used for a single-user blog	No

Name	Description	Enabled by Standard Installation Profile?
Book	Creates a section of a web site to organize, display, and navigate content using an outline format	No
Color	Allows users to change the color scheme of certain themes, such as the Bartik theme	Yes
Comment	Allows users to comment on published content	Yes
Contact	Creates a "Contact Us" form for individual users and the entire web site	No
Content translation	Allows user-submitted content to be translated into different languages	No
Contextual links	Provides links that perform actions related to elements on a page, such as the block and node gear icon	Yes
Dashboard	Provides a dashboard page in the administrative section	Yes
Database logging	Logs system events such as error messages to the database	Yes
Field	API to add fields to objects like nodes and users	Yes
Field SQL storage	Stores field data in a SQL database	Yes
Field UI	Creates the user interface to manage and display fields	Yes
File	Creates a field to upload files and images	Yes
Filter	Filters content before it is displayed	Yes
Forum	Creates forums for users to post and discuss topics	No
Help	Displays help messages provided by modules	Yes
Image	Allows Drupal to manipulate images	Yes
List	Defines list field types; used with the Options module to create selection fields	Yes
Locale	Allows the user interface to be translated into multiple languages using GNU gettext Portable Object files (.po)	No

Name	Description	Enabled by Standard Installation Profile?
Menu	Allows the creation and customization of site navigation and menu links	Yes
Node	Allows content to be submitted and displayed on pages	Yes
Number	Defines numeric field types	Yes
OpenID	Allows users to log into your site using OpenID	No
Overlay	Displays the Drupal administration interface using a jQuery-based overlay	Yes
Path	Allows users to create customized URLs to access a web page	Yes
PHP filter	Allows users to enter PHP code in content	No
Poll	Allows users to post polls and automatically calculates the results	No
Profile	Supports configurable user profiles used when people register for an account on your site; will eventually be superseded by the Profile2 module (http://drupal.org/project/profile2).	No
RDF	Enriches site content with metadata to let other applications better understand page content	Yes
Search	Enables searching of content for keywords	Yes
Shortcut	Provides the shortcuts menu in the administration toolbar	Yes
Statistics	Logs access statistics for your site, such as the number of times a page has been viewed, along with a number of reporting pages	No
Syslog	Logs system events to a server's syslog	No
Taxonomy	Allows the categorization and organization of content	Yes
Testing	Provides functional testing of Drupal functions	No
Text	Defines text field types	Yes

Name	Description	Enabled by Standard Installation Profile?
Toolbar	Enables an administration toolbar at the top of every web page	Yes
Tracker	Allows users to track content they or others have posted	No
Trigger	Allows actions to be fired on system events, such as when a new account is created	No
Update manager	Checks Drupal.org for available updates to the core system, contributed modules, and themes; allows for updates via the web interface	Yes
User	Manages user registration and login	Yes

Drupal users from across the globe write and contribute modules, resulting in a large foundation of code from which to build your site. There are thousands of modules to use depending on your version of Drupal; modules can help you animate content, improve site security, protect against spam, integrate Google AdSense, run an e-commerce store, display Twitter posts, and more. Modules are also used to integrate non-Drupal systems within the Drupal framework, such as the Google Maps API or your own custom script. People who write and contribute modules are called **Drupal developers** (which is beyond the scope of this book). Adding, enabling, and configuring contributed modules are all discussed in Chapter 7.

Themes

Everything mentioned up to this point can be configured through the administrative interface. You can create content, add users, move blocks, and enable advanced functionality all through a web browser without requiring any programming. **Theming** a web site, which is the process of creating HTML templates and CSS files to display content, is the exception. A theme is responsible for the layout and presentation of all content. It contains a number of HTML templates, CSS files, image files, JavaScript files, and more. Because all content is saved in a database and separate from the theme, it is easy to switch themes and update the look and feel of a web site. The default Drupal web site contains two active themes, one for the live site (Bartik, as shown in Figure 1-2) and one for the administration overlay (Seven, as shown in Figure 1-1).

Navigating the administrative interface

Log into the Drupal system by using the login block or by navigating to example.com/user (or www.FoundationDrupal7.com/user if you're following along online). Logging in gives you access to the administrative interface and a number of tools to create and manage your site. As shown in Figure 1-3, a toolbar with several links appears at the top of the screen on every page of the site.

- The administration toolbar, located in the upper-left corner, contains links to each of the major administrative sections (**Dashboard**, **Content**, **Structure**, **Appearance**, and so on).
- The user menu contains links to your account page (**Hello RJ** in Figure 1-3) and lets you log out.
- The shortcuts menu is where you can add links to commonly visited pages. The shortcuts menu is preconfigured with two links, **Add content** and **Find content**, and can be opened and closed by clicking the arrow to the right of the user menu **Log out** link.
- Note the homepage icon in the upper-left corner of the menu; this will always take you to the site's homepage.

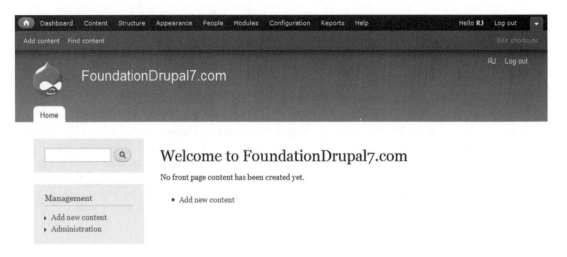

Figure 1-3. The administration toolbar is located at the top of every page and contains links to manage your site, your user account, and shortcuts to various pages.

After you log in, Drupal provides you with a number of links to different pages of the site to help with editing blocks and nodes. Place your mouse pointer over the Management block, and a gear icon appears in the upper-right corner of the block; clicking this block displays several links (see Figure 1-4), which takes you to the administrative page to configure the block. This same gear appears when you place your mouse pointer over menu blocks, node content, and other areas of the site.

Figure 1-4. Place your mouse pointer over a block, and click the gear icon to quickly navigate to the administrative page to edit the block.

Click the **Administer** link in the Management menu to navigate to the main administrative section of the site. Everything you need to manage your site should be within one or two clicks of this page. You'll notice that the title for each box corresponds to a link in the upper section of the administration toolbar; you'll see **appearance**, **people**, **modules**, and so on (see Figure 1-5). This is by design; the administrative section simply displays links and link descriptions from the administration toolbar. This means you have several ways to access the dashboard and other administrative areas.

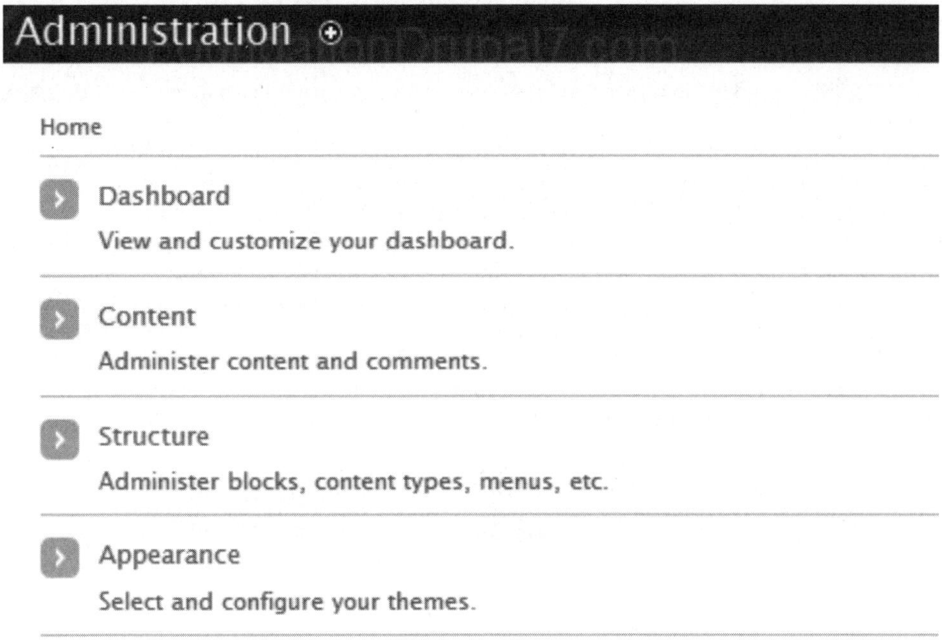

Figure 1-5. Click the **Administer** link in the Management menu to navigate to the main administration section of the site.

The two links at the top right of the page directly below the administration toolbar (**TASKS** and **INDEX**) are called **tabs** (see Figure 1-6). Tabs are used in certain administration pages to provide additional configuration options. In the main administration section, for example, these tabs allow you to view a high-level overview of configuration options available or view an index of all configuration options. I recommend using the INDEX page of the administrative section to configure your site when you first start using Drupal to help build your knowledge of how Drupal works. You'll also notice a circular icon with an *X* in the center; click this icon to close the administration section.

Figure 1-6. Tabs are located in the upper-right section of the administration area and provide additional configuration options.

When browsing the various administrative sections of the site, you'll notice that the page title always has a circular icon with a plus sign in it. Placing your mouse pointer over this icon causes an **Add to** *Default* **shortcuts** link to appear (see Figure 1-7). This allows you to add the currently viewed page to the shortcuts menu in the lower section of the administration toolbar. You can add up to seven links to the shortcuts menu. I frequently change the shortcuts I place in this menu depending on the task I need to perform. If I find myself frequently configuring and reconfiguring the same module or adding a specific content type, for instance, I'll add that module or node creation page to the shortcuts menu. When I'm done with that specific task, I click the **Edit shortcuts** link and delete the shortcut. There's no right or wrong way to do this—only what works best for you.

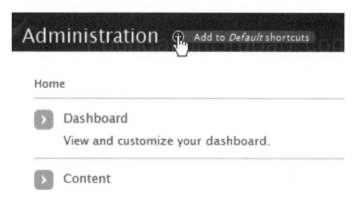

Figure 1-7. Place your mouse pointer over the icon next to the page title to add the page to the shortcuts menu.

Drupal also comes with a customizable **Dashboard** to which you can add and remove blocks of information. These are the same blocks I discussed earlier, except that they are displayed through the **Dashboard** instead of in the main site. This gives you some pretty cool options for what you can add and display on this page. For example, you can add a **Who's new** block to your **Dashboard** to quickly view new people who have registered with your site. Another option is to look outside the core modules and see what blocks are available through contributed modules. If you've enabled the core statistics module and installed the views module (www.drupal.org/project/views), you can create a block that displays the number of page views from the previous day, week, or month. Wicked awesome! While viewing the **Dashboard**, click the **Customize Dashboard** link to view and add blocks (see Figure 1-8).

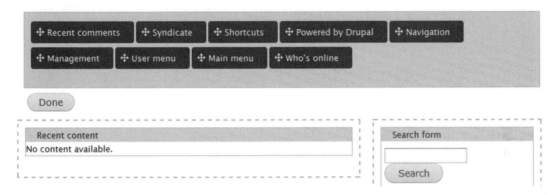

Figure 1-8. Click the **Dashboard** icon, and click the **Customize Dashboard** link to add blocks to the **Dashboard**.

Creating a web page

Creating a web page in Drupal is pretty straightforward. In this section, you're going to create a basic page from start to finish. You'll learn how to create a page, add a menu link, set a custom URL path, and promote it to the front page. You'll also add a block to one of the sidebars so you can get a complete picture of how to create a web page. I won't go into it in detail; this section is more to help you become familiar with the administrative interface and to understand the process. I highly recommend you follow along at www.FoundationDrupal7.com or on your own installation. Let's go!

How to create a basic page

In Drupal, a **basic page** has two fields: the title and the body. Other content types may have additional fields, such as the **article** content type, which has a field to upload and display images. By default, the title is displayed at the top of the node, and the body is displayed directly below it (which can all be changed by configuring the content type, discussed in Chapter 5).

1.   Click the **Add content** button in the shortcuts menu.

2.   A list of all available content types appears. Click the **Basic page** link.

3.   You are now on the page to create a basic web page. Fill in the **Title** and **Body** fields.

4.   Click **Edit summary** to change the body text that appears in the teaser view (such as the default front page).

5. **Text format** refers to the HTML tags allowed in the body field (refer to Chapter 3 for details on how to configure this). For now, leave it on its default value. Selecting the different values in the drop-down displays the different HTML tags allowed in the body.

6. There are six vertical tabs in the area below the body; make sure **Menu settings** is selected.

7. Click the **Provide a menu link** box; several fields appear, including **Menu link title, Description**, **Parent item**, and **Weight** (see Figure 1-9); all are discussed in length in Chapter 3. Enter a name in **Menu link title**, which will appear at the top of the page in the main menu.

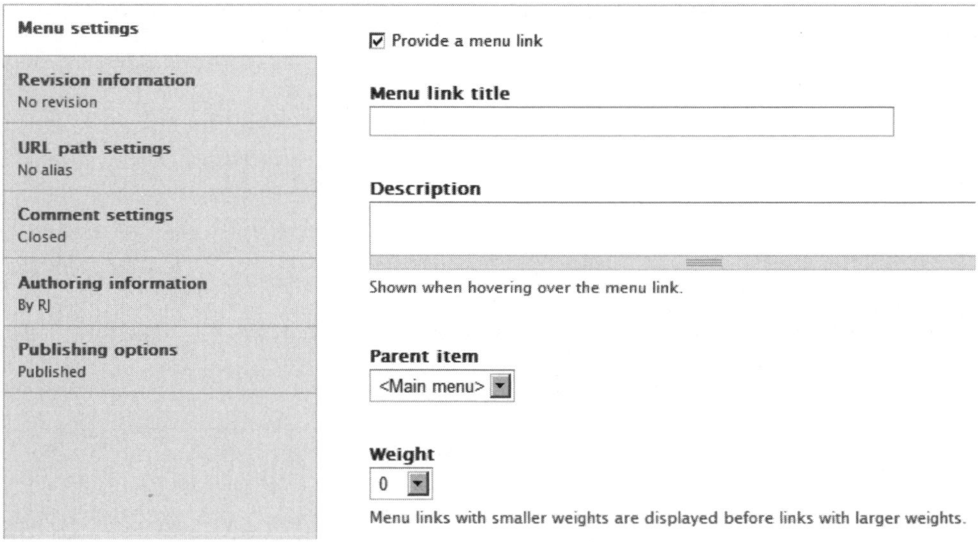

Figure 1-9. Enter a name in **Menu link title**.

8. Revision information is used for previously created content. You will not need to select the **Create new revision** check box if you are creating a node (see Figure 1-10).

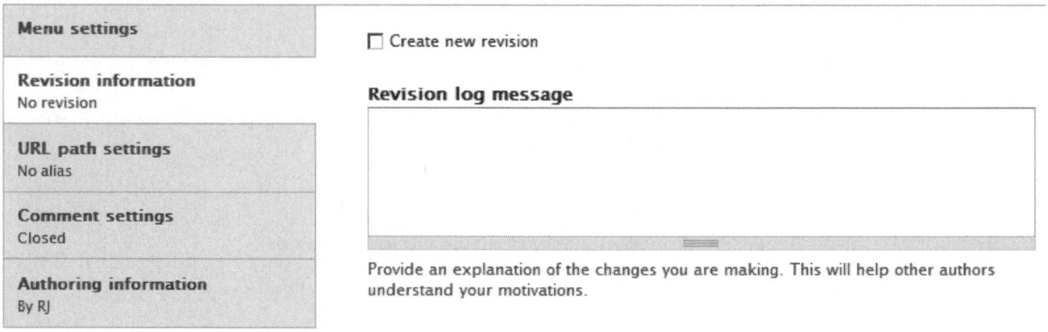

Figure 1-10. Don't select **Create new revision** if you are creating a node.

9. Select the **URL path settings** box, and enter an optional URL alias (see Figure 1-11). A **URL alias** is how you access the web page, such as www.FoundationDrupal7.com/example-page. If you *do not* create a URL alias, then the page will be made available at www.FoundationDrupal7.com/node/nid, where nid is the numerical ID of the node.

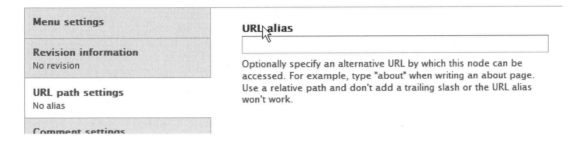

Figure 1-11. Enter a URL alias if you'd like.

10. **Comment settings** allows users with the proper permissions to comment on your web page (see Figure 1-12). For now, no changes need to be made. Note that if you are creating an article, **comment settings** will be set to **Open**.

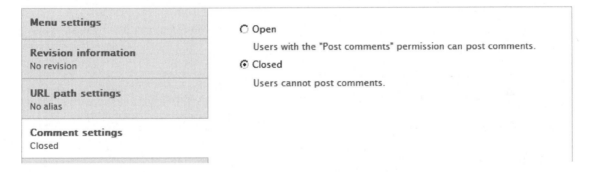

Figure 1-12. Comment settings allow users with the proper permissions to comment on your web page.

11. Notice that **Authoring information** is prefilled with the name of the author (that is, the name of the user) and the time at which the node was submitted (see Figure 1-13). You don't need to do anything here.

Figure 1-13. Authoring information contains the name of the user who created the node and the date the node was created.

12. Several publishing options are available, including **Published**, **Promoted to front page**, and **Sticky at top of lists** (see Figure 1-14). **Published** means the node is available to all users. **Promoted to front page** means the node is listed on the default front page. A node that is set to **Sticky at top of lists** will appear at the top of lists whenever there is a listing of nodes, such as the front page.

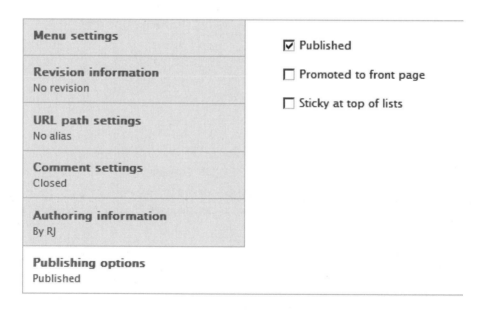

Figure 1-14. Choose your publishing option here.

13. Click **Save** at the bottom of the page, or click **Preview** to view the node before you save it.

Your page is now live!

How to create a block

Now that you've created a node, you may want to add a block to it. A block appears in a region of the web site, such as the left sidebar, right sidebar, header, or footer. If you're creating a "Contact Us" block, then you'll probably want to add the region to the left sidebar, whereas if you're creating a copyright block, you'll want to add it to the footer. Most times, when you add a block, it will not appear exactly the way you want it to appear. You may want to add an image to the header or a color behind the block; this is discussed in detail in Chapter 8.

1. Navigate to **Structure ➤ Blocks**, and click **Add block**.

2. Fill in the **Block description** field (see Figure 1-15). This appears on the block administration page, not on the web page itself.

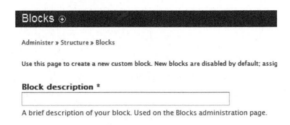

Figure 1-15. Fill in the **Block description** field.

3. Fill in the **Block title** field (see Figure 1-16). This appears on the web page at the top of the blog. Enter **<none>** if you do not want a block title to appear.

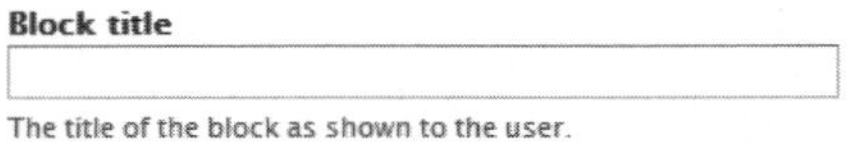

Block title

The title of the block as shown to the user.

Figure 1-16. Fill in the **Block title** field.

4. Fill in the **Block body** field (see Figure 1-17). This is the main area of the block and is similar to the node body in that you can format the text using the **Text format** drop-down menu.

Figure 1-17. Fill in the **Block body** field.

5. **Region Settings** refers to both the theme and region in which the block will appear (see Figure 1-18). Because you want this to appear in the main site and not the admin section, select a region for the Bartik theme (probably the sidebar first or sidebar second).

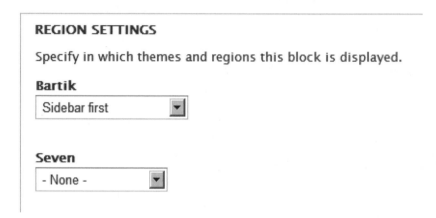

Figure 1-18. Select a region for the Bartik theme.

6. The visibility settings are covered in Chapter 4 (see Figure 1-19). If you do not select any of these settings, the block will appear on every page for every user.

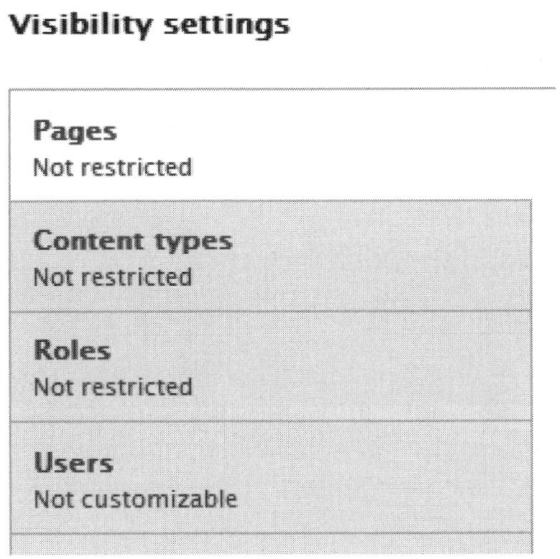

Visibility settings

Pages
Not restricted

Content types
Not restricted

Roles
Not restricted

Users
Not customizable

Figure 1-19. Don't select anything if you want the block to appear on every page for every user.

7.   Click **Save block**. Your block is now live and will appear on every page on the site!

Chapter 2

Setting Up a Web Host and Installing Drupal

This chapter will teach you, step-by-step, how to set up a web host and install Drupal for either a single-site installation or a multisite installation. I cover several important topics, including meeting the system requirements, selecting a web host, and using cPanel to install Drupal. Single-site and multisite installations are covered in detail with instructions to configure your site for both.

How to select a web host

Selecting a web host is key to your Drupal experience. It's very easy to ignore this step and just pick a web host that promises the most bang for the buck; after all, what could go wrong with a web host that offers unlimited storage, unlimited bandwidth, and a free domain name? For the love of Drupal and Tastykakes, please take time selecting a host and don't buy the least expensive hosting package you find. Drupal will not run on most inexpensive hosting plans. I went through four hosts in my first year of business until I finally found a company that offers the perfect mix of server performance, price, and customer service. In this section, I cover what I learned during this process, including Drupal's requirements and questions to ask a hosting company. Some of this may seem a little confusing, especially if you've never worked with a server before and are not familiar with frequently used terms. I'll do my best to explain as I go along.

System requirements

Drupal requires an operating system, a web server, a database server, and PHP. Drupal works on a number of operating systems, including both Microsoft and Linux. It was developed to be web server independent; it has been successfully used on both the Apache and Microsoft IIS web servers. Drupal recommends MySQL for the database server but also supports PostgreSQL. (See Table 2-1 for Drupal's system requirements (refer to http://drupal.org/requirements for more information.)

Table 2-1. Drupal system requirements

Requirements	Minimum specifications
Operating system	Various, although the majority of development is performed on Linux-based operating systems
Web server	Recommended: Apache 1.3 or 2.*x*
	Microsoft IIS 5, 6, or 7
Database server	Recommended: MySQL 5.0 or newer (`max_allowed_packet` greater than 16MB)
	PostgreSQL 8.3 or newer
PHP	PHP 5.2 or newer
	Minimum 30MB PHP memory limit, more depending on the number and type of installed modules (96MB to 128MB recommended)
	GD library (for image manipulation)
	PECL `uploadprogress` library (to display file upload progress)
	PHP Data Objects (PDO) extension
	`DomDocument` class
	`Mbstring` extension (for Unicode support)
	`mysql`, `mysqli`, or `pgsql` extension
	`register_globals` disabled
	`session.save_handler = user`
	`safe_mode = off`
	`session.cache_limiter = nocache`

I recommend using a LAMP-based host (LAMP stands for **L**inux, **A**pache, **M**ySQL, and **P**HP). It is usually less expensive than Microsoft products, and because the majority of Drupal development and deployment is done on LAMP, there is more testing and higher reliability. Generally speaking, you will need to use a virtual private server (VPS) to achieve the best performance with Drupal, which is usually more expensive. Unfortunately, Drupal will not work on most inexpensive hosts.

When selecting a VPS, you will want to find a host with a minimum of 512MB of RAM. Although PHP may require only 30MB to 90MB of memory, additional memory is needed for other services, such as MySQL, Apache, SFTP, and more. If your server has too little RAM or not enough memory for PHP, you'll find that your web site is slow or may result in server timeout errors. Personally, I run two different server configurations—one type for development and testing and one type for production. My development servers have 768MB of RAM, and I definitely notice a slowdown in site responsiveness when two or more developers are working on the same server. On the other hand, I hardly notice any slowdown when my production servers receive significant traffic, which have 8GB RAM and host 20+ sites apiece. Although a number of factors contribute to server speed, increasing the amount of RAM in your host will significantly improve site performance.

Web host requirements

There are thousands of web hosts offering a number of hosting plans. Some hosts even offer to install Drupal for you. I do not recommend using automated installation scripts because they will frequently install an outdated version of Drupal. The best way to install Drupal is by using the packages available at the Drupal web site, as discussed later in this chapter.

Configuring MySQL, PHP, and your web server (Apache or IIS) can be a challenging process, especially for those without server administration experience. My recommendation is to find a host that provides an 800 number with 24/7 support and will configure it for you. These are some questions you should ask your host to ensure Drupal will run on their servers:

- Can you edit the `php.ini` configuration file and add extensions/libraries? If not, does the server meet minimum the PHP requirements listed in Table 2-1?
- Can you set the MySQL system variable `max_allowed_packet` to at least 16MB? Many contributed modules require this.
- Do database accounts support the following rights: select, create, insert, alter, update, delete, drop, index, lock, and create temporary tables? Core modules and some contributed modules require these rights.
- Does the web server (Apache or IIS) provide a `mod_rewrite` extension or URL rewrite module? You will need this for clean URLs.

There are also a few things you will need to consider if you are hosting more than one site:

- Can you park multiple domains or subdomains? You need this to run a multisite installation.
- Can you create more than one database? You need this to run a multisite installation.
- Can you access the host via Secure Shell (SSH)? This is the easiest way to create symlinks, change folder permissions, and install Drupal.
- Can you access databases using phpMyAdmin or some other application? Sometimes you need to look at actual database data when troubleshooting a site.

You should also consider the type of control panel the host offers. Installing a Drupal site requires a few operations: adding a database, parking a domain, uploading files (via SFTP or SSH), and changing permissions on a few files and folders. Many hosts offer cPanel and Plesk, two of the more popular systems, which will allow you to do all this and more. Some hosts offer proprietary in-house applications for managing your host; check with the host to see how easy it is to perform required operations.

Setting up a web host with cPanel and WHM

After you've selected a host, the next step is to configure it for Drupal, which includes pointing a domain to the server and creating a database. Your host may do this for you, or they may provide you with tools to do this yourself. cPanel is popular server administration software that provides you with a graphical user interface to easily create databases, park domains, and more. cPanel is frequently used in tandem with Web Host Manager (WHM), an application used to create cPanel accounts and manage many other server tasks. When you create an account with a host, the host will either provide you with a single cPanel account or provide you with access to WHM so you can create multiple cPanel accounts.

Create a cPanel account with WHM

Many hosts will automatically create a cPanel account for you and may not give you access to WHM. If you already have a cPanel account to which you can log in, you can safely ignore this step. If you're unsure of the difference between WHM and cPanel and which system you're using, there are a few ways to find out:

- Log in and look at the web page header or browser title. Does it say WHM or cPanel?
- Examine the URL used to log in. Does it have a port number at the end of the URL (such as example.com:2083), and if so, what is the number? cPanel usually uses port 2083, while WHM uses port 2087.

To create a cPanel account in WHM, click **Account Functions ➤ Create a New Account**. You are presented with a number of options, including domain information, package, options, settings, and more (see Figure 2-1).

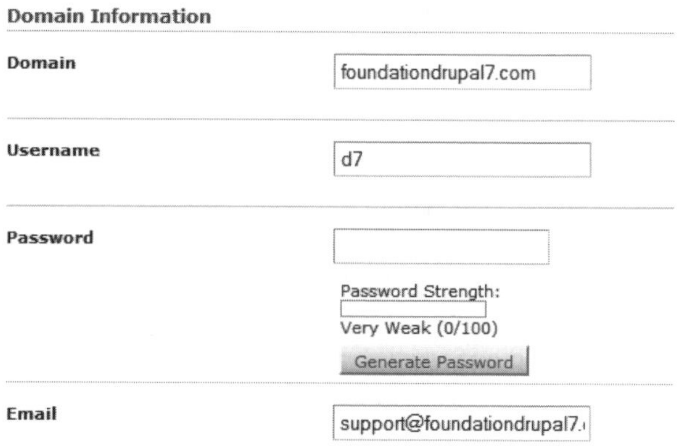

Domain Information

Domain	foundationdrupal7.com
Username	d7
Password	
	Password Strength:
	Very Weak (0/100)
	Generate Password
Email	support@foundationdrupal7.

Figure 2-1. Creating a new account in WHM

1. Add the domain name without the http or www. If you use a multisite configuration (discussed later in the chapter), this is the domain on which you will park domains.

2. Add the cPanel user name. This is the name of the folder in the /home directory, so create a user name that is short and relevant.

3. Generate a password.

4. Add an e-mail address. This is the default e-mail address to which all system e-mails are sent.

5. Click **Select Options Manually** to configure additional options.

6. The **Manual Resource Options** box contains many options. You will need to set the **Max SQL Databases** and **Max Parked Domains** options to greater than 1 if you plan to use a multisite configuration (see Figure 2-2).

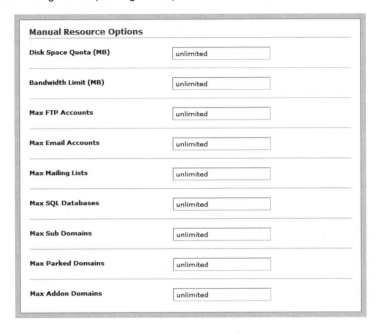

Figure 2-2. Click Select Options Manually to configure the maximum number of databases, parked domains, and more for each cPanel account.

7. Select **Shell Access** under **Settings**, as shown in Figure 2-3. Drupal does not require FrontPage Extensions or CGI access.

Figure 2-3. Make sure the cPanel account allows for shell access.

8. Click the **Create** button, and you're ready to go.

Adding a database and MySQL user with cPanel

Next, log in to your cPanel account, and click **MySQL Databases** to add a database (**MySQL Databases** is usually on the cPanel account homepage). This form allows you to create databases and add users to databases.

1. Enter the name of the database under **Create New Database**. cPanel automatically prepends the cPanel user name to the database name, such that if the cPanel user name is **d7** and the entered database name is **fd7**, as shown in Figure 2-4, then the actual database name is **d7_fd7**. Write down the name of the database, because Drupal requires this.

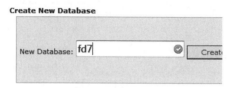

Figure 2-4. Enter the name of the database under **Create New Database**.

2. As with databases, cPanel also prepends the cPanel user name to the MySQL user name, such that if the entered MySQL user name is **cmd**, as shown in Figure 2-5, then the actual MySQL user name is **d7_cmd**. Write down the name of the user name and password.

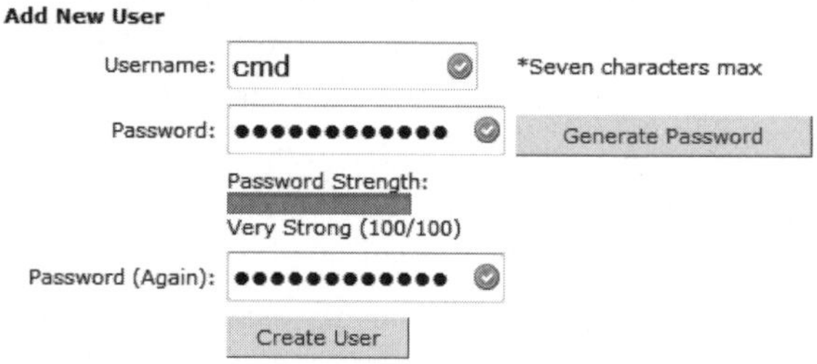

Add New User

Username: cmd   *Seven characters max

Password: ••••••••••••   Generate Password

Password Strength:
Very Strong (100/100)

Password (Again): ••••••••••••

Create User

Figure 2-5. Enter the MySQL user name and password.

3. Under **Add User To Database**, select the correct user and database, and click **Add**, as shown in Figure 2-6.

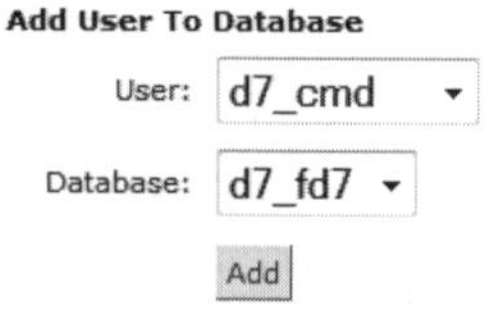

Add User To Database

User: d7_cmd ▾

Database: d7_fd7 ▾

Add

Figure 2-6. Add the user to the database.

4. The following page allows you to manage user privileges. Select **ALL PRIVILEGES**, and click **Make Changes**, as shown in Figure 2-7.

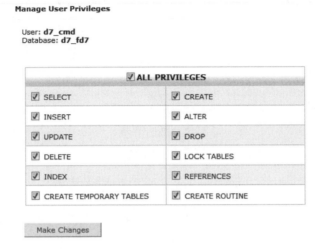

Figure 2-7. Select **ALL PRIVILEGES** when adding a user to a database.

Congrats, you are ready to download and install Drupal. Please note that this process may differ depending on your host and how it has cPanel configured. This should give you enough information to extrapolate to your own host; it's a relatively simple process of creating the cPanel account, pointing the domain to the account, and creating a database with a user who has the proper permissions.

Drupal's file and folder layout

Once you have set up your host, you are ready to download and install Drupal. In this section, I discuss important files and folders in the downloaded Drupal package. I talk about the difference between core files and site files and what should be placed in each. I also discuss how Drupal uses a domain to serve a web site. In closing, I'll discuss the difference between multisite and single-site installs and how each works.

Core files

You can download the latest release of Drupal from Drupal.org. The download contains a number of files and folders, all of which are considered "core" (see Figure 2-8 for all the folders included with core). For the most part, the only folder to which you will add files and images is the `sites` folder (advanced Drupalers may add one or more install profiles to the `profiles` directory). This brings up a big point: do not hack any folders other than the `sites` folder unless you know what you are doing. Modifying files outside of the `sites` folder can lead to problems, especially when you update your site, as discussed in Chapter 11.

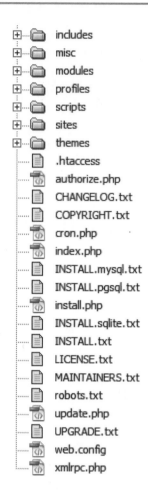

Figure 2-8. Drupal's folders and files located in the download package

I should point out the `modules` folder as another folder of interest. In Chapter 1, I briefly discussed how Drupal is a modular system; that is, modules can be added to Drupal to add or improve current functionality. The `modules` folder contains all of Drupal's core modules; that means users, content types, node creation, and so on, are all located in this folder. When developing a Drupal site, you may find additional "contributed" modules that need to be added to the site. Contributed modules are not added to this folder.

The sites directory

The `sites` folder contains modules, themes, images, scripts, and more, specific to one or more sites (see the "Multisite" section for further discussion of running two or more sites off one installation of Drupal core). In Figure 2-9, you'll notice the `sites` directory contains two folders, `all` and `default`, with a directory for `modules` and `themes` within the `all` directory. Understanding how Drupal uses these directories requires an understanding of how Drupal serves a site. When Drupal receives a request for a web page, it searches the `sites` folder for a configuration directory with a corresponding domain name.

For example, if I plan to create the site www.FoundationDrupal7.com, I will create a configuration directory named foundationdrupal7.com in the sites directory. When the web server receives a request for foundationdrupal7.com, Drupal searches the sites directory for a directory named foundationdrupal7.com. If this directory does not exist, then Drupal uses the sites/default folder.

Several files and folders are located within a configuration directory (see Figure 2-9). Each directory contains a number of files and folders for each site, including the following:

- Publicly available files in the files directory
- Site-specific contributed modules
- Site-specific contributed themes
- settings.php (also named default.settings.php in the default site folder)

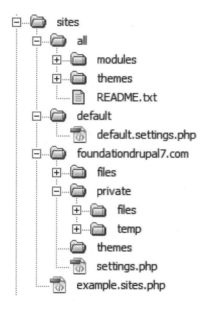

Figure 2-9. Site-specific directory as configured for foundationdrupal7.com

Remember, if you do not create a site-specific configuration directory, then Drupal will use the default folder. This means the default folder is also a site-specific directory and can contain any of the folders and files located in the foundationdrupal7.com directory in Figure 2-9. You'll also notice that the file default.settings.php is located in the default folder.

The all directory contains contributed modules and themes. You may ask, "If modules and themes are added to this directory and they're also added to the configuration directory, which directory should I place them in?" I don't believe there's any right or wrong answer to this, so here's what I do. I place contributed modules and themes in the all/modules or all/themes folder. If I ever hack a contributed or core module, I copy it to the site-specific modules directory and do my hacks there. Here's the reason to my madness: when Drupal is searching for contributed modules and themes, it first searches the site-specific configuration directory, then the all/modules and all/themes directories, and finally the core modules directory. If I hack a module or theme, copying it to the site-specific configuration directory allows two versions of it to exist: the original and modified versions. Then I simply reinstall the module, and

Drupal "finds" the hacked version first, because it exists in the site-specific configuration directory. This is also beneficial when running a multisite setup.

Various Drupal modules use the public and private folders to create and manage files and images accessed on your site. When configuring the file system for your site, you are required to set the default download method as public or private and set the folder locations for each. All folders must be configured to allow Drupal to read, write and execute permissions (see the section "Downloading and installing Drupal" later in this chapter). Configuring private downloads is discussed in depth in Chapter 3.

Note that if you change the default download method from public to private, or vice versa, Drupal switches which folders are used, and you may lose data. For this reason, it is not recommended that you switch the default download method after a site is in production.

The settings.php file is a configuration file responsible for a number of settings, including database connections. Configuring the settings.php file is discussed in the section "Downloading and installing Drupal" later in this chapter.

Single-site and multisite installs

Drupal's core code can be used to host more than one web site, known as **multisite**. That is, site-specific information resides in the sites folder (that is, foundationdrupal7.com from Figure 2-9), and all other core files are shared between sites. You can potentially run an unlimited number of web sites off one instance of Drupal core. Drupal's multisite feature is another reason not to modify Drupal core. If you modify Drupal core, your changes will affect all sites on the multisite installation.

In a multisite setup, all domains point to a single directory on your host. When you created the cPanel account and set the domain, you configured the web server to point the domain to the public_html folder. With a multisite configuration, you park a domain to accomplish the same thing; parking a domain points the parked domain to the same folder as the cPanel account domain. When Drupal receives a request for a web page, it uses the domain to determine which sites folder to serve.

Drupal discovers the configuration directory by stripping the hostname from left to right (that is, everything before the .com) and the path name from right to left (that is, everything after the .com). This gives you a wide variety of domains, subdomains, and paths that can point to unique Drupal sites, all running off the same core code but with unique configuration settings. Drupal searches the sites directory for the configuration folder name in the following order:

1. First, the entire path is used, and the hostname is stripped from left to right:

   - www.example.com.demo.d7
   - example.com.demo.d7
   - com.demo.d7

2. Next, the path name is stripped of the rightmost path, and the hostname is again stripped from left to right:

   - www.example.com.demo
   - example.com.demo
   - com.demo

3. Again, the path name is stripped of the rightmost path, and the hostname is stripped from left to right:

    *   www.example.com
    *   example.com
    *   com

4. If the configuration directory is not found, Drupal uses the sites/default folder.

Drupal searches each configuration directory for a configuration file named settings.php and uses the first one found. This means a single domain can host a number of installations depending on how you name your directories, such as example.com, example.com/d7, dev.example.com, and more.

When using a multisite configuration, themes and modules in the all/modules and all/themes directories are available across all sites. Let's say you have two sites running off a multisite configuration, foundationdrupal7.com and drupalfordesigners.com, meaning you have a site-specific directory for each. If you place a module in all/modules or a theme in all/themes, then this module or theme will be available for both foundationdrupal7.com and drupalfordesigners.com. Remember if you hack a contributed module, you should place it in the site-specific directory. If you were to place a hacked contrib module in the all/modules folder, then any changes made to that module will appear across all sites. Do not place site-specific modules or themes in the all directory if you plan to use a multisite configuration.

The main benefit of using a multisite configuration is the ease of updating. During an update (such as from 7.1 to 7.2), core files and folders are updated for security or bug fixes. When each site is running its own set of core code, each site must be updated individually. A multisite configuration allows you to update all sites at once by simply copying the sites folder (which contains all site-specific information) from the old version to the new version.

Downloading and installing Drupal

By now you should have an understanding of the various files and folders in the Drupal package and how they work. In this section, the rubber meets the road and I discuss how to download, install, and configure Drupal.

Download Drupal to your host

You can download Drupal to your host in two ways: via Secure File Transfer Protocol (SFTP; also called SSH File Transfer Protocol) and via SSH. Each method has its pros and cons. If you've never used the command prompt before, SFTP is by far the easiest method to load Drupal onto your host; you simply download it from Drupal.org to your machine and then upload it to your web host. This is the process to load Drupal on your host using an SFTP client:

1. Go to Drupal.org, and download the latest version of Drupal to your desktop. There is a link on the homepage.

2. Decompress the files. The downloaded files have a tar.gz file format, commonly called a **tarball**, and require a special program such as 7-zip (7-zip.org) to decompress.

3. Use an SFTP client such as FileZilla or Secure Shell Client to connect to your server.

4. Navigate to the web directory. This is usually located in the home directory and may be called `public_html`.

5. Upload all Drupal files into this directory.

Although this process will work if you're building only one site, it can become lengthy and cumbersome if you find yourself frequently building new sites and/or adding contrib modules. My recommendation is to use an SSH client (the command prompt) to download Drupal to your host.

The command prompt allows you to quickly load files from Drupal's servers to your server by typing a few lines of code. Instead of downloading the file from Drupal.org to your desktop and then to your server, you simply download it from Drupal to your host, skipping the middle step. Some of you may be scratching your head and asking, "What's wrong with the first method? It sounds easier." It is easy, and there's absolutely nothing wrong with it. However, there are others who are thinking, "I love saving time by using the command prompt." Personally, I prefer the command prompt when downloading contrib modules because I can download and untar a module in a matter of seconds.

Here is the process to load Drupal onto your server via SSH:

1. Use an SSH client such as PuTTY Secure Shell Client to access your server.

2. Navigate to the home directory where you want to install Drupal. From the command prompt, type `cd ~` (if cPanel) or `cd /home/username`, where `username` is the name of the folder in which the public web folder is located.

3. Load Drupal onto your host by typing the following, changing X to the most current Drupal version: `wget http://ftp.drupal.org/files/projects/drupal-7.X.tar.gz`. Drupal is now saved at `/home/username/drupal-7.X.tar.gz`.

4. Next, you need to untar Drupal to your `public_html` directory using the following: `tar -zxvf drupal-7.x-dev.tar.gz -C public_html --strip=1`.

5. At this point, Drupal core is now loaded on your host. Your next step is to add a site configuration directory and then any contributed modules.

Creating a site-specific directory

Whether you are using Drupal for a single site or multisite, each site lives in a site-specific folder, which I often call the **configuration directory**. The first step in building your Drupal site is to create this directory, update the configuration file, and set permissions. As previously discussed, the name of the folder is the domain URL (for example, `example.com`). Creating a folder using an SFTP client such as Secure Shell Client is relatively easy:

1. First, open your SFTP client, and navigate to the `/home/username/public_html/sites` folder.

2. Click the **New Folder** icon.

3. Enter the name of the folder as `domain.com`.

4. You now need to change the permissions of this folder so that Drupal (that is, your web server) has permission to create new folders. Right-click the folder, and select **Properties**, as shown in Figure 2-10.

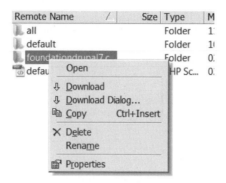

Figure 2-10. Select **Properties** in this list.

    5.   Change the permissions to **777**, as shown in Figure 2-11, and click **OK**.

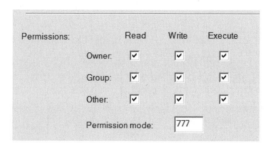

Figure 2-11. Change the permissions to **777**.

    6.   Next, you need to copy default.settings.php from the default folder into the domain.com folder, changing the name from default.settings.php to settings.php.

    7.   Finally, change the permissions of the settings.php file to **666**, as shown in Figure 2-12.

Figure 2-12. Change the permissions to **666**.

Installing Drupal

You're all set to install Drupal. You've set up your host, downloaded Drupal, added a configuration directory, and set permissions. Navigate to example.com/install.php to begin the install process. Select the **Standard** installation profile, as shown in Figure 2-13.

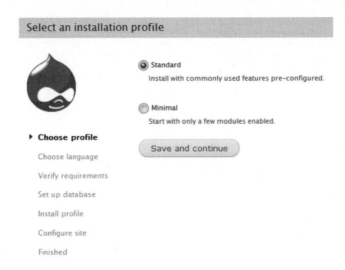

Figure 2-13. Navigate to `example.com/install.php` to begin the installation process.

Next, you can select your language preference and install Drupal in a language other than English. This can be performed after Drupal has been installed and is covered in Chapter 6. Select **Install Drupal in English**, and click **Save and continue** (see Figure 2-14).

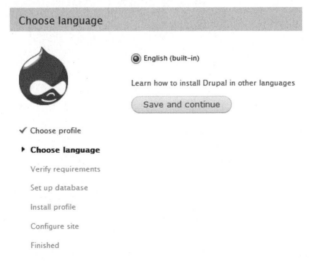

Figure 2-14. You can choose your language during installation or afterward.

After selecting the language, Drupal checks your server to ensure requirements are met and provides you with a report of any problems. Drupal will automatically continue to set up the database once all requirements are met.

In Figure 2-15, the permissions for the file system and settings file have not been properly set, as discussed in the previous section. Once all error messages are fixed, Drupal will automatically progress to the **set up database** screen. As a note, some error messages may need to be resolved by your server host, such as installing a PDO or JSON library.

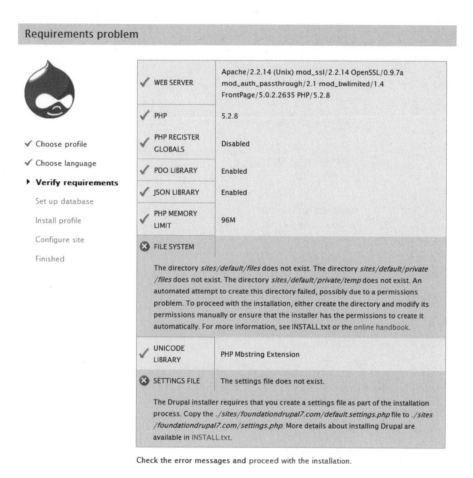

Requirements problem		
✓ WEB SERVER	Apache/2.2.14 (Unix) mod_ssl/2.2.14 OpenSSL/0.9.7a mod_auth_passthrough/2.1 mod_bwlimited/1.4 FrontPage/5.0.2.2635 PHP/5.2.8	
✓ PHP	5.2.8	
✓ PHP REGISTER GLOBALS	Disabled	
✓ PDO LIBRARY	Enabled	
✓ JSON LIBRARY	Enabled	
✓ PHP MEMORY LIMIT	96M	
✗ FILE SYSTEM		
The directory *sites/default/files* does not exist. The directory *sites/default/private /files* does not exist. The directory *sites/default/private/temp* does not exist. An automated attempt to create this directory failed, possibly due to a permissions problem. To proceed with the installation, either create the directory and modify its permissions manually or ensure that the installer has the permissions to create it automatically. For more information, see INSTALL.txt or the online handbook.		
✓ UNICODE LIBRARY	PHP Mbstring Extension	
✗ SETTINGS FILE	The settings file does not exist.	
The Drupal installer requires that you create a settings file as part of the installation process. Copy the *./sites/foundationdrupal7.com/default.settings.php* file to *./sites /foundationdrupal7.com/settings.php*. More details about installing Drupal are available in INSTALL.txt.		

Choose profile ✓
Choose language ✓
▸ **Verify requirements**
Set up database
Install profile
Configure site
Finished

Check the error messages and proceed with the installation.

Figure 2-15. Drupal verifies system requirements and provides you with a report of problems.

Earlier you added the `settings.php` file to the `foundationdrupal7.com` directory. The next step automatically configures the `setting.php` file by adding the database name, user name, and password values from values you enter. You will enter the database values from when you created the database on cPanel, as shown in Figure 2-16.

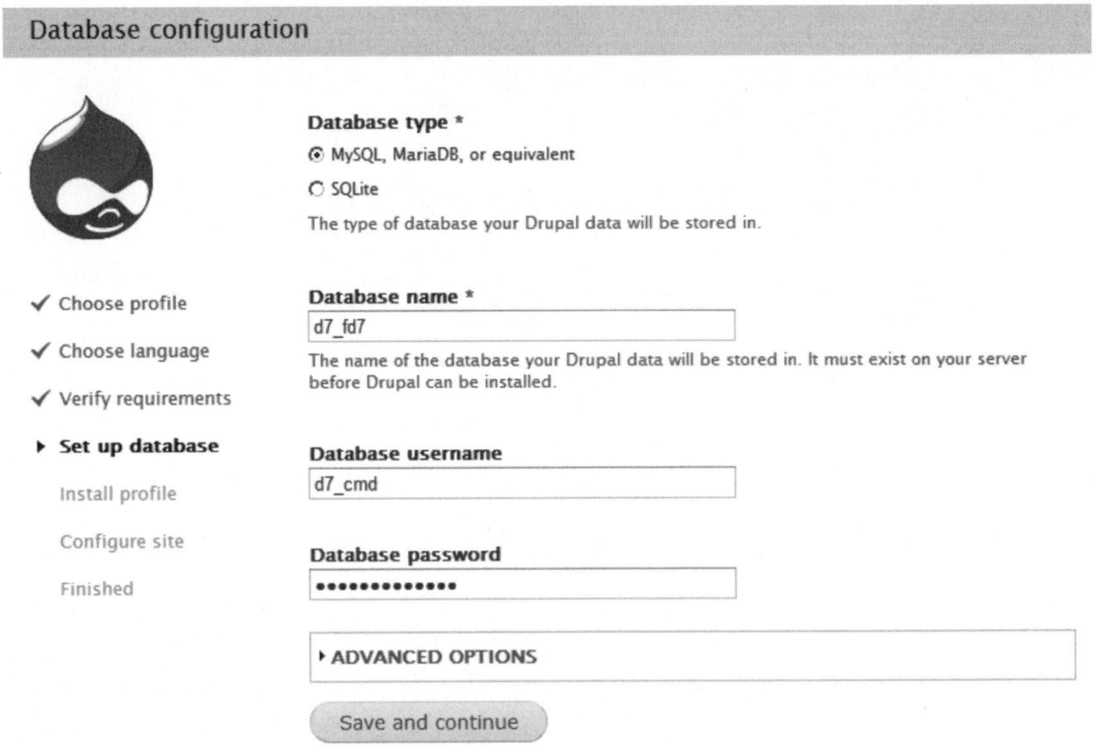

Database configuration

Database type *

◉ MySQL, MariaDB, or equivalent

○ SQLite

The type of database your Drupal data will be stored in.

✓ Choose profile

✓ Choose language

✓ Verify requirements

▸ **Set up database**

Install profile

Configure site

Finished

Database name *

```
d7_fd7
```

The name of the database your Drupal data will be stored in. It must exist on your server before Drupal can be installed.

Database username

```
d7_cmd
```

Database password

```
••••••••••••
```

▸ **ADVANCED OPTIONS**

Save and continue

Figure 2-16. Entering database information during installation automatically configures the `setting.php` file.

After entering the database information, the install profile enables modules and configures the site. You are now ready to enter site-specific information, including the site name, site e-mail address, and main administrator user name (see Figure 2-17). The site name appears at the top of the site on the homepage and, depending on your theme, may appear in the browser's page title.

You'll notice the orange error message at the top of the screen, telling you that write permissions need to be changed on the site. You'll take care of that in a few paragraphs, but let's continue installing.

A quick note about the account you're creating: this is the main site administrator, user #1, and in Drupal it has special permissions. I try to be careful about the user name and e-mail address I use, just to avoid the possibility of someone hacking the superadmin account. I never use the name **admin**, and I always have either a randomly generated password or a hard-to-guess one.

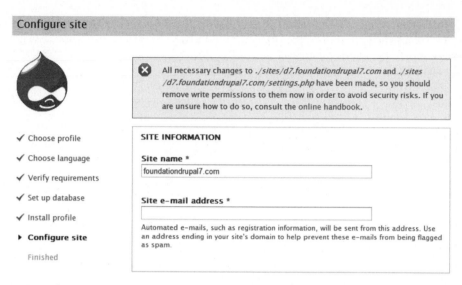

Configure site

❌ All necessary changes to *./sites/d7.foundationdrupal7.com* and *./sites /d7.foundationdrupal7.com/settings.php* have been made, so you should remove write permissions to them now in order to avoid security risks. If you are unsure how to do so, consult the online handbook.

✓ Choose profile

✓ Choose language

✓ Verify requirements

✓ Set up database

✓ Install profile

▸ **Configure site**

  Finished

SITE INFORMATION

Site name *

foundationdrupal7.com

Site e-mail address *

Automated e-mails, such as registration information, will be sent from this address. Use an address ending in your site's domain to help prevent these e-mails from being flagged as spam.

Figure 2-17. Site information and the main administrator account are entered when configuring your site.

Server settings and update notifications must be configured, as shown in Figure 2-18. Select your default country and time zone. This can be any time zone of your choosing; it is used by a number of modules, so I usually pick the time zone in which the client is located. You can also enable both **Check for updates automatically** and **Receive e-mail notifications** to receive e-mails to the main administrator account when either core Drupal or a contributed module has an update (in other words, Drupal 7-1 to 7-2).

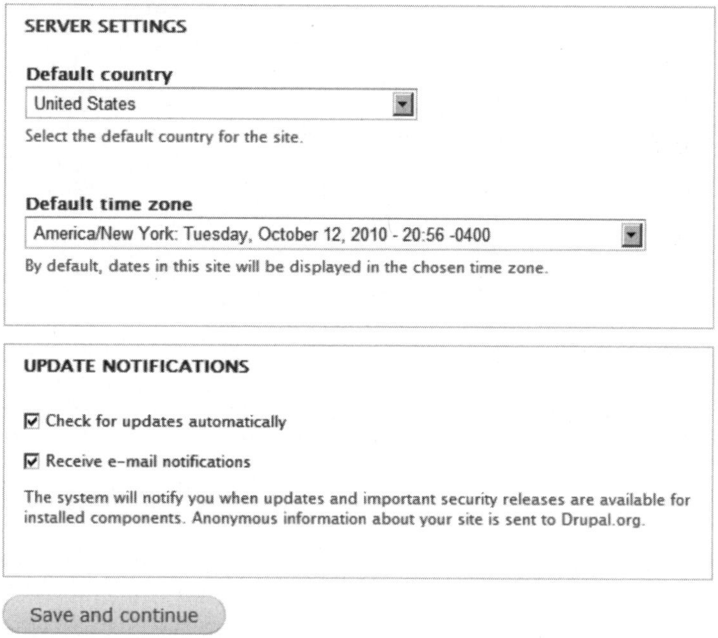

SERVER SETTINGS

Default country

United States

Select the default country for the site.

Default time zone

America/New York: Tuesday, October 12, 2010 - 20:56 -0400

By default, dates in this site will be displayed in the chosen time zone.

UPDATE NOTIFICATIONS

☑ Check for updates automatically

☑ Receive e-mail notifications

The system will notify you when updates and important security releases are available for installed components. Anonymous information about your site is sent to Drupal.org.

(Save and continue)

Figure 2-18. Server settings and update notifications must be entered when configuring your site.

After Drupal has been successfully installed and configured, you now need to fix the orange message by changing the permissions of a few folders and files. Using SSH Secure Client, navigate to the `foundationdrupal7.com` folder, right-click, and select **Properties**; then set the permission to **755**, as shown in Figure 2-19.

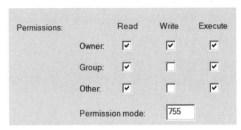

Figure 2-19. The site configuration directory's permissions must be reset to 755 after install.

You also need to change the permissions of `settings.php` back to **644**, as shown in Figure 2-20.

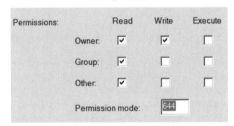

Figure 2-20. The site's `settings.php` file must be set back to 644 after install.

Congratulations, your Drupal installation is complete (see Figure 2-21).

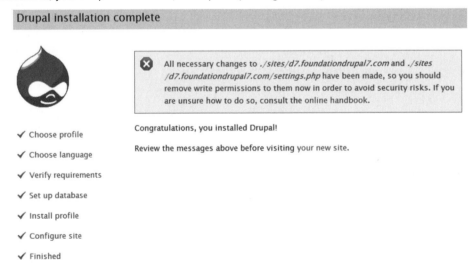

Figure 2-21. The **Drupal installation complete** page

You can now continue to your new site. If you do not follow any of the preceding steps or your host does not meet minimum Drupal requirements, an error message will appear at the top of the admin section (see Figure 2-22). Click the **Configuration** link in the administrative toolbar to see whether you have an error message. Click the **status report** link to view all errors.

Figure 2-22. After installing Drupal and continuing to the site, an error message will appear if any problems are detected.

Summary

I covered quite a bit of material about installing Drupal in this chapter. I started at the very beginning: how to select a web host and minimum requirements your host will need to meet. I then talked through how to set up your host using cPanel, touching upon topics such as creating a database and pointing the domain at your host. I discussed downloading and installing Drupal, the significance of the sites directory, and how a web site's domain name is used as the folder's name. After changing folder and file permissions, I talked you through the various steps required to configure a site during installation.

Chapter 3

Configuring a Basic Drupal Web Site

In this chapter, I review *almost* everything you need to know to build a basic web site in Drupal. I start with a basic review of the development processes that I use to develop sites and explain how I tend to divide site building into two phases, development and theming. I then talk about several important Drupal topics, including blocks, menus, and themes. My goal is to give you a solid foundation so you can go forth and create. You may want to skim Chapter 4 and Chapter 8 before reading this chapter, just to help you understand some of the other details. I also recommend installing your own version of Drupal and following along, or you can log in at www.FoundationDrupal7.com.

An iterative approach

An iterative approach to software development describes the method in which an application is developed. The basic idea is to create an application in iterations, starting from a working prototype and adding features incrementally. A new piece of functionality is delivered through each iteration. Several software development methodologies use an iterative approach, including IBM's Rational Unified Process and methods based on the agile development framework. The model places an emphasis on learning, adaptation, and teamwork, allowing developers to build on what was learned during the development of earlier versions of the system.

There are many insights gained from iterative development methods that apply to building a Drupal-powered web site:

- An installed Drupal web site is a working prototype that you can add features to incrementally.
- Every enabled module adds a new piece of functionality.
- Sections and features should be developed incrementally, not all at once.

Building a Drupal site is different from building an HTML/CSS site in many aspects. Primarily, there is a clear distinction between content and markup. Because content is managed separately from graphics,

I've found that it's much easier to create your content first and then build the theme around it. My recommendation is to configure as much of the site as possible before theming, with the goal of creating content, blocks, menus, and page views that can transfer between themes. When it comes time to theme, you then devote your time to arranging markup and displaying graphics using HTML and CSS. This logical distinction makes it easier to update graphics in the future by simply dropping a new theme in the `themes` folder.

Practically speaking, this means a site takes on two different stages. In the first stage, I am simply adding content, arranging blocks, adding menu links, enabling modules, and more. Once I am finished with this stage, I have a "blank" site that has all the content and functionality but no graphics; it is simply white and black with some blue links (see Figure 3-1). Note that this site is using the Zen theme and not the default Garland theme.

Figure 3-1. The site RocBoxing.com after it has been configured but before it has been themed. Note that this site is using the Zen theme and not the default Garland theme.

There are times when it's fine to add images to your content. My general rule of thumb is that if a graphic is uploaded through Drupal, then the graphic should be added while configuring your site. For example, the Article content type includes a field to upload an image. Or you may upload an image through your WYSIWYG editor. These are fields and graphics controlled and displayed by Drupal, not through CSS.

You will spend the remainder of this chapter focusing on creating content, menu links, and blocks. Although there is no right or wrong way to configure a site, I have found that following a basic site-development outline helps improve my proficiency and reduce the number of mistakes made. Here are the basic steps to take when configuring a site:

1. Make sure all the basic site settings are accurate, such as the file system, default e-mail address, and so on.

2. Set up sitewide blocks and menu blocks (do not add links), and assign them to regions, including those entered manually and those provided by a module.

3. Create content using Drupal's default content types (covered in Chapter 1), or alternately create your own content type (covered in Chapter 4).

4. Set up content type–specific blocks and assign them to regions.

5. Do you have another content type to add such as a blog or forum? Repeat steps 3 and 4.

6. Set up the front page.

Basic configuration settings

When you first installed Drupal, the installation script required a number of fields, such as default country, site name, e-mail address, and more. Always double-check these settings before configuring a site just to make sure you've entered all the information correctly. In this section, I will cover basic configuration settings such as site information, regional settings, date and time, clean URLs, and the file system. Site configuration settings are available by clicking the **Configuration** link in the administrative toolbar.

Site information

You can access site information by navigating to **Configuration ➤ Site information.** Many of the settings on this page are configured during the initial site installation, such as the site name and e-mail address. The site name is used in a number of places in your web site, including the page title, header (if the theme is configured to display the site name), and registration and cancellation e-mails. The e-mail address is used as the From address in all automated e-mails. I usually set up an e-mail account such as admin@example.com or webmaster@example.com for this field. It is also recommended that you use the web site's domain URL to reduce e-mails being tagged as spam. The slogan is displayed in the page title on the homepage or, if the theme is configured, in the header (see Figure 3-2). I have found that writing a slogan using search-relevant keywords helps increase search engine ranking.

Figure 3-2. The site name and slogan are displayed as the page title and header.

Default front page, as shown in Figure 3-3, determines the content displayed on the front page. The default **node** setting displays nodes in a list on the front page depending on the **Number of posts on front page** setting. With this set, all you need to do is select the check box **promoted to front page** when creating or editing a node for the node to appear on the front page. If you want a specific node to display as the homepage, simply enter node/nid, where nid equals the ID of the node. The **number of posts on front page** setting is the maximum number of nodes displayed on the homepage, including sticky content. This is covered in depth later in the section "Setting up your front page."

SITE DETAILS

Site name *

FoundationDrupal7.com

Slogan

Everywhere Drupal!

How this is used depends on your site's theme.

E-mail address *

rj@cultivatetechnologies.com

The *From* address in automated e-mails sent during registration and new password reques

FRONT PAGE

Number of posts on front page

10

The maximum number of posts displayed on overview pages such as the front page.

Default front page

http://foundationdrupal7.com/

Optionally, specify a relative URL to display as the front page. Leave blank to display the de

ERROR PAGES

Default 403 (access denied) page

http://foundationdrupal7.com/

Figure 3-3. Site information is accessed by navigating to **Configuration ➤ Site information.**

You can configure the default 403 Access Denied page and 404 Not Found page by entering `node/nid`, where `nid` equals the ID of the node. If these fields are blank, Drupal displays a generic Access Denied or Not Found page using the theme as the background. Drupal does not use the browser's default Access Denied or Not Found page.

Cron

Cron is similar to crontab in Linux and other Unix-based operating systems in that it executes commands at specified intervals. Some modules hook into cron to run required jobs that do not need to run each time a page is refreshed. For example, the core update status module, which checks with Drupal.org once a day to see whether any enabled modules have been updated, requires cron to function. Drupal will automatically run cron when a page is requested if cron has not been run since the **Run cron every** interval. Setting a longer interval helps reduce server load but can also cause some modules to not function properly. I recommend setting this no higher than one day.

Cron is configured by navigating to **Configuration ➤ Cron**, as shown in Figure 3-4. Clicking the **Run cron** button immediately runs cron, which can be useful when testing or troubleshooting cron-related issues. Cron can also be run from outsite the site by entering a unique URL; navigate to **Reports ➤ Status report** to view the URL for your site.

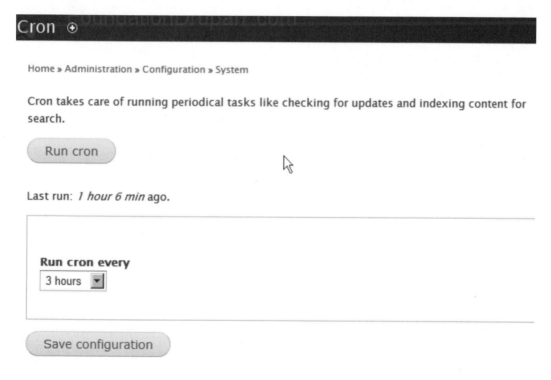

Figure 3-4. Cron is configured by navigating to **Configuration ➤ Cron**.

Regional settings

Regional settings are accessed at **Configuration ➤ Regional settings**, as shown in Figure 3-5. The **Default country** field has the goal of supporting country-specific language, date, and number formats. For example, a user could register for an account from France, and the user's time zone and language preference would be adjusted accordingly. **Default time zone** sets the time for the site and is displayed in a number of places, including comments and content (if **display post information** has been enabled on the content type). If a user is logged in and **Users may set their own time zone** is selected, then the date and time will be converted to the user's time zone (provided the user has set their time zone). Users can be reminded to set their time zone by selecting **Remind users at login if their time zone is not set**. There are three settings for setting a user's time zone when they register for an account. **Empty time zone** leaves the time zone field blank, while **Default time zone** uses the default value; selecting either value displays the site default time on comments and content until the user updates their time zone. Selecting **Users may set their own time zone at registration** displays a field to enter the time zone on the user registration page.

Figure 3-5. Access **Regional Settings** by navigating to **Configuration ➤ Regional settings**.

Date and time

Drupal gives you the ability to customize the way dates and times are displayed on your site. Navigate to **Configuration ➤ Date and time** to view the three default date types: **Long**, **Medium**, and **Short**. Each date type has a drop-down selector under **OPERATIONS** allowing you to customize the output, as shown in Figure 3-6.

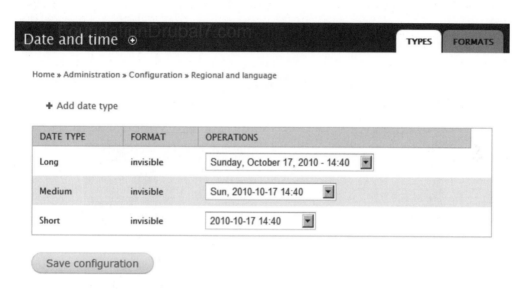

Figure 3-6. Navigate to **Configuration ➤ Date and time** to view and add date types.

Additional date types can be added by selecting the **Add date type** link, as shown in Figure 3-7. There are a number of data formats available in the drop-down; however, sometimes you may want to add a more customized format using PHP's date() function. Navigate to **Configuration ➤ Date and time**, and click the **FORMATS** tab to view all custom formats. To create a new format, click the **Add format link**, and enter date parameters in the **Format string** field, as shown in Figure 3-8. Click the **PHP manual** link to view all available parameters.

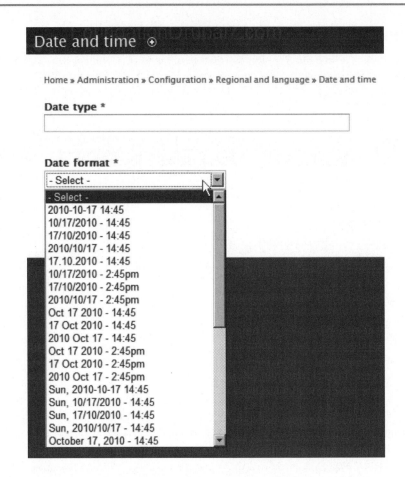

Figure 3-7. Click the **Add date type** link to add additional date types.

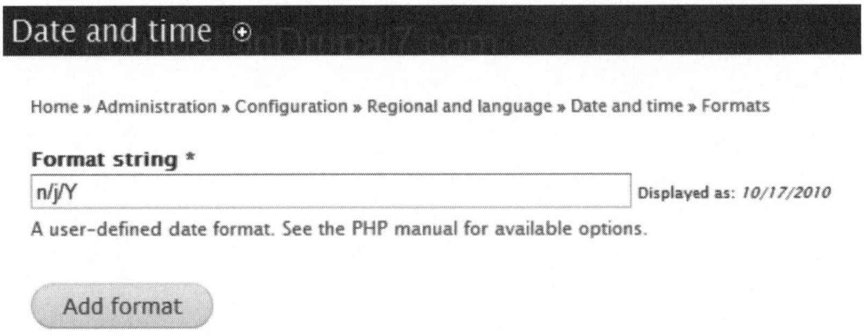

Figure 3-8. Click the **FORMATS** tab to add a format using PHP date() parameters.

Clean URLs

Drupal displays URLs in one of two formats depending on the capabilities of your web server: as a clean URL (for example, `example.com/node/1`) or as a default URL (`example.com/?q=node/1`). Clean URLs require your web server to have URL rewriting enabled. During installation, Drupal automatically checks to see whether your server is capable of using clean URLs and enables this if it can. Navigate to **Configuration ➤ Clean URLs** to enable clean URLs (see Figure 3-9).

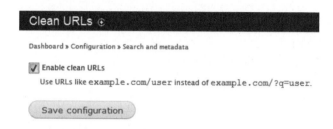

Figure 3-9. Navigate to **Configuration ➤ Clean URLs** to enable clean URLs.

Configuring the file system and private downloads

By default, all files uploaded to the server through Drupal are accessible on the public Internet in either the `sites/default/files` directory or the `sites/example.com/files` directory, depending on how your site is set up. Optionally, you can configure private downloads, such that Drupal stores all files in a directory outside the publically available Drupal root. Navigate to **Configuration ➤ File system**, as shown in Figure 3-10. In this example, the **Private file system path** setting has been set relative to the Drupal root; the `private` directory is located immediately outside the `public_html` directory.

Note you will need to create the directory for private downloads and make it writable by Drupal in order for the **Private local files served by Drupal** option under **Default download method** to become available. It is not recommended that you change this value after the site has gone into production.

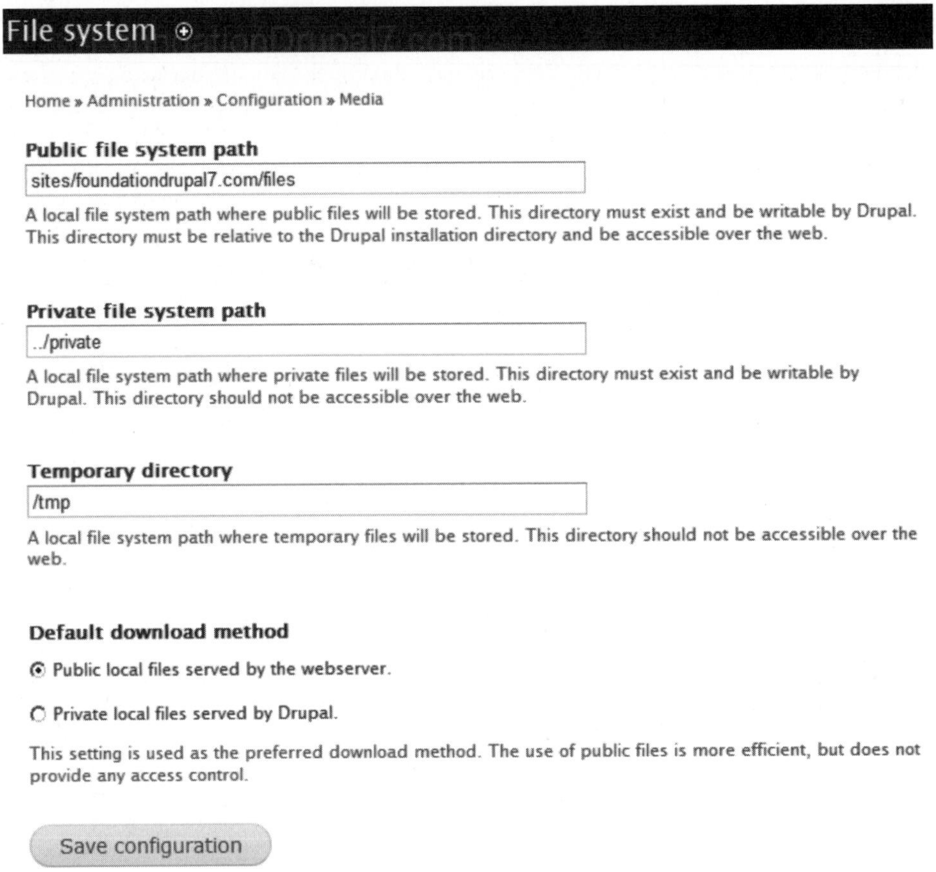

File system ⊕

Home » Administration » Configuration » Media

Public file system path

sites/foundationdrupal7.com/files

A local file system path where public files will be stored. This directory must exist and be writable by Drupal. This directory must be relative to the Drupal installation directory and be accessible over the web.

Private file system path

../private

A local file system path where private files will be stored. This directory must exist and be writable by Drupal. This directory should not be accessible over the web.

Temporary directory

/tmp

A local file system path where temporary files will be stored. This directory should not be accessible over the web.

Default download method

⦿ Public local files served by the webserver.

○ Private local files served by Drupal.

This setting is used as the preferred download method. The use of public files is more efficient, but does not provide any access control.

(Save configuration)

Figure 3-10. Navigate to **Configuration ➤ File system to configure private downloads.**

Blocks

Blocks are the foundation of displaying content in Drupal, because they display content from a wide variety of sources, including menus. I take an in-depth look at blocks in this section, covering how they work and their many different configuration settings. I discuss how blocks can be displayed to a user based on a number of settings, including the node's content type, URL, user's role, and user. Menus, which are displayed through blocks, are covered in the next section.

How blocks work

A **block** is a section of a page that displays content; it can be any size or shape and can display any type of content. You can manually create a block and add content, similar to creating a node, resulting in a block with static content. Modules can also create blocks, such as recent comments or a recent content block, resulting in a block with dynamic and changing content. Menus are also blocks, as discussed in the previous section. When you're trying to find a way to display content in Drupal, you'll probably want to do it through a block.

Blocks are located in regions, which are areas of a page such as the footer, content, or left sidebar. If you navigate to **Structure ➤ Blocks** to view the block configuration page, available regions are in bold on the left side of the screen (see Figure 3-11). You can also click the **Demonstrate block regions** link to view available regions. Although it is not required that a block is output through a region, outputting a block through a region using the block configuration page has a major benefit: you can easily adjust the order of blocks within a region through the drag-and-drop interface.

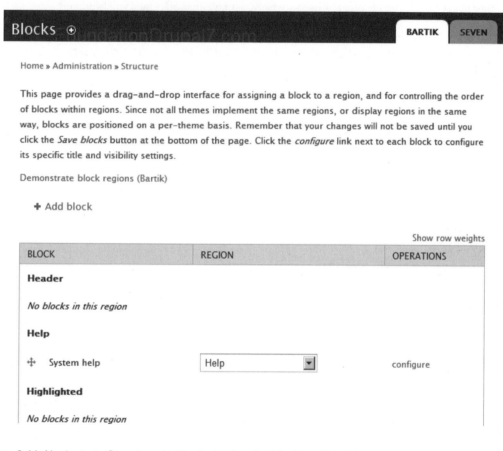

Figure 3-11. Navigate to **Structure ➤ Blocks** to view the block configuration page.

Every theme has different regions, so blocks are assigned to regions on a per-theme basis. This means you may assign a block to the left sidebar region in one theme and place it in the header region in another theme. Every theme must have two important regions:

- The content region that by default contains the main page content block
- The help region that by default contains the system help block

The default Drupal installation includes a number of blocks, including recent comments, user information, and several menus. Blocks are usually added by modules, although you can also create a block and write content to appear within it. The downside to creating content in a block is that it will not appear in search results. Navigate to **Structure ➤ Blocks ➤ Add block** to create a block.

One or more blocks can appear in a single region, but a block cannot be configured through the Drupal interface to appear in multiple regions. There are exceptions to this, of course, most of which require placing custom code in your theme template (see Chapter 8). Another exception involves the main menu, secondary menu, and other various elements, which can be configured by the theme to display as page elements by navigating to **Appearance ➤ Settings ➤ TOGGLE DISPLAY**. The main difference between blocks and page elements is that you cannot control the location of page elements through the Drupal interface; the location of a page element is defined by the theme. By default Drupal enables all page elements.

Moving and arranging blocks

Whenever you add a new block or enable a module with blocks, you will need to place the block in a region for it to display. Drupal's interface allows you to drag and drop the order of blocks within a region or move blocks between regions. Navigate to **Structure ➤ Blocks**, click the plus icon to the left of the block name, and drag up or down. Remember to click the **Save Blocks** link at the bottom of the page, because changes are not automatically saved.

Configuring a block

A block can be displayed on one page, across a number of pages, to a specific user group, or only when a node of a specific content type is displayed. There are a plethora of other configuration options as well, including block title and module-specific settings. Click the **configure** link on the block administration page next to the block you need to configure these settings (see Figure 3-12).

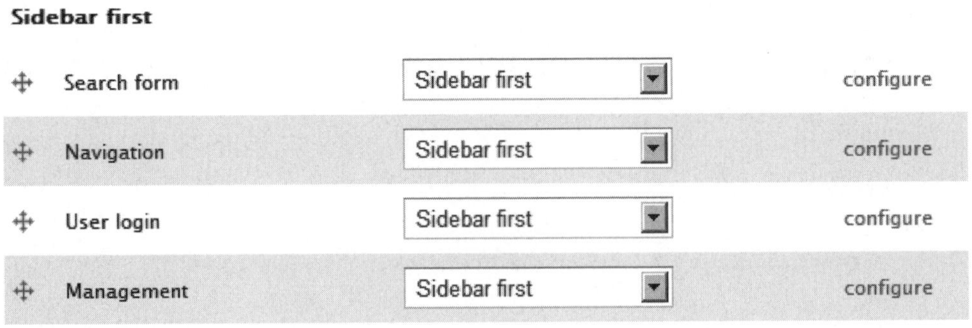

Sidebar first

✛	Search form	Sidebar first ▼	configure
✛	Navigation	Sidebar first ▼	configure
✛	User login	Sidebar first ▼	configure
✛	Management	Sidebar first ▼	configure

Figure 3-12. Click the **configure** link on the block administration page next to the block you need to adjust these settings.

Block-specific settings

Every block has a default title that appears in the block header when the block is displayed. Entering a block title in this form overrides the default title. You can also enter `<none>` to hide the default title.

Modules may or may not insert additional configuration settings in this form. For example, the forum module inserts a drop-down box to enter the number of forum topics the block should display, as shown in Figure 3-13.

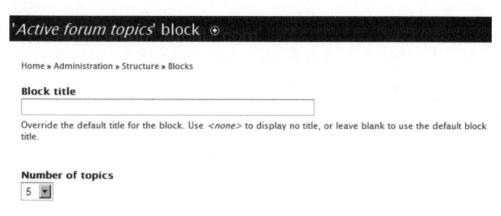

Figure 3-13. The forum module inserts a drop-down field in the block-specific settings tab.

Region settings

Region settings allow you to see the location of a block in every theme. Although you will normally use the block administration page to arrange the location of blocks, this is a quick way to see the themes and regions in which a block is active (see Figure 3-14).

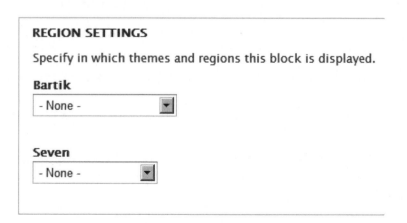

Figure 3-14. Region settings determine where a block is placed in each theme.

Page-specific visibility settings

Blocks can be configured to appear on select pages or on every page except for select pages. The URL wildcard (*) allows you to display blocks across a number of pages. For example, to make the most recent blog block display on all blog pages, you would enter `blog/*`. Use `<front>` only if you want the block to appear on the front page. See Figure 3-15 for an example.

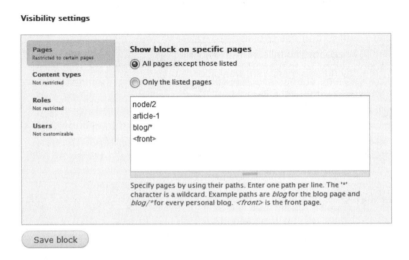

Figure 3-15. Page-specific visibility settings

You can enter the path either as the system URL (for example, `node/2`) or as the path alias (for example, `article-1`). See Chapter 7 for a discussion on path aliases. Drupal differentiates between the two, which means you may run into display problems if you use a path alias and the alias changes at some point. For example, if a block is configured to display only when the alias equals `about` and at some point the alias is changed from `about` to `about-us`, then the block will no longer display on the `about` page. Using the system URL overcomes this because a node's system URL never changes, but it also has its own limitations. For example, you may have ten pages you want the block to display on, which means you must enter ten different system URLs and cannot use the URL wildcard. Automating path aliases can help alleviate this to a certain extent (covered in Chapter 8), but it also has its limitations. Regardless, you will need to think through how you structure your content and URLs before you decide on your page-specific visibility settings.

Content type-specific visibility settings

Blocks can be configured to appear only when a node of a specific content type is being viewed, as shown in Figure 3-16. For example, you may want the active forum topics block to appear only when a user is browsing the forums.

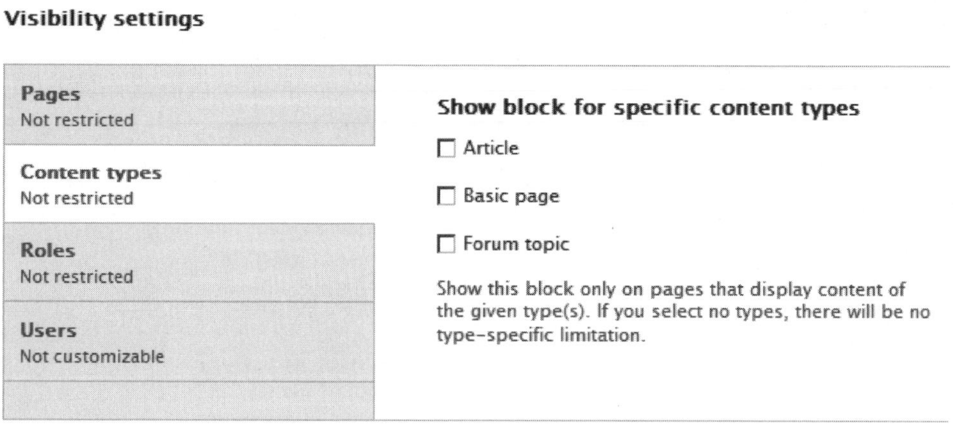

Visibility settings

Pages Not restricted	**Show block for specific content types** ☐ Article ☐ Basic page ☐ Forum topic Show this block only on pages that display content of the given type(s). If you select no types, there will be no type-specific limitation.
Content types Not restricted	
Roles Not restricted	
Users Not customizable	

Figure 3-16. Content-type specific visibility settings

Role-specific visibility settings

This setting allows you to restrict a block to users of a specific role and only give them permission to view it (see Figure 3-17). If a role is not selected, then the block is available to all roles.

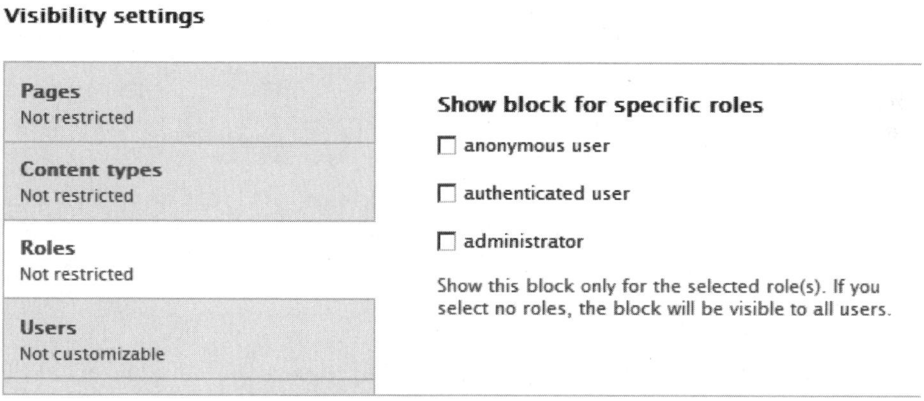

Visibility settings

Pages Not restricted	**Show block for specific roles** ☐ anonymous user ☐ authenticated user ☐ administrator Show this block only for the selected role(s). If you select no roles, the block will be visible to all users.
Content types Not restricted	
Roles Not restricted	
Users Not customizable	

Figure 3-17. Role-specific visibility settings

User-specific visibility settings

If enabled, users have the option to hide or view a block from displaying (see Figure 3-18). Users must log in and edit their account page to enable or disable a block.

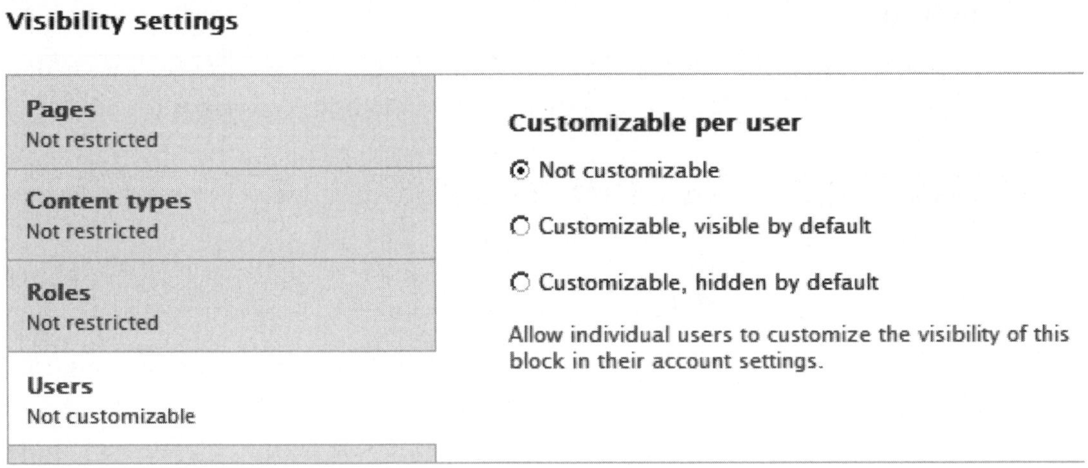

Visibility settings

Pages
Not restricted

Content types
Not restricted

Roles
Not restricted

Users
Not customizable

Customizable per user

◉ Not customizable

○ Customizable, visible by default

○ Customizable, hidden by default

Allow individual users to customize the visibility of this block in their account settings.

Figure 3-18. User-specific visibility settings

Menus and menu links

In this section, I discuss Drupal's built-in mechanism to add and organize menus and menu links. I talk about Drupal's default menus, accessed at **Structure ➤ Menus**, and review the easy process of creating a menu and adding menu links. I also discuss Drupal's default menus and the many configuration options available. After reading this section, you will be a menu-creating and link-moving superstar!

Overview of Drupal's menu system

Navigate to **Structure ➤ Menus** to access the form used to create menus and menu links. The process for creating a menu and adding menu links is relatively straightforward:

1. Add a menu.

2. Add menu links.

3. Navigate to the blocks administration page to move the menu block to a region.

The key thing I want to point out about menus is that every menu has a corresponding block managed using the **Structure ➤ Blocks** form. This means a menu block has the same functionality as a regular block. You can move a menu to any region in your site. You have the ability to show it on specific content types, pages, or user groups. Please note that although you can hide a menu from a specific user group, this does not mean the user group cannot access the pages to which the menu links point.

By default, Drupal displays links vertically, which means CSS must be used to display links horizontally (see Chapter 8). When you are configuring your site, it is easy to get sidetracked and say, "I'm just going to fix these menu links really quickly so they display correctly, and then I'll continue configuring the site." Don't do it! Run away! Stick with configuration and then theme!

Default menus

The default Drupal installation has five menus, each with a specific purpose, as discussed in the following sections. Navigate to **Structure ➤ Menus** to view the full list of menus. You can also use this page to list links, add links, and edit menu settings (see Figure 3-19).

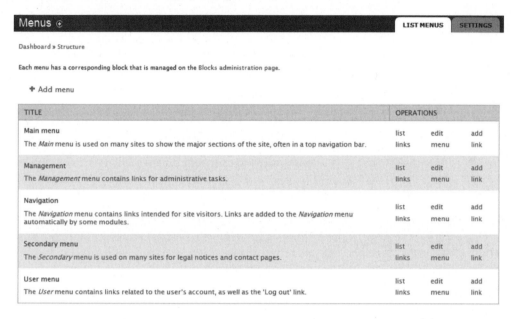

Figure 3-19. Navigate to **Structure ➤ Menus** to view the full list of menus.

Main menu

This is the primary menu for adding links to major sections of the web site, usually displayed in the header or near the top of a page. Themes commonly display this menu as a page element, discussed in further detail in the "Themes" section of this chapter.

Management

The management menu is located in the upper toolbar and contains links to administrative pages. It is also displayed in the left sidebar in the default Garland theme.

Navigation

Modules add links intended for site visitors and users to the navigation menu by default. It is located in the left sidebar of the default Garland theme and may or may not appear depending on whether a module has added a link to the menu.

Secondary menu

The secondary menu is used for links that play a smaller role than main menu links and may be displayed in the footer or underneath the main menu. Themes often display this menu as a page element.

User menu

The user menu is displayed in the administrative toolbar and contains links to the user's account page and to log out.

Global menu settings

A number of global menu settings are available at **Structure ➤ Menus ➤ SETTINGS**, as shown in Figure 3-20. (I call these **global menu settings** to differentiate them from individual menu settings; Drupal refers to both as **menu settings**.) The **Default menu for content** drop-down determines which menu is preselected as the menu setting's parent item on the content creation form. I usually set this to the same menu selected in the **Source for the Main links** drop-down.

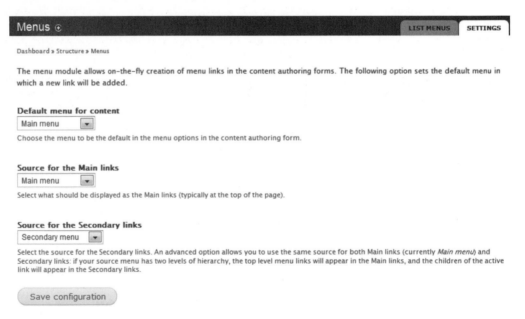

Figure 3-20. Menu settings that apply to all menus are accessed at **Structure ➤ Menus ➤ Settings**.

The **Source for Main links** setting is used by many themes to determine which menu it should use as the main menu. Any menu can be used as the source for main links, which depending on your theme may be displayed as a page element. The **Source for Secondary links** is much the same; any menu can be used, and your theme may display it as a page element. However, an advanced option allows you to set the source for main links and secondary links to the same menu. If you do this, then the secondary menu will display any links nested under an active link. For example, say your menu looks like this:

- Home
- About
    - People
    - Strengths
    - Investors
- Contact Us

When a user selects the about link, three links will appear in the secondary menu: **People**, **Strengths**, and **Investors**. When a user clicks the **Home** or **Contact Us** link, the secondary menu will be empty.

Adding a menu

You can add or edit a menu by navigating to **Structure ➤ Menus** and selecting **Add menu** (see Figure 3-21). Only one field is required, **title**, which appears in many locations: on the main menu administration page, in the content creation form under menu settings, and as the block title. The description appears only on the main menu administration page. After you create a new menu, a block is added to the block administration page. You will need to enable and configure the block on the block administration page at **Structure ➤ Blocks**.

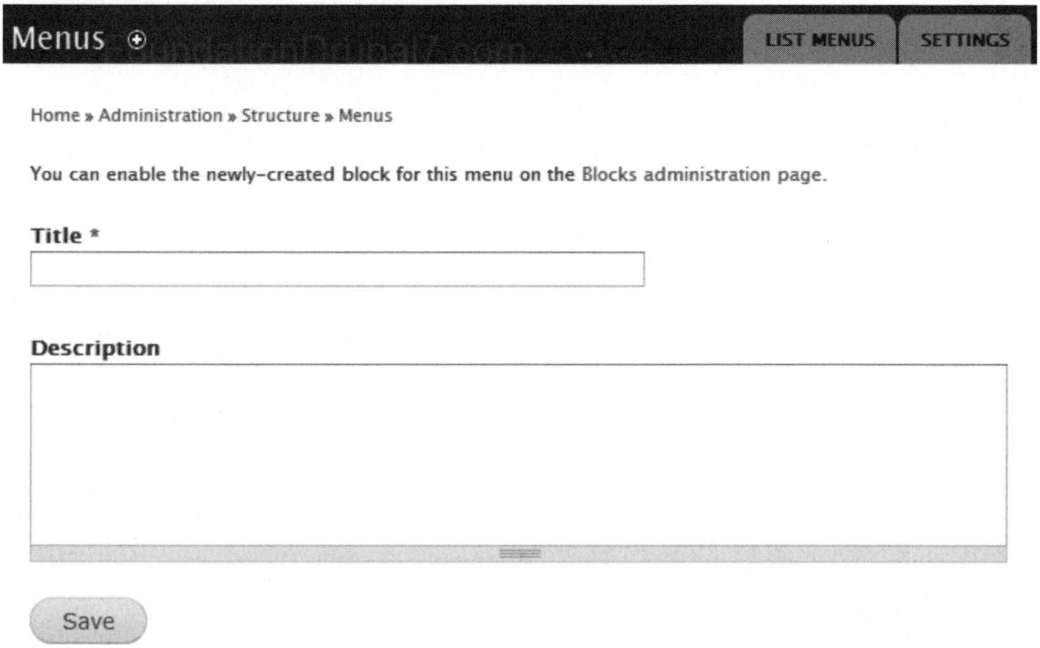

Figure 3-21. Navigate to **Structure ➤ Menus**, and select **Add menu** for the form to add a menu.

Listing links

Each menu has a menu link administration form accessed at **Structure ➤ Menus ➤ LIST LINKS**. This form allows you to rearrange the order of menu links via drag-and-drop. This is a much simpler way to manage link order when compared to the menu link weight box on the content creation form. If you have horizontal menu links, moving links up or down on this form causes links to move right to left in the menu (see Figure 3-22).

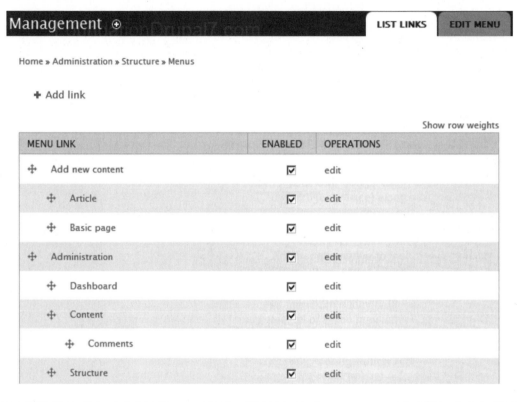

Figure 3-22. Menu link administration page for the **Management** menu, accessed at **Structure ➤ Menus ➤ LIST LINKS**

Menu links are enabled by default; when disabled, they disappear from the menu block but still appear in the administration form. Links can be nested under each other up to nine levels deep. Selecting **show as expanded** means that when a link is active (in other words, the user is on the page to which the link points), all links nested underneath it are displayed. As expected, selecting the **delete** link under operations deletes the link, while selecting **edit** brings you to a form to edit the link.

Creating a menu link

Menu links can be created through the content creation form or by navigating to **Structure ➤ Menus** and clicking **Add link** next to the appropriate menu. A number of fields are required for a menu link (see Figure 3-23).

The **Menu link title** setting contains the text of the link, while the **Path** setting is the location to which the link points. The **Description** field is the text that appears when a mouse pointer hovers over a link. I recommend writing a description using search engine–relevant keywords, because search engines frequently use this field when crawling sites. By default, a link is enabled; this can also be changed on the menu administration page. The **Show as expanded** check box, which determines whether child links should be displayed when the parent links are active, can also be changed on the menu administration page. You must select a parent link for the link to appear. As a note, the only way to move a link from one menu to another is by changing the parent link.

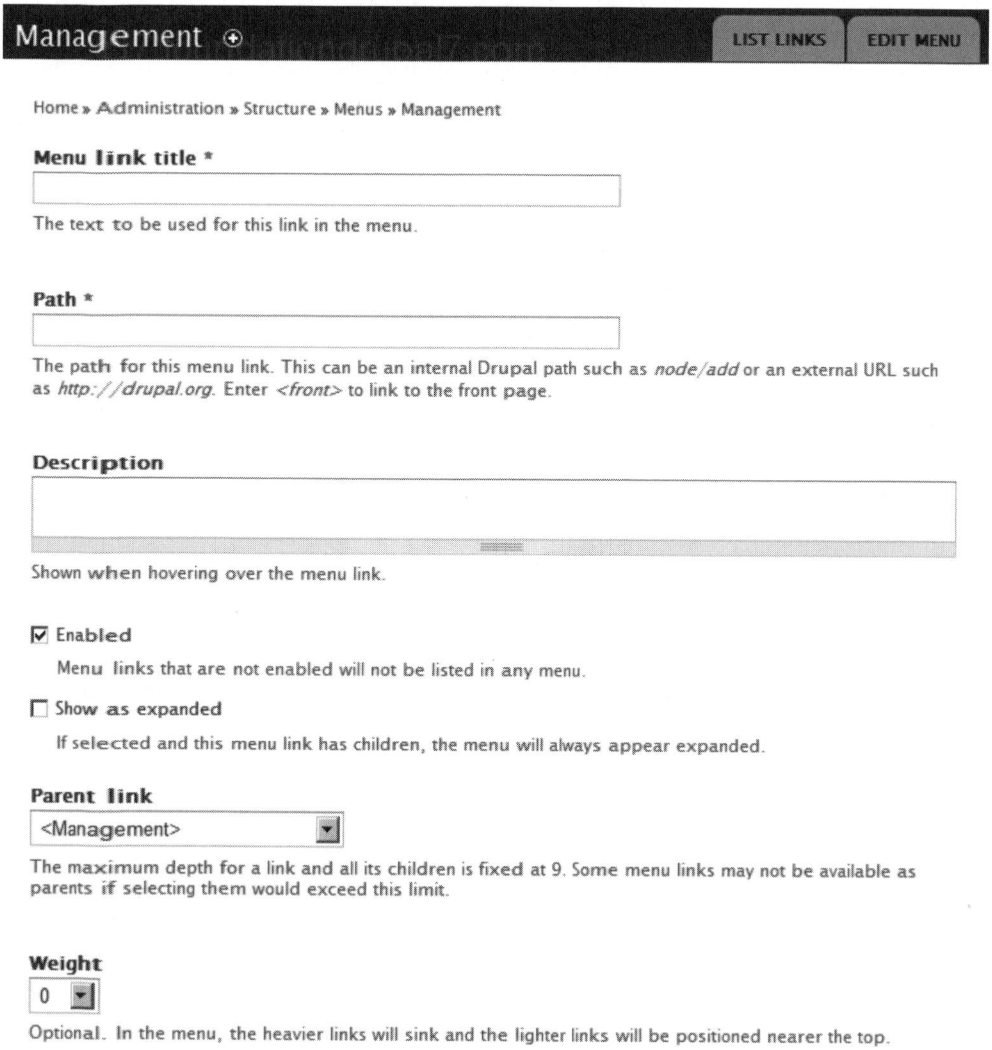

Management ⊕   LIST LINKS   EDIT MENU

Home » Administration » Structure » Menus » Management

Menu link title *

_____

The text to be used for this link in the menu.

Path *

_____

The path for this menu link. This can be an internal Drupal path such as *node/add* or an external URL such as *http://drupal.org*. Enter *<front>* to link to the front page.

Description

_____

Shown when hovering over the menu link.

☑ Enabled

   Menu links that are not enabled will not be listed in any menu.

☐ Show as expanded

   If selected and this menu link has children, the menu will always appear expanded.

Parent link

   <Management>   ▼

The maximum depth for a link and all its children is fixed at 9. Some menu links may not be available as parents if selecting them would exceed this limit.

Weight

   0 ▼

Optional. In the menu, the heavier links will sink and the lighter links will be positioned nearer the top.

Figure 3-23. The edit menu link form is accessed by navigating to **Structure ➤ Menus** and clicking **Add** link next to the appropriate menu.

One potential issue with using **promoted** is that multiple nodes may have this selected. You can use **sticky at top of lists** to ensure one specific node was always displayed, but multiple nodes could also select this as well. In this case, it would be a simple task of navigating to **content** and mass updating the publishing options.

Note that any page can be the site's front page. You can use taxonomy term listings, pages generated by modules, views, and more. Be creative!

Appearance

Drupal uses themes to lay out and mark up content. A theme contains a number of HTML templates, CSS files, image files, JavaScript files, and more. A web site can have more than one theme and by default uses two: one for the admin section and one for main site content. You can easily switch themes to update the look and feel of a web site, but you cannot edit a theme from a browser. As such, it is often difficult for new Drupal users to understand what is changed through the administrative section and what is coded in the theme. A conceptual understanding of themes helps, but often it takes experience and problem-solving skills. The process of creating and editing a theme is called **theming** and is covered in Chapter 8.

Selecting a theme

Click the **Appearance** link in the administrative toolbar to navigate to the theme administration page. This page contains a list of all available themes with a screenshot and a number of available options for each (see Figure 3-28). The default Drupal installation enables the Bartik theme for the main content section and the Seven theme for the administration section.

The **set default** option controls which theme is used for the main content section of the site (**set default** is available only on themes that are not default). Selecting another default theme means you will change the appearance and layout of the site. A theme must be enabled before it can become the default theme. Enabling a theme allows other modules and administrative sections of the web site to interact with it. For example, the block admin page (**Structure ➤ Blocks**) allows you to manage blocks on a per-theme basis. Once a theme is enabled, a link to the theme's block administration page appears underneath the block title. If a theme is not enabled, there is no link, and you are not able to add and manage blocks.

Appearance ⊕

LIST | SETTINGS

Home » Administration

Set and configure the default theme for your website. Alternative themes are available.

ENABLED THEMES

Bartik 7.x–dev (default theme)

A flexible, recolorable theme with many regions.

Settings

Seven 7.x–dev

A simple one–column, tableless, fluid width administration theme.

Settings | Disable | Set default

Figure 3-28. *The theme administration page is accessed by selecting* **Appearance** *in the administrative toolbar.*

Click the **Administration theme** drop-down to set the theme for the admin section. The default Drupal installation sets the Seven theme as the administration theme. Optionally, you can set the Minnelli theme as the administration theme or download a user-contributed theme from Drupal.org. Selecting **default** uses the same theme as the rest of the site, which in this case would be the Garland theme. Selecting the **Use the administration theme...** check box controls which theme is used on the content creation form (see Figure 3-29).

ADMINISTRATION THEME

Administration theme

Seven ▾

Choose "Default theme" to always use the same theme as the rest of the site.

☑ Use the administration theme when editing or creating content

Save configuration

Figure 3-29. Click the **Use the administration theme...** check box at the bottom of the theme administration page to select the theme for administration pages.

Global and individual theme settings

Drupal has a number of theme settings that can be configured through the admin section. Navigate to **appearance** and click the **settings** tab to view global settings, or click the **settings** link next to a theme to view individual theme settings.

Themes display a number of page elements that can be toggled on or off, such as a logo, site name, search box, and main menu (see Figure 3-30 for full list). These settings can be configured at the global level or overridden at the individual theme level. As a note, the search box, main menu, and secondary menu can be displayed as a block, a page element, or both at the same time.

TOGGLE DISPLAY
Enable or disable the display of certain page elements.

☑ Logo

☑ Site name

☑ Site slogan

☑ User pictures in posts

☑ User pictures in comments

☑ User verification status in comments

☑ Shortcut icon

☑ Main menu

☑ Secondary menu

Figure 3-30. List of page elements that can be toggled on or off

By default, Drupal uses the duplicon for both the site logo, which appears in the web site header, and the favicon, which appears in the browser. You can upload a new logo or favicon by deselecting the **Use the default logo** or **Use the default shortcut icon** check boxes (see Figure 3-31). The logo image settings and shortcut icon settings are covered in detail in Chapter 8.

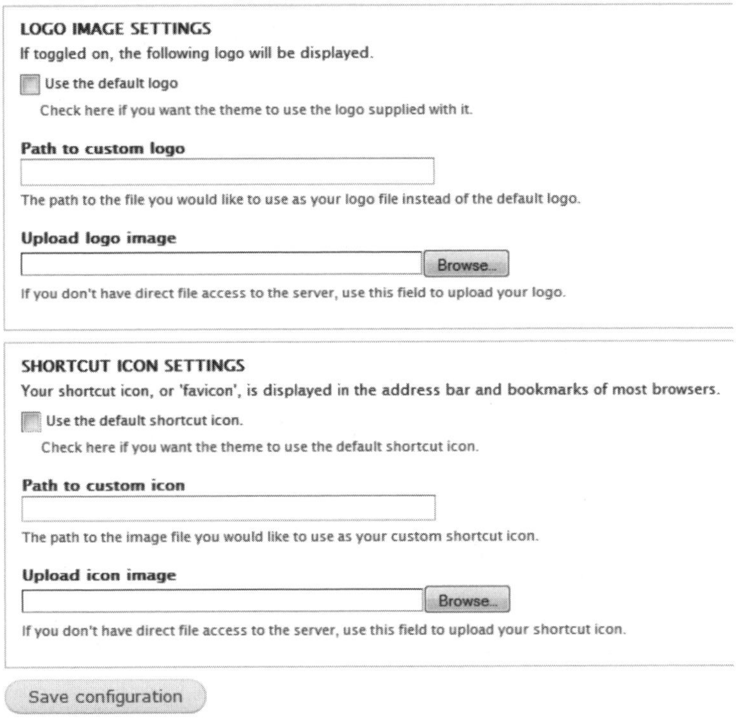

Figure 3-31. List of page elements that can be toggled on or off

Summary

I started the chapter covering development processes and how I tend to develop a site in two phases: development and theming. During the development phase, I configure modules, set up blocks, add content, and upload images before I even begin to think about adding HTML or CSS. I talked about how I develop incrementally, installing Drupal and then building one section (that is, content type + blocks) at a time.

I then talked about several important Drupal topics, including blocks, menus, and themes. You learned that blocks are displayed in regions and can be easily arranged through the block configuration form. You also learned that blocks display content from a number of sources, such as menus, modules, and user-entered content. They also have a number of settings to determine which page and to whom the block is displayed. I closed the chapter discussing themes and how you can easily switch a theme and configure a theme to display various page elements.

Chapter 4

Adding Content Types and Fields

Content types are probably one of the most important things to understand about Drupal. In this chapter, I discuss what content types are, how you can use them to your advantage, and how to create one. Content types also have fields associated with them, and I take an in-depth look at the various fields provided by Drupal. I close the chapter by discussing taxonomy terms, also called **tagging**, and how you can use tagging to relate one or more pieces of content.

What is a content type?

I talked about the concept of a node in Chapter 1 and described how most content in Drupal is entered as a node (blocks and comments are the exception). A **content type** is a logical grouping of nodes that have many shared attributes, such as publishing options, display settings, comment settings, and more. A node belongs to only one content type, but a content type can have an unlimited number of nodes. Content types can also have an unlimited number of fields attached to them, such as image uploads, select fields, text boxes, tags, and others. The result is a powerful mechanism to enter, organize, and display content.

I tend to think of nodes as objects, in the object-oriented programming sense. That is, nodes are data structures that have a set of data fields and instructions on how to use those data fields when required. In this sense, a content type is the node's class, defining the characteristics of the node and the operations it can perform. The article content type, for example, has several characteristics: a title, an image, a body, and category tags. When an article node is created, the content type tells Drupal what to do with it, such as publish it to the front page, allow comments, set a custom URL path, create a revision, and so on.

Modules are used to tell Drupal what to do with a node. Many of Drupal's most popular and powerful contributed modules are based upon content types. The Ubercart e-commerce module is a great example. When enabled, the module creates a content type called Product with a number of fields, including a product description, price, image, shipping weight, and more. The module then displays Product nodes in an online catalog, allows you to add them to a cart, and creates a pretty nifty administrative section to manage all nodes.

Knowing when to add a content type

There is no perfect number to the number of content types a web site should have. I have seen awesome Drupal sites using only the default node types and also have been involved in projects where the site had more than 30 content types (note that I frequently use *node type* and *content type* interchangeably to refer to the same thing).

Adding a content type is a matter of functionality and preference. When I say *functionality*, I mean a few things. First, does the node require one or more special fields? In many cases, you will want to use the **Basic Page** content type for static pages while using another content type for, say, a project portfolio, catalog, or restaurant menu. This additional content type has extra fields, such as image uploads and category tags, that differentiate it from a **Basic Page**. Second, does the content type require a special feature or module, such as allowing user ratings or comments? Because modules tend to affect all nodes of a specific content type, it can sometimes be very difficult to use a module on a specific node. Third, how many nodes with the same settings do you require? If you need a large number of nodes with the same settings for each, then I highly recommend creating a content type. A portfolio is a great example; each portfolio node should have identical functionality, such as images, commenting, and tagging. Of course, you could modify one of the core content types to meet your needs, but then you must manually adjust node settings each time you use the content type for something other than a portfolio. Fourth, do users need to have a specific role assigned to them to post the node? Roles are covered in detail in the next chapter. Finally, does the node require a significantly different layout than another content type? As discussed in Chapter 8, it is much easier to theme the layout for nodes of a specific content type than for individual nodes of single content type.

Adding a content type is also a matter of preference. When you create a content type, it is available on the **Add New Content** page. How many content types do you want on this page? Does it make logical sense for you or the client to have three or more content types? How would you explain the content type you added to someone who doesn't use the site?

Knowing when to add a content type takes both experience and foresight. It involves understanding how your site will work and how users will add content. My general rule of thumb is that if a content type is part of a section (that is, part of the forums, blogs, products, catalog items, and so on), requires a specific module, or has multiple nodes with multiple settings or fields, then you should probably create a content type. Content types can also help solve problems. For example, you can sit and stare at the screen for hours asking the question, "How do I get a specific field to appear at this specific place?" Frequently, creating a content type will solve this problem.

Adding a content type

So, you've decided to add a content type. Now what? Many times a module will create a content type for you, but what if you need to add one yourself? In this section, I cover how to create a content type and the various settings you will need to configure. Content types are created and administered by navigating to **Structure ➤ Content Types** (see Figure 4-1).

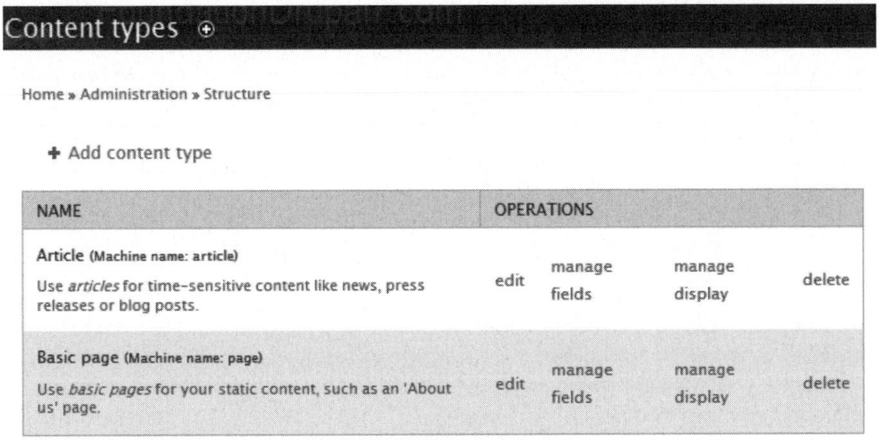

Figure 4-1. The page to create and administer content types is accessed by navigating to **Structure ➤ Content types**.

Every content type has two names: a human-readable name and a machine name (see Figure 4-2). The human-readable name, along with the description, appears when creating a content type on the **Add content type** page; several other options are available in vertical tabs. You'll use the machine name primarily when theming the site. If you create a content type (see Figure 4-2), Drupal will create the machine name for you automatically based on the human-readable name. There is also an **Edit** link to change the machine name. I recommend shortening the machine name to one word with less than eight letters; otherwise, typing the name can become a tedious task when theming.

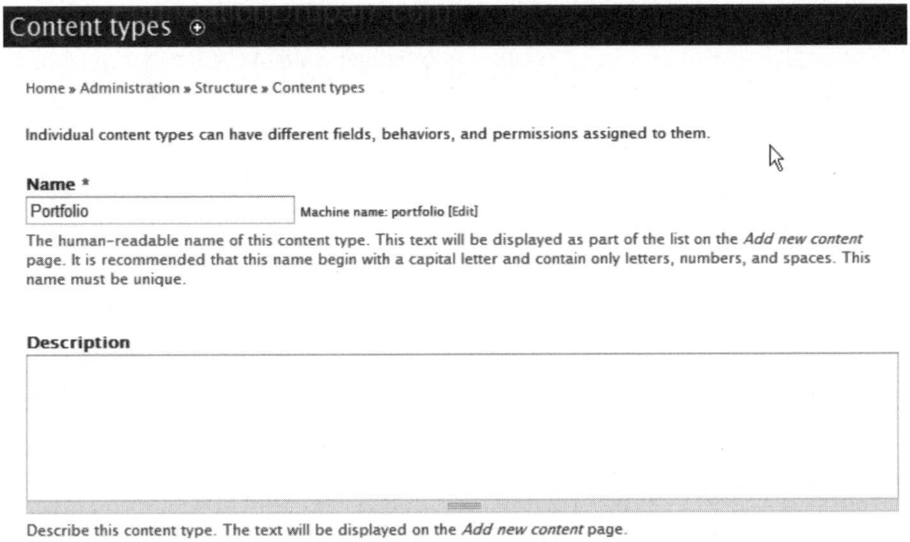

Figure 4-2. Create a new content type by navigating to **Structure ➤ Content types**.

Fields and form settings available to a content type

Underneath the **Description** text area are a number of vertical tabs that control many of the default settings when creating a node (see Figure 4-3 for details). The first vertical tab is **Submission form settings**, which controls many settings on the content creation page (in other words, `example.com/node/add`). You can give the **Title field label** setting any arbitrary name. If **Preview before submitting** is set to **Disabled**, the preview link at the bottom of the content creation form will not appear. If set to **Optional**, which is the default, a **Preview** link will appear and allow users to preview the node before the form is submitted. The **Explanation or submission guidelines** setting appears at the top of the content creation form.

Every content type created is automatically given a **Body** field, which is (usually) used for main or primary data. When creating a node, the **Body** field allows you to enter the full body text used when the node is displayed. Optionally, you can edit the summary view of the **Body** field, which is displayed in lists and (frequently) through the Views module.

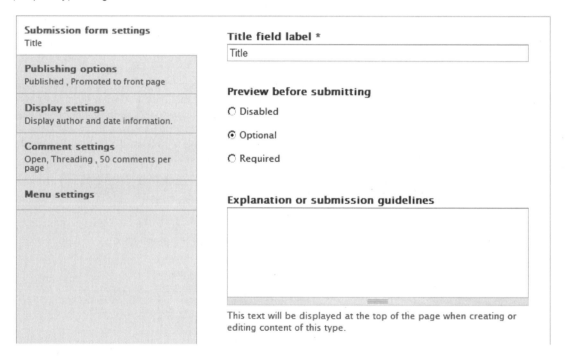

Figure 4-3. The **Submission form settings** tab is located in the vertical tabs at the bottom of the content type (in other words, `example.com/node/add`) edit page.

Content publishing options

Drupal provides four default publishing options. When creating a node, these four publishing options are spread across two tabs: **Revision information** and **Publishing options**. If users do not have the **administer nodes** permission, discussed in the next chapter, they may or may not be able to change these settings when creating a node (see Figure 4-4).

The only reason you do not want to select **Published** as the default option is if the site administrator (or someone else) needs to approve content before it is published. The **Promoted to front page** check box works only when the site is configured with the default homepage (or when a view is configured to use the check box, covered in Chapter 7). Selecting the **Sticky at top of lists** check box sends the node to the top of a list (once again, if configured with the default homepage; see Chapter 7 for exceptions). If **Create new revision** is selected, every time a node is edited, a revision is created. This can become very cumbersome to manage on sites where content is frequently updated, especially if there are more than ten revisions of a node. However, note that many developers frequently turn this on and forget about it, relying on the end user to manage and delete revisions.

Figure 4-4. The settings on the **Publishing options** tab determine the default publishing options on the content creation form.

Displaying the author and publication date

When a node is created, the user name of the author and the time it was created is saved. Selecting **Display author and date information** shows this information underneath the node's title whenever the full-page node is viewed (see Figure 4-5).

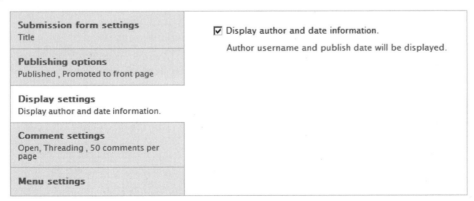

Figure 4-5. Display settings determine if author and date information will be automatically displayed on a node.

Displaying comments

The **Comment settings** tab has a number of options that can be configured at the content type level (see Figure 4-6); keep in mind these are default settings and can be updated by users with the appropriate permissions. Comments can either be **Open**, **Closed**, or **Hidden**. Hidden comments means users cannot add or view comments, while **Closed** comments means users can view previous comments but cannot add one; I recommend setting this as either **Open** or **Hidden** and then allowing site administrators to close comments if required. Please note that changing this setting to **Closed** (or vice versa) will not affect previously created nodes.

Comments can be displayed either as a straight list or as threaded. A threaded list groups comments according to replies; if a user posts a comment and three people reply to that comment, those four posts are considered a thread and grouped together.

When displaying comments, Drupal automatically includes a **pager** (that is, it includes links to page 1 of comments, page 2 of comments, and so on) to view additional comments when the number in the **Comments per page** setting is exceeded. The **Allow comment title** check box adds a comment title field in the comment form, allowing users to create a custom title for their comment. If the check box is deselected, Drupal creates a title for the comment based on the first 29 characters of the comment.

The comment form can appear either on the same page as the node or on a separate page. Deselecting the **Show reply form on the same page as comments** check box displays an **Add new comment** link at the bottom of a node directing users to a second page to add comments. If this is selected, then the comment form will appear at the bottom of the full-page node.

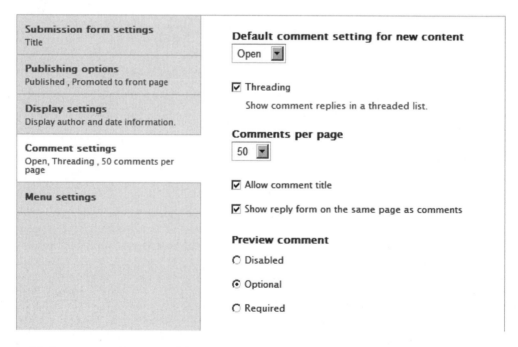

Figure 4-6. Comment settings control the way comments are displayed underneath nodes.

You can also change whether a user must preview a comment before submitting it by selecting **Disabled**, **Optional**, or **Required** under **Preview comment**. If you select either **Optional** or **Required**, then a **Preview Comment** button appears under the comment form.

Menu settings

The **Menu settings** tab allows you to add a link to the node to any of the available menus on the site. When a node is added to a Drupal site and the user has permission to add a menu link, the user is presented with a single drop-down field to select to which menu the node link belongs. The **Menu settings** tab allows you to select which menus appear in the drop-down (see Figure 4-7). If more than one menu is selected, then the **Default parent item** setting controls which menu is displayed as the default, that is, which menu link is selected by default when a node is created. This drop-down automatically updates when additional **Available menus** options are selected.

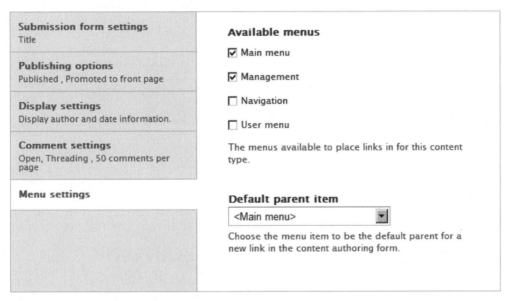

Figure 4-7. The **Menu settings** tab allows you to select which menus appear in the drop-down.

Adding fields to a content type

Content fields are added to content types to create customized forms. Multiple field types are available, such as check boxes, radio buttons, drop-down lists, text fields, images, file uploads, and more. This means that whenever someone creates a node, you can add custom fields to that form, which are displayed (and available for display) when viewing the node. You can add an unlimited number of fields to a content type. For example, the **Article** content type contains two added fields: a taxonomy **Tags** field for tagging and categorizing content and an **Image** field for uploading images (see Figure 4-8). You can create multiple example.com/node/add/content_type forms with customizable fields.

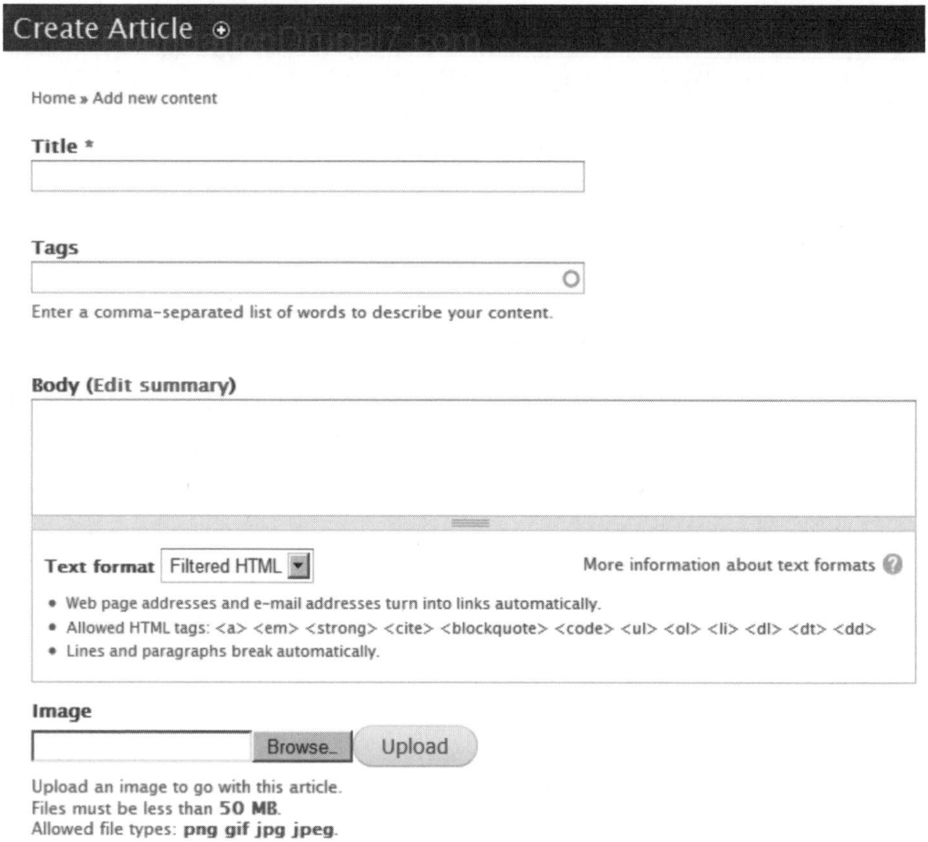

Create Article ⊕

Home » Add new content

Title *

Tags

○

Enter a comma-separated list of words to describe your content.

Body (Edit summary)

Text format Filtered HTML ▾   More information about text formats ❓

- Web page addresses and e-mail addresses turn into links automatically.
- Allowed HTML tags: \<a\> \<em\> \<strong\> \<cite\> \<blockquote\> \<code\> \<ul\> \<ol\> \<li\> \<dl\> \<dt\> \<dd\>
- Lines and paragraphs break automatically.

Image

[Browse...] (Upload)

Upload an image to go with this article.
Files must be less than **50 MB**.
Allowed file types: **png gif jpg jpeg**.

Figure 4-8. The **Article** content type contains two added fields: **Image** and **Tags**.

When creating a node, fields can be required, optional, or hidden. Field values are then output on full-page, teaser, RSS, and search views and have a number of options to configure how they are displayed; see the section "Managing the display of fields in multiple locations" later in this chapter. If required, JavaScript can be used to control field display behaviors (that is, displaying a field if a check box is selected, prefilling fields, and so on).

Navigate to **Structure ➤ Content types**, and click the **MANAGE FIELDS** tab to manage and add fields to a content type (see Figure 4-9). Note that you can add fields only after the content has been created. The form lists all fields and field types added to a content type. The order of fields is the same order they are displayed in the node creation form and in the full-page display. The form contains a drag-and-drop interface to change the order of fields; click the field's label and drag up or down. The label is the human-readable name of the field and appears with the field value. Depending on **MANAGE DISPLAY** settings, the label can appear above the field, can be to the left, or can be hidden. Click **edit** or **delete** to manage the field settings for the individual content type.

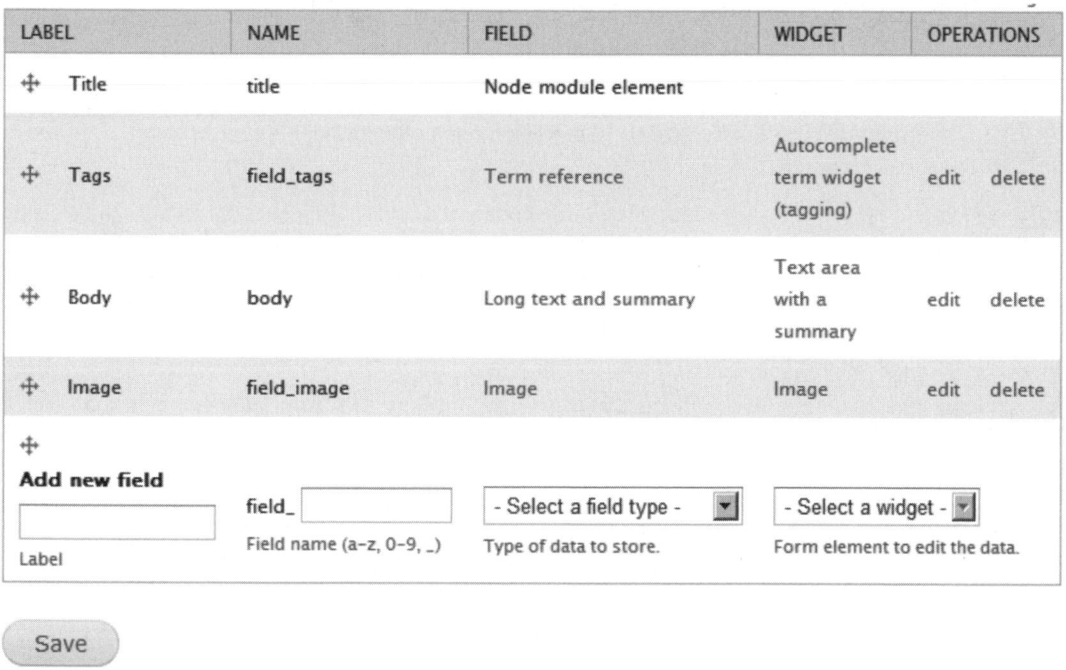

LABEL	NAME	FIELD	WIDGET	OPERATIONS
✛ Title	title	Node module element		
✛ Tags	field_tags	Term reference	Autocomplete term widget (tagging)	edit delete
✛ Body	body	Long text and summary	Text area with a summary	edit delete
✛ Image	field_image	Image	Image	edit delete
✛ **Add new field**	field_	- Select a field type - ▼	- Select a widget - ▼	
Label	Field name (a-z, 0-9, _)	Type of data to store.	Form element to edit the data.	

Save

Figure 4-9. The form to add, edit, and order fields within a content type is accessed by navigating to **Structure ➤ Content types ➤ MANAGE FIELDS.**

Each field has a number of configuration settings depending on the field type. Some settings are used across all field types, such as **value is required**, **number of values**, and **help text**. Other settings are specific to the field type; for example, radio buttons require values for each button, while an image upload field requires a location for the images to be saved. Content fields integrate with language translations so that each field can be either translatable or language neutral (that is, not translatable). If a field is translatable, the content translation and locale modules are used to manage language translations, covered in Chapter 6.

Adding field types

Fields are added by navigating to **Structure ➤ Content types**, clicking the **MANAGE FIELDS** tab, and filling out the fields under **Add new field**. The label is the human-readable name of the field and can contain any variation of letters, numbers, spaces, and symbols. The field name is the machine-readable name and cannot contain symbols or spaces. You can use the machine-readable name when theming the site or dealing with PHP arrays, so keep it short and related to the label name. The field type and widget drop-downs, discussed in a moment, determine several options configured on the next page after clicking **Save**. The Label and widget can usually be changed, so proceed with caution.

If you are new to working with database-powered web sites, the number of fields and widgets may be overwhelming. At its core, there are three types of fields:

- Text fields and areas for entering user-submitted content
- Select lists, check boxes, and radio buttons for selecting per-configured values
- File and image uploads

Data are stored in tables in a database; each table consists of rows and columns. Every time a field is added to a Drupal site, a column is added to a table to store field values. When a node is submitted, a new row is created, and all fields, including the node title, body text, and added fields, are saved in the row (it's a little more complex than that, but you get the general idea of how it works). Database columns must be configured to hold specific data types, such as numbers, date and time, text, and more. Drupal configures this for you when you select the field type.

After selecting the field type and clicking **Save**, you are brought to a form containing all the required values for the field type (see Figure 4-10). These values cannot change after you click **Save field settings**. The remaining values on this form are specific to field types and discussed in the following sections.

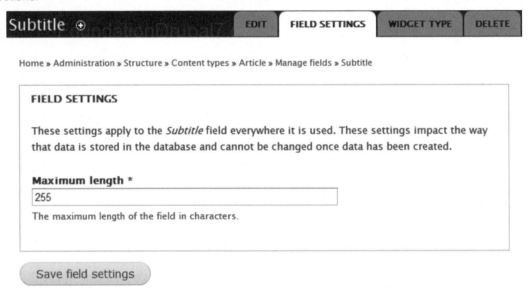

Figure 4-10. After selecting a **Text FIELD** type and a **WIDGET Text Field** type and then clicking **Save**, you are brought to a form containing all the required values for the field type.

The remaining section takes you through the various **FIELD** and **WIDGET** types available. Note that contributed modules may add additional fields to this page, such as name (`drupal.org/project/name`) and link (`drupal.org/project/link`).

Text fields and boxes

Text fields and text boxes are a very common method of collecting user-submitted data on forms. Text fields are selected based on the type of data a user will enter and how data should be stored and handled in the database. The **Text**, **Long text**, and **Long text and summary** field types are used when field values are non-numerical; that is, a user may type a sentence containing numbers, letters, and symbols. **Text** is a simple one-row field (see Figure 4-11), while **Long text** and **Long text and summary** are text boxes similar to a node's body field. When adding a text field or long text, you can optionally enter the maximum number of characters that can be entered in the field. You cannot change this after you create the field.

Text Field

Figure 4-11. A text field is a simple one-row field.

Drupal provides three types of fields for numbers (that is, 1234567890; no letters or symbols): integer, decimal, and float. Integer is used when the number does not have a decimal and falls between the range of −2,147,683,648 and 2,147,483,647. I do not recommend using the integer field for phone numbers; either use a text field or the phone module (www.drupal.org/project/phone) for this. Decimal and float are similar in that they both allow a user to enter a number with a decimal (optionally, users may enter a comma or space in place of the decimal if configured). Decimal allows up to 32 total digits, including the number of digits to the right of the decimal. The decimal is fixed, meaning it will always have the number of digits to the right of the decimal, regardless of what the user inputs. Float allows up to ten total digits, including the decimal. The decimal point floats, meaning the stored value will have between zero and nine digits to the right of the decimal depending on what the user enters. The difference between the two is accuracy vs. efficiency. Decimal is very accurate when the server is making computations but at a loss of efficiency (speed). Financial transactions most commonly use the decimal type. Float is very efficient for computations because there are fewer digits to compute. However, numbers may be round when making computations and can potentially result in inaccurate results. See Figure 4-12 for details.

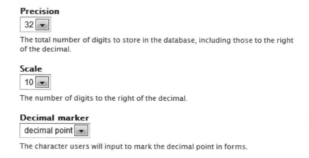

Precision

32

The total number of digits to store in the database, including those to the right of the decimal.

Scale

10

The number of digits to the right of the decimal.

Decimal marker

decimal point

The character users will input to mark the decimal point in forms.

Figure 4-12. A decimal field requires the total number of digits to save in the database (**Precision**) and the number of digits to the right of the decimal (**Scale**).

Taxonomy terms, discussed later in the chapter, provide another type of text field you can add to content types called **Term reference**. Taxonomy terms allow you to organize and categorize content with one or more words. The **Term reference** field provides a unique widget called **Autocomplete term widget (tagging)** that searches for and displays previously entered terms as you type so you can easily select a tag; see Figure 4-13 for details. It also allows you to easily enter taxonomy terms; otherwise, you must go to the **taxonomy term** section to add terms.

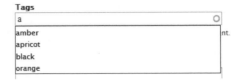

Figure 4-13. The **Term reference** widget **Autocomplete term widget (tagging)** searches for words matching text entered into the text field.

Drop-down lists, check boxes, and radio buttons

When adding a **FIELD**, a number of **WIDGET** options are available that configure how a user can enter content. Select lists, check boxes and radio buttons are used when a user must select a predetermined value; see Figure 4-14 for an example of each. Each field type can be configured so a user is forced to select a single value from the field or multiple values. A select list with **Number of values** set to **1** returns a drop-down field list, while values greater than **1** return a box-style selector. Similarly, check boxes are displayed when multiple values are allowed, and radio buttons are displayed when a single value is required. A single on/off or yes/no check box is also available.

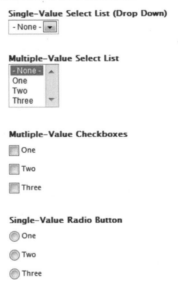

Figure 4-14. There are four different types of select lists, check boxes, and radio buttons depending on configuration settings. Note that this is a composite image displaying all the available configuration settings.

Select lists, check boxes, and radio buttons consist of a label and a key. The label is the value the user selects; in Figure 4-15, the words **One**, **Two**, and **Three** are labels. The key is the value saved in the database and is not shown to the user. The value saved can be either numeric or text but needs to be selected when creating the field and cannot change afterward. Generally speaking, saving the value as a number is preferred, although either will work fine.

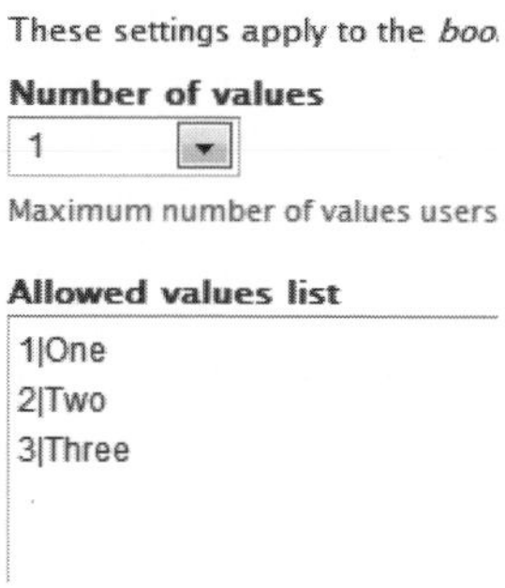

These settings apply to the *boo*

Number of values

1

Maximum number of values users

Allowed values list

1|One
2|Two
3|Three

Figure 4-15. Number of values determines the number of selections a user can make, while the **Allowed values list** contains the key (the value saved in database) and label (the value displayed to user).

There are three different field types you can select: boolean, list, and term reference. Boolean is the only field type with an on/off check box that saves one value if the user selects the check box and another value if the check box is not selected. You can also use a list to create a single check box, but it will save a value only if the check box is selected; if the check box is not selected, then a value is not saved. **List** (text) is the only field type allowing text to be saved in the database.

Files and images

Files and images can be added to content types allowing for multiple files and images to be associated with a single node. Files and images are uploaded into a folder on the server, and Drupal saves file information (file name, type, and so on) in a database table. This is important to note: files and images are not saved in a database. Rather, they are saved in a specific folder within the `files` directory. This is important because it can cause a lot of problems if you change the file directory after files have been uploaded. See Figure 4-16 for a file uploaded to a node with the **Description** and **Include file in display** fields enabled.

file

README.txt (4.92 KB) Remove

☑ Include file in display

Description

The description may be used as the label of the link to the file.

Figure 4-16. The **file** upload field with **Description** and **Include file in display** fields enabled

Configuring files and images are similar in many aspects. Both share the following settings:

- Allowed file extensions
- File directory
- Maximum upload size (note that maximum size also depends on settings in the `php.ini` config file)
- Upload destination

Any number of **Allowed file extensions** can be added and must be separated with a space or comma; do not include the leading dot (for example, use **pdf** rather than **.pdf**). See Figure 4-17 for an example. The **File directory** setting is the location on your server where uploaded files are stored. Depending on upload destination, a file or image may be uploaded to the private or public directory (see Chapter 2 for details). This brings up another good point: if you change a field from public files to private files (or vice versa), files do not automatically transfer from one folder to the other. This means you will need to move the files or images yourself, or users will receive an error message when they try to download. I recommend saving each file type or image field type in its own directory. Otherwise, files from multiple fields will live in the same directory and will cause havoc if you ever need to update a field or content type.

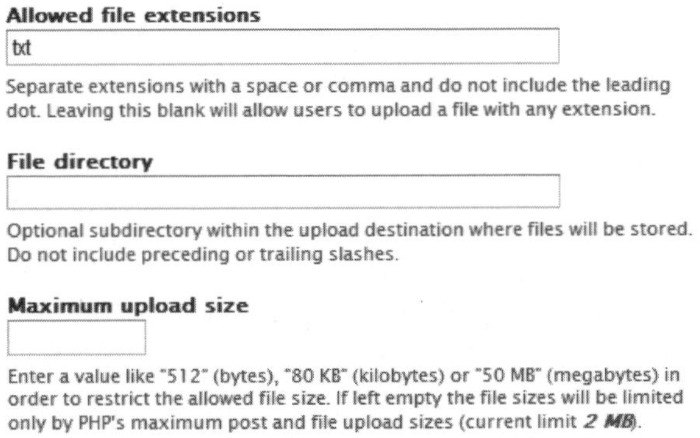

Allowed file extensions

txt

Separate extensions with a space or comma and do not include the leading dot. Leaving this blank will allow users to upload a file with any extension.

File directory

Optional subdirectory within the upload destination where files will be stored. Do not include preceding or trailing slashes.

Maximum upload size

Enter a value like "512" (bytes), "80 KB" (kilobytes) or "50 MB" (megabytes) in order to restrict the allowed file size. If left empty the file sizes will be limited only by PHP's maximum post and file upload sizes (current limit *2 MB*).

Figure 4-17. Shared settings between image and file field types

Maximum file size can be entered as bytes (such as 1024), kilobytes (such as 500KB), or megabytes (such as 10MB). You are also limited by the maximum upload size as configured in the php.ini file, which overrides any settings in Drupal. For example, you may set a 100MB maximum upload size in Drupal, but if php.ini is configured for a maximum 2MB upload, then you can upload only a 2MB file.

See Figure 4-18 for an example image upload with the **Alternate text** and **Title** fields enabled. The **Image** field type has several settings specific to images. The minimum and maximum image size can be set in pixels. If an image is larger than the maximum image resolution allowed, the file is resized to the entered width and height. Images smaller than minimum image resolution are not allowed for upload; see Figure 4-19 for details. Select **Enable *Alt* field** and **Enable *Title* field** to display the alternate text and title fields on the image upload field. Alternate text is displayed when the image is not available and is often used by search engines to categorize images. The title is displayed when the mouse pointer is placed over the image. The **Preview image style** setting determines how the image displays on the node creation form after it is uploaded.

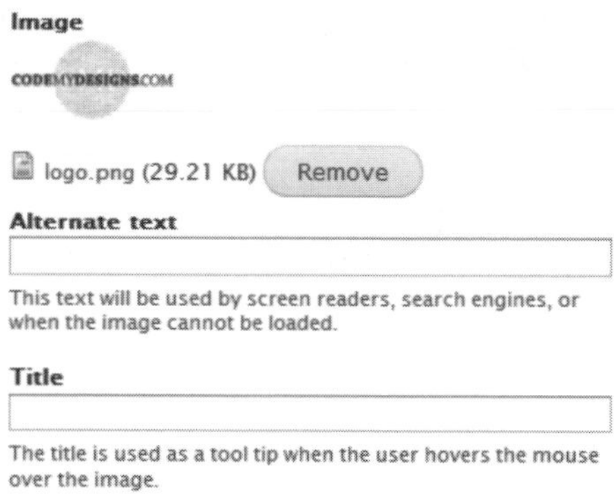

Image

CODEMYDESIGNS.COM

📄 logo.png (29.21 KB) (Remove)

Alternate text

[   ]

This text will be used by screen readers, search engines, or when the image cannot be loaded.

Title

[   ]

The title is used as a tool tip when the user hovers the mouse over the image.

Figure 4-18. The **Image** upload field with the **Alternate text** and **Title** fields enabled

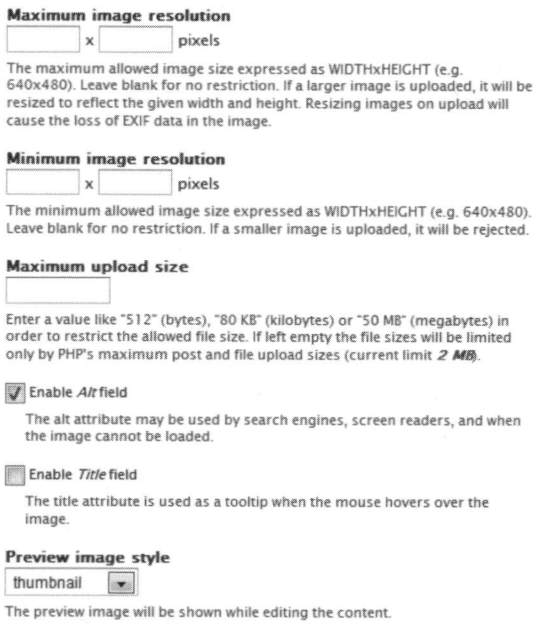

Maximum image resolution

[   ] x [   ] pixels

The maximum allowed image size expressed as WIDTHxHEIGHT (e.g. 640x480). Leave blank for no restriction. If a larger image is uploaded, it will be resized to reflect the given width and height. Resizing images on upload will cause the loss of EXIF data in the image.

Minimum image resolution

[   ] x [   ] pixels

The minimum allowed image size expressed as WIDTHxHEIGHT (e.g. 640x480). Leave blank for no restriction. If a smaller image is uploaded, it will be rejected.

Maximum upload size

[   ]

Enter a value like "512" (bytes), "80 KB" (kilobytes) or "50 MB" (megabytes) in order to restrict the allowed file size. If left empty the file sizes will be limited only by PHP's maximum post and file upload sizes (current limit *2 MB*).

☑ Enable *Alt* field
  The alt attribute may be used by search engines, screen readers, and when the image cannot be loaded.

☐ Enable *Title* field
  The title attribute is used as a tooltip when the mouse hovers over the image.

Preview image style

[thumbnail ▼]

The preview image will be shown while editing the content.

Figure 4-19. Configuration options for the **Image** field type

The file image type has several settings specific to files (see Figure 4-20). The **Enable *Description* field** option allows users to enter a description of the file that is then used as the name of the link to the file. **Enable *Display* field** allows users to choose whether a link to the file should be displayed, and **Files displayed by default** causes the **Include file in display** check box to be preselected (see Figure 4-16 for an example).

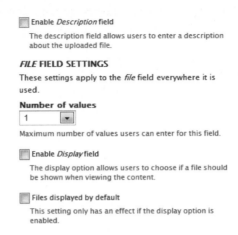

Enable *Description* field

The description field allows users to enter a description about the uploaded file.

FILE FIELD SETTINGS

These settings apply to the *file* field everywhere it is used.

Number of values

1 ▾

Maximum number of values users can enter for this field.

Enable *Display* field

The display option allows users to choose if a file should be shown when viewing the content.

Files displayed by default

This setting only has an effect if the display option is enabled.

Figure 4-20. Configuration options for the **file** field type

Managing the display of fields in multiple locations

You can view a node and node data in a number of locations across a site, including a full-page node view, list views, an RSS feed, and search results. When viewing a node in these different locations, you may want to format the node's fields to display according to the context of the location. For example, a node appearing in search page results should contain only a short, trimmed version of the node's body field. On the other hand, the full-page view of a node should contain all the information, including the full body text and any added fields. Alternatively, you may want to hide certain fields from showing in an RSS feed. The **Manage display** tab configures which fields are displayed and how they are formatted in various locations across your site.

Default view mode

The **Structure ➤ Content types ➤ MANAGE DISPLAY** form controls how a node's fields are output in a full page and teaser (see Figure 4-21). This form has a number of options and needs a little explanation to help understand how it works. Two buttons, **Default** and **Teaser**, appear in the upper right of the screen and switch between the different view modes you can configure. Default configures how fields are output across all view modes, including the full-page node view (for example, `example.com/node/1`). The teaser view is a shorter, alternative view of a node that typically displays the summary version of the body's text. For example, the summary view is displayed by default on the site's default homepage with a **Read More** link. Clicking the **CUSTOM DISPLAY SETTINGS** link opens a fieldset with several check boxes allowing you to customize additional view modes. Selecting a check box and clicking **Save** results in the view mode's button appearing in the upper-right corner of the form.

Figure 4-21. The form to adjust the various view modes of a node includes any fields added to the content type, such as the image field added to this content type.

Every field added to the content type is listed in the basic view. Each field has two values:

- **LABEL**, the human-readable name of the field, such as body or image
- **FORMAT**, the style in which the field is output

A **LABEL** will always have three basic options: **Hidden**, **Inline**, and **Above**. An **Inline** label is placed to the left of the field value, while an **Above** label is placed immediately above the field value, as shown in Figure 4-22. The **FORMAT** drop-down contains a number of options depending on the type of field; a text area such as the body has different formatting options than a check box or an image. The body has five available options:

- Default
- Plain text, which removes all HTML from the body
- Trimmed, a short version of the body
- Summary or trimmed, which displays the summary version if entered by user
- Hidden, which hides the field from view

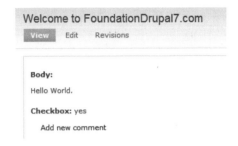

Figure 4-22. In this full-page view, the body label is placed above the body content while the check box label is placed inline.

RSS view mode

Drupal's default RSS feed is available at `http://example.com/rss.xml`. You need to select the **RSS** check box underneath the **CUSTOM DISPLAY SETTINGS** fieldset for the **RSS** button to appear at the top right of the default view mode form, as shown in Figure 4-23. All fields are listed and have options to configure both the label and the format. As a note, by default all fields are hidden from display.

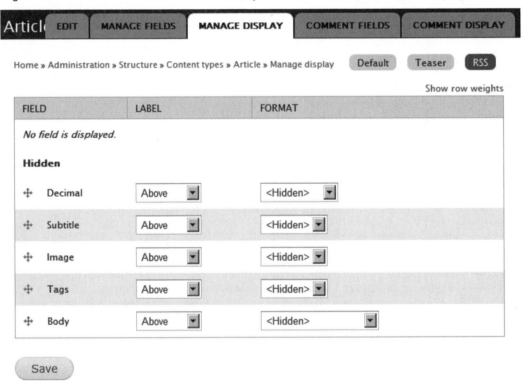

Figure 4-23. The form to edit the output of RSS feeds has similar configuration options as the basic view.

Additional configuration settings for the RSS feed are available at **Configuration ➤ RSS publishing**. This page allows you to place a description of your web site at the top of the feed and determine the number of nodes that appear in the feed. There is also a setting called **Feed content**, which allows you to switch the output between titles only, titles plus teaser, and full text. I do not recommend using this; you can attain the same results by configuring the RSS view from the **MANAGE DISPLAY** form.

Search index and search result view modes

Drupal has a built-in search module that is used to search content. When a node is created, Drupal indexes content from that node. That is, it determines and scores the most relevant key words and phrases in the content and saves them in a table in the database. The **Search index** view mode controls which fields are indexed, while the **Search results** form controls how which fields appear in search results.

You need to select the **Search index** or **Search result** check box underneath the **CUSTOM DISPLAY SETTINGS** fieldset for the search buttons to appear at the top right of the default view mode form, as shown in Figure 4-24. The default settings for search indexing and search results are usually adequate for most people's needs, although you may want to make adjustments if you have added additional fields. For example, the value entered in a check box may not be relevant to a user's search and can be hidden from indexing. Note that all search fields are hidden by default when either search view node is enabled.

> ***Search indexing*** *refers to how Drupal saves and retrieves data during search queries. Refer to* `http://drupal.org/handbook/modules/search` *for a description of how search indexing works.*

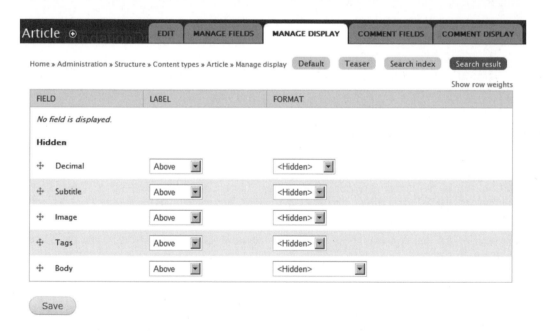

Figure 4-24. The **Search result** and **Search index** view modes configures how Drupal indexes content and displays search results.

Adding comment fields and controlling how they display

The cool thing about Drupal 7 is the ability to add fields to almost any piece of content, including comments. The process to add fields and adjust display settings on comment fields are the same as the **MANAGE FIELDS** and **MANAGE DISPLAY** forms; see Figure 4-25 for the form to add comment fields.

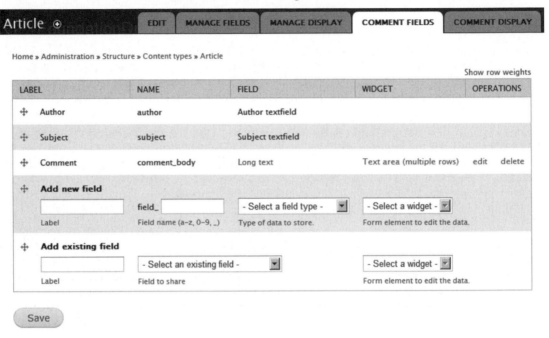

Figure 4-25. The **COMMENT FIELDS** form configures how Drupal indexes content and displays search results.

Designing the taxonomy of your site

In science, **taxonomy** refers to the classification of plants and animals based on relationships. Drupal uses this same principle to relate, organize, and display content through vocabularies and vocabulary terms. For example, the vocabulary *automobiles* might have *Chevrolet*, *Ford*, *Nissan*, and *Toyota* as terms. Terms can be nested as well so that *Explorer* and *Taurus* would be nested under *Ford*, while *Camry* and *4Runner* would be nested under *Toyota*.

Drupal organizes and displays content based on the relationships between terms. Using the automobile vocabulary as an example, say a web site has ten nodes tagged as a Ford Explorer and ten as a Ford Taurus. If a user navigates to the Ford Taurus taxonomy URL, Drupal will create and display a list of all ten Taurus instances. If a user navigates to the Ford taxonomy URL, then Drupal displays a list of 20 automobiles. Remember how I related a Ford Explorer to a Toyota 4Runner? If a user navigates to the Ford Explorer URL, then Drupal displays both Explorers and 4Runners. Navigate to **Structure ➤ Taxonomy** to view and edit vocabularies and vocabulary terms (see Figure 4-26).

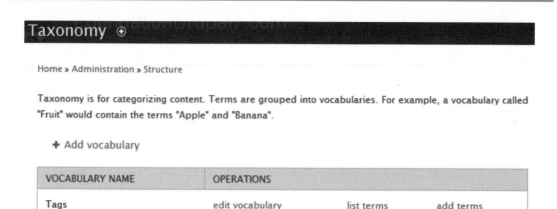

Figure 4-26. Navigate to **Structure ➤ Taxonomy** to view and edit vocabularies and vocabulary terms.

Adding a vocabulary

Vocabularies are added by navigating to **Structure ➤ Taxonomy** and clicking the **Add vocabulary** link, as shown in Figure 4-27. Every vocabulary term requires a human-readable name that Drupal converts into a machine name. Because the machine name is sometimes used when theming, I recommend keeping it to less than eight characters. The description is used by modules.

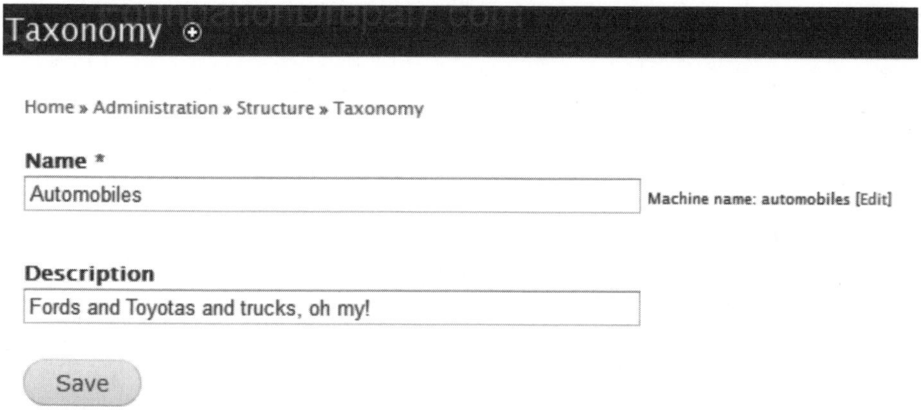

Figure 4-27. A view of the form to add a vocabulary, available at **Structure ➤ Taxonomy** and by clicking the **Add Vocabulary** link.

Adding terms

Terms are added to a specific vocabulary by navigating to **Structure ➤ Taxonomy** page and selecting the **Add terms** link, as shown in Figure 4-28. Terms can also be added in the content creation form if the vocabulary has been configured with tags, although only the term name can be added.

All terms contain a unique ID called the **term ID**, or tid for short. Drupal uses the term ID to assign a system path to a term. For example, navigate to `http://example.com/taxonomy/term/1` to view all content associated with term 1. A URL alias can be used to access the term content in place of the system URL. Alternatively, the module PathAuto can create path aliases automatically, discussed in Chapter 7. This is ideal, for example, when users add vocabulary terms using the content creation form and do not have the ability to create URL aliases.

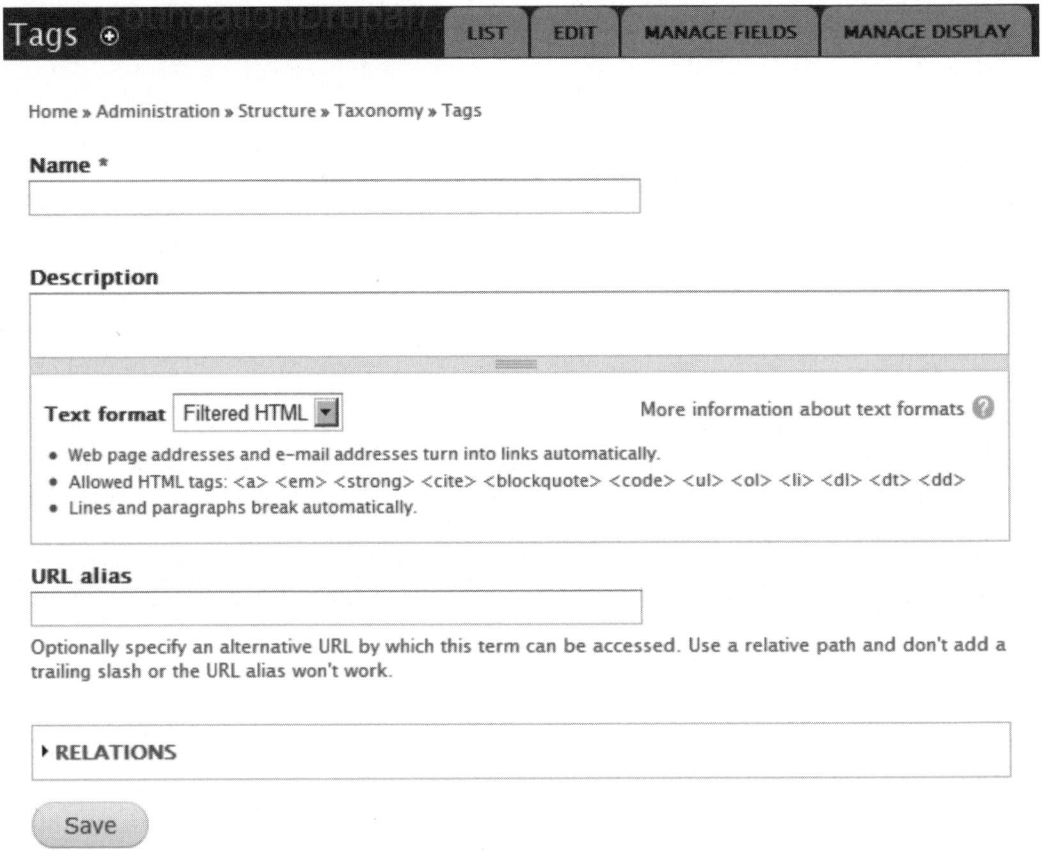

Figure 4-28. The form to add terms to a vocabulary, accessed at **Structure ➤ Taxonomy** and clicking the **Add terms** link.

Clicking **RELATIONS** at the bottom of the form opens a number of additional settings. The **Parent terms** box allows you to nest one term under another, as shown in Figure 4-29. As described earlier, all children terms nested under a parent term are related. If a user navigates to the parent term, all content tagged with the children terms are displayed.

The **Weight** field controls the order in which terms are displayed in the content creation form. The easiest way to manage the order of fields is to use the drag-and-drop feature available by navigating to **Structure ➤ Taxonomy** and selecting the **List** link. Keeping the weight at zero sorts the list of terms alphabetically.

Figure 4-29. Click the **Relations** link on the add terms form to view additional options.

Managing terms

Navigate to **Structure ➤ Taxonomy** and select **List** to view and manage all terms associated with a vocabulary, as shown in Figure 4-30. The order of vocabulary terms are managed via drag and drop.

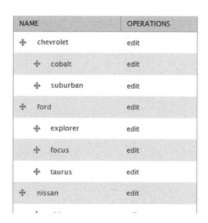

Figure 4-30. Access the page to manage links by navigating to **Structure ➤ Taxonomy** and selecting the **List** link.

Summary

We started off the chapter discussing content types and how they're used to organize and interact with nodes. A content type is responsible for a node's data fields; you first add fields to a content type, which are then entered when creating a node. Many modules also hook in to a content type, giving the node advanced functionality. One module we briefly discussed was the Ubercart module, which turns a node into a product that can be purchased and supplies the back end for managing both product nodes and product purchases.

We then discussed fields that can be added to content types. There are three basic types of fields:

- Text fields and areas for entering user-submitted content
- Select lists, check boxes, and radio buttons for selecting preconfigured values
- File and image uploads

We also discussed how to adjust field display settings when fields are output with a node, including the node view, RSS feed, and search results.

We closed by talking about taxonomy terms and the ability to tag content with categories. A taxonomy, also called a **vocabulary**, is a mechanism for categorizing content. It is also a field that can be added to both content and comments.

Chapter 5

People, Roles, and Permissions

In this chapter, I review the concepts of people, roles, and permissions and how you can customize the way your site interacts with the people who use it. People are added to your site and are assigned one or more roles, giving them permission to access various features such as commenting or creating a web page. I discuss several topics, such as how to add a user, how to create a role, and how to change permissions. I cover the many different sections and screens available in Drupal to configure your site, including the account settings page and the IP address blocking page. By the end of this chapter, you will know how to change system-generated e-mails, how to change who can register for an account, how to change what happens when people cancel their account, and more. Let's go!

An overview

A Drupal web site allows people to log in to the site and perform various tasks depending on their role and the permissions assigned to that role. Every user has a unique ID, called the **user ID** (or **uid** for short), starting at the number 1 (but note that user #1 is a special user, which I'll discuss shortly). Users have a corresponding account page accessed through a system-generated URL at http://example.com/user/uid; see Figure 5-1 for a screenshot of this page. You can easily navigate to this page by clicking your user name in the administration toolbar, located next to the **Log out** link, or by navigating to example.com/user. Users can update their own information from this page, and they may or may not access other user account pages depending on the permissions assigned to them.

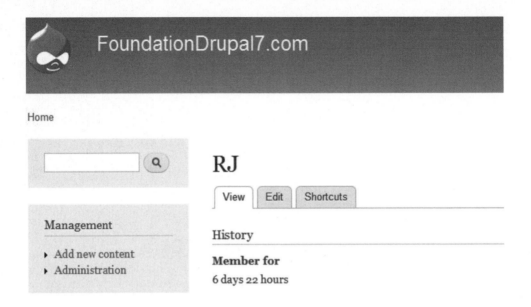

Figure 5-1. Your account page is accessed by navigating to `http://example.com/user` or by clicking your user name in the administration toolbar.

Drupal manages users in much the same way as nodes. Three pieces of information are required to create a user account: a user name, an e-mail address, and a password. Additional fields can be added to user accounts by navigating to **Configuration ➤ Account** settings and clicking the **MANAGE FIELDS** and **MANAGE DISPLAY** tabs, following the process described in Chapter 4. This means, for example, you can require people to enter contact information, text boxes, and more after signing up for an account on your site. Note that these fields do *not* appear on the user registration page; they appear only when a user edits their account settings. You will need to use the core profile module to add fields to the user registration form, discussed in Chapter 6.

Drupal allows you to assign roles and permissions to people who visit and interact with your web site. A **role** is a set of permissions assigned to a user, and **permissions** determine what a user can and cannot do on your web site. For example, you may want to give users who register for an account the permission to post comments. The default Drupal web site has three roles: anonymous, authenticated, and administrator (of course you can add more), with varying permissions assigned to each group of users. See Figure 5-2 for a partial view of the form used to add or remove permissions, accessed by navigating to **People** and clicking the **PERMISSIONS** tab. An anonymous user is someone who is not logged in to the site and has limited permissions. On most web sites, for example, an anonymous user does not have the permission to post comments. All users who log in to the site are considered authenticated; that is, they have an account on the web site and have correctly entered their user name and password. Authenticated users are usually given additional permissions, such as the ability to post content or comments. The administrator is a special role that has full access to edit and update the site.

A couple of things should be noted about the administrator role. Essentially administrators are superusers given permission to do anything and everything on a site. As discussed later in this chapter in the "Customizing account settings" section, you can change this "superadmin" role to any role. This is a high-level role and should be given only to trusted and technically literate users.

PERMISSION	ANONYMOUS USER	AUTHENTICATED USER	ADMINISTRATOR
Block			
Administer blocks	☐	☐	☑
Comment			
Administer comments and comment settings	☐	☐	☑
View comments	☐	☑	☑
Post comments with approval	☐	☑	☑
Post comments without approval	☐	☑	☑
Edit own comments	☐	☐	☑

Figure 5-2. A partial view of the page to add or remove permissions to roles, available by navigating to **People** and clicking the **PERMISSIONS** tab

Drupal recognizes the first user as a special user, sometimes called the **administrator**. The first user is the person who created the web site and has a user ID of 1. This user has access to all administrative sections and configuration settings. The default Drupal installation also has a special role called administrator, discussed earlier. Users assigned to the administrator role are usually given access to all administrative sections and configuration settings.

The user management page, available by clicking the **People** link in the administration toolbar, is similar to the content management page (see Figure 5-3). The list of users can be filtered by a number of fields (**role**, **permission**, and **status**, all discussed in the following sections), and mass updates can be performed on selected users.

Figure 5-3. List of all users available by clicking **People** in the administration toolbar

How to add people

People have the ability to register for accounts themselves by navigating to /user/register; disabling this is discussed later in the next section. To manually add a user, navigate to **People ➤ Add user** (see Figure 5-4). Three fields are required when adding a user: **Username**, **E-mail address**, and **Password**. The user name and e-mail address must be unique and are not case sensitive. When entering the user's password, Drupal will provide you with a number of hints to make the password stronger. The **status** field allows you to block and unblock a user. You will probably never create a blocked user, but because the **Add user** form is the same as the **Edit user** form, you may use this field when editing a user. Roles are added manually when creating a user. The default Drupal installation has three roles (anonymous, authenticated, and administrator), and any additional roles will appear here as well. Finally, selecting the **Notify user of new account** check box will send the user an e-mail. Customizing this e-mail is discussed in the next section.

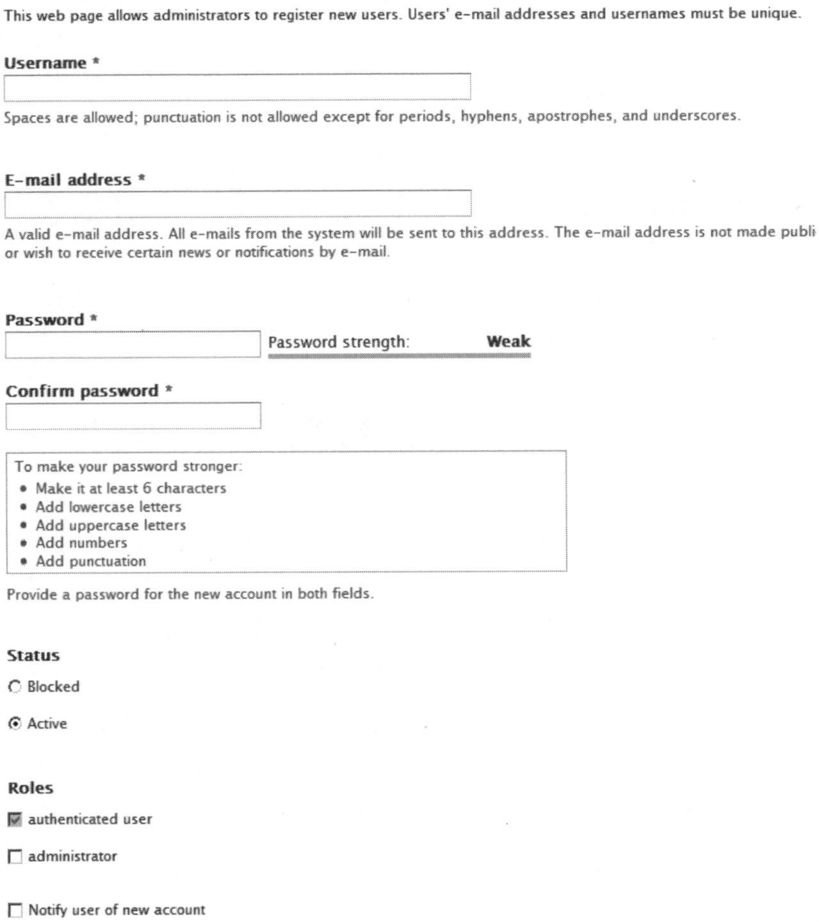

This web page allows administrators to register new users. Users' e-mail addresses and usernames must be unique.

Username *

Spaces are allowed; punctuation is not allowed except for periods, hyphens, apostrophes, and underscores.

E-mail address *

A valid e-mail address. All e-mails from the system will be sent to this address. The e-mail address is not made publi
or wish to receive certain news or notifications by e-mail.

Password *

Password strength: **Weak**

Confirm password *

To make your password stronger:
- Make it at least 6 characters
- Add lowercase letters
- Add uppercase letters
- Add numbers
- Add punctuation

Provide a password for the new account in both fields.

Status

○ Blocked

◉ Active

Roles

☑ authenticated user

☐ administrator

☐ Notify user of new account

Figure 5-4. You can access the form to add people to your site by navigating to **People** and selecting the **Add user** link.

Customizing account settings

You can customize a number of settings for people, including the registration process, e-mail text, user pictures, and more. Navigate to **Configuration ➤ Account settings** to view the account settings page. This form is also used to add fields to the user edit form; see Chapter 4 to learn how to add, manage, and display fields.

Anonymous users and administrator role

The **ANONYMOUS USERS** field determines the name given to users not logged in to the site (see Figure 5-5). Drupal uses this value in a number of places, such as database logs or the "submitted by" label on a post if anonymous users have permission to post content. I rarely change this unless a client requests it. By default Drupal gives the name **anonymous** to anonymous users. I should point out that the name given to anonymous users does not change the name of the anonymous users role, and vice versa.

The **ADMINISTRATOR ROLE** field is a special setting for administrators of the site. If a role is selected, then the selected role is automatically assigned new permissions whenever a module is enabled. This is useful if you want a role to have full access to administrate a site, meaning that every permission check box is selected. This is discussed in further depth later in this chapter.

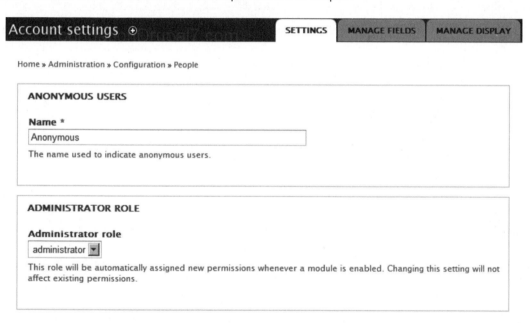

Figure 5-5. The account settings form is accessed at **Configuration ➤ Account settings**.

Registration and cancellation

REGISTRATION AND CANCELLATION controls how people sign up for accounts and what happens when an account is deleted. The fields under **Who can register accounts?** determines how new users are added to the site (see Figure 5-6). Selecting **Visitors** or **Visitors, but administrator approval is**

required allows users to register for the site. If **Administrators only** is selected, only users assigned to the administrator role can create accounts. You will probably select this if you are creating a web site that is managed by a few people, such as a personal web site or an online brochure. Selecting this also removes the **Create New Account** link on the user login form. **Visitors, but administrator approval is required** is selected by default, which means that anyone can create an account. If creating an account requires administrator approval, an e-mail is sent to all users assigned to the administrator role. The user's account is blocked, and a site administrator must edit the user's account and activate the account. When the account is activated, Drupal can be configured to send the user an e-mail with login information.

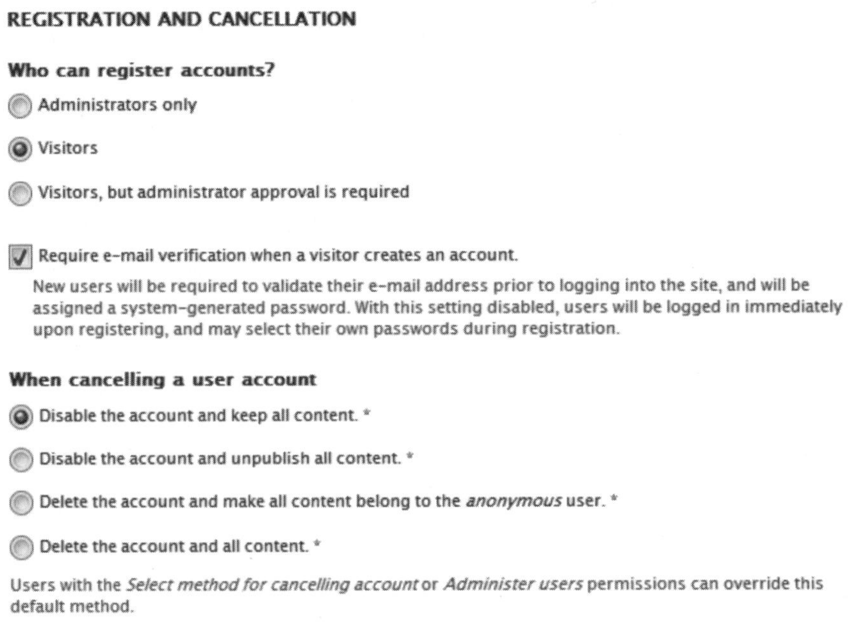

REGISTRATION AND CANCELLATION

Who can register accounts?

◯ Administrators only

◉ Visitors

◯ Visitors, but administrator approval is required

☑ Require e-mail verification when a visitor creates an account.
New users will be required to validate their e-mail address prior to logging into the site, and will be assigned a system-generated password. With this setting disabled, users will be logged in immediately upon registering, and may select their own passwords during registration.

When cancelling a user account

◉ Disable the account and keep all content. *

◯ Disable the account and unpublish all content. *

◯ Delete the account and make all content belong to the *anonymous* user. *

◯ Delete the account and all content. *

Users with the *Select method for cancelling account* or *Administer users* permissions can override this default method.

Figure 5-6. Registration and cancellation options are accessed at **Configuration ➤ Account settings**.

Selecting **Require e-mail verification...** configures Drupal to send e-mails to users to verify their e-mail address. The e-mail contains login information, including a system-generated password. Additionally, selecting this field removes the **Password** field from the account registration page. See the user registration form in Figure 5-7 with **Require e-mail verification...** disabled.

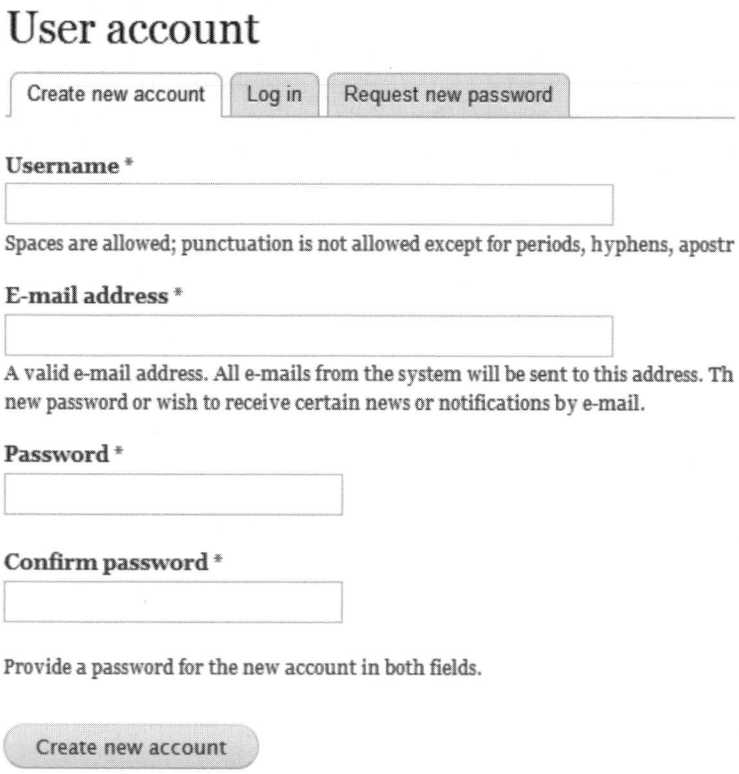

User account

| Create new account | Log in | Request new password |

Username *

Spaces are allowed; punctuation is not allowed except for periods, hyphens, apostr

E-mail address *

A valid e-mail address. All e-mails from the system will be sent to this address. Th
new password or wish to receive certain news or notifications by e-mail.

Password *

Confirm password *

Provide a password for the new account in both fields.

Create new account

Figure 5-7. The user registration form is accessed at `http://example.com/user/register`. Requiring e-mail verification removes the password from this form and e-mails a system-generated password to the user.

You can add additional fields to the registration form by using the profile module, discussed in the next chapter.

User accounts are deleted by clicking the **People** link, selecting the user(s) you want to delete, and selecting **Cancel the selected user accounts** from the **UPDATE OPTIONS** drop-down. Alternatively, you can give users the permission to cancel their own user account, meaning they can edit their account from their account page and delete it. Drupal provides a number of options if an account is cancelled, as shown in Figure 5-6. A disabled account means the account is blocked and can be activated by an admin at a future point. Additionally, the user's page cannot be accessed. Deleting an account permanently removes it from the site. If the option **Disable the account and keep all content** is selected, then content will remain live on the site with the user's name as the author; this is the default Drupal setting. **Disable the account and unpublish all content** should be used only if unpublishing the user's content will not disrupt other user's content. For example, unpublishing a blog post with comments from other users will remove those comments as well. **Delete the account and keep all content** is the default Drupal setting and what you will probably use if your web site allows users to register for accounts. Finally, **Delete the account and all content** deletes all content, including comments users have posted.

Personalization

You can allow users to personalize their accounts with either a signature or a picture (see Figure 5-8). Signatures are small snippets of text added to the end of comments. They can only contain text and must have 255 characters or less. When the **Enable signatures** check box is selected, a text box appears on the edit user page where users can add a signature. Some modules place this signature at the end of content, such as in forums or comments.

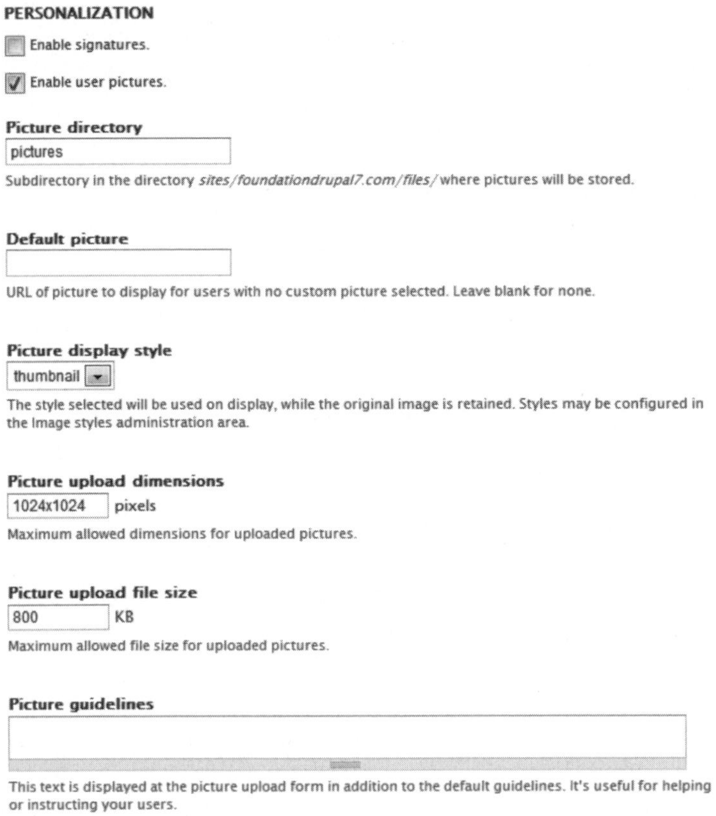

PERSONALIZATION

☐ Enable signatures.

☑ Enable user pictures.

Picture directory

| pictures |

Subdirectory in the directory *sites/foundationdrupal7.com/files/* where pictures will be stored.

Default picture

| |

URL of picture to display for users with no custom picture selected. Leave blank for none.

Picture display style

| thumbnail ▾ |

The style selected will be used on display, while the original image is retained. Styles may be configured in the Image styles administration area.

Picture upload dimensions

| 1024x1024 | pixels

Maximum allowed dimensions for uploaded pictures.

Picture upload file size

| 800 | KB

Maximum allowed file size for uploaded pictures.

Picture guidelines

| |

This text is displayed at the picture upload form in addition to the default guidelines. It's useful for helping or instructing your users.

Figure 5-8. Accounts can be personalized with signatures or pictures by navigating to **Configuration ➤ Account settings**.

User pictures are enabled by default. All images are saved in the **Picture directory**, which Drupal will automatically create if the directory does not exist (the file directory is discussed in detail in Chapter 2). The **Picture display style** determines the dimensions Drupal resizes the image, which by default is 85 pixels by 85 pixels; picture display styles are discussed in further detail in Chapter 4. You will need to update the theme if you use a larger picture. The **Picture upload dimensions** and **Picture upload file size** settings are the maximum file size for the image; leaving these blank allows for an unlimited dimensions and/or size. **Picture guidelines** are displayed on the user edit form underneath the upload picture field, as shown in Figure 5-9.

Figure 5-9. When **Enable signatures** and **Enable pictures** are enabled, users can upload pictures and add signatures to their account.

E-mails

Drupal sends out a number of emails during the account registration and cancellation process. The text of each email is customizable and allows for a number of variables to be inserted into both the subject and body. See Tables 5-1 and 5-2 for more information.

Table 5-1. Variables for e-mails sent during the account registration and cancellation process

Variable	Description
[site:name]	The name of the web site as defined at **Configuration ➤ Site Information**
[site:url]	A link to the web site, such as http://foundationdrupal7.com
[site:login-url]	A link to log in to the web site, such as http://foundationdrupal7.com/user
[user:name]	The name of the user as seen on the user account page
[user:mail]	The e-mail address of the user
[user:edit-url]	The link to edit the user's account

Variable	Description
`[user:one-time-login-url]`	The link to log in and reset the user's password
`[user:cancel-url]`	The link to cancel the user's account

Table 5-2. E-mails sent during the account registration and cancellation process

E-mail	Description
Welcome (new user created by administrator)	Sent to users when an administrator creates an account and selects **Notify user of new account**.
Welcome (awaiting approval)	Sent to users when they create a new account and administrator approval is required.
Welcome (no approval required)	Sent to users when they create a new account and administrator approval is not required.
Account activation	Sent to users when an administrator changes the status of an account from blocked to active. This e-mail is enabled by default and can be disabled by deselecting **Notify user when account is activated**.
Account blocked	Sent to users when an administrator changes the status of an account from active to blocked. This e-mail is disabled by default and can be enabled by selecting **Notify user when account is blocked**.
Account cancellation confirmation	Sent to users when they cancel their account. Users must follow the **[user:cancel-url]** link.
Account canceled	Sent to users when their accounts are canceled. This e-mail is disabled by default and can be enabled by selecting **Notify user when account is canceled.**
Password recovery	Sent to users who have forgotten their password and request a new one.

Roles and permissions

Roles are added by navigating to **People**, selecting the **PERMISSIONS** tab, and then selecting the **Roles** link in the upper-right corner. Creating a new role is a simple process of entering a human-readable name and clicking **Add role** (see Figure 5-10). You can click the **edit permissions** link to update permissions for that specific role.

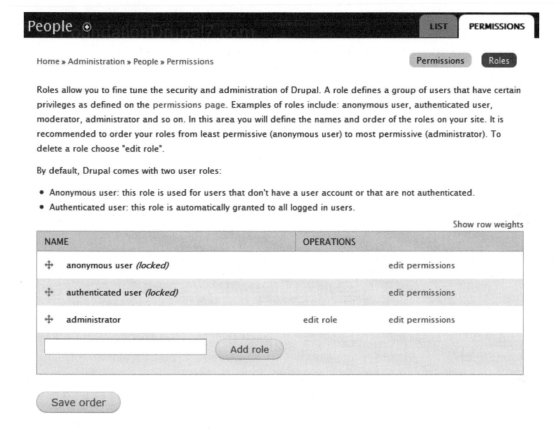

Figure 5-10. Roles are added by navigating to **People**, selecting the **PERMISSIONS** tab, and then clicking the **Roles** link in the upper-right corner.

You can also select **People** and click the **PERMISSIONS** tab to view the permissions of all roles side by side (see Figure 5-11). I typically use this page when configuring permissions because it allows me to easily compare permissions of roles to each other.

People ⊕   LIST   PERMISSIONS

Home » Administration » People   Permissions   Roles

Permissions let you control what users can do and see on your site. You can define a specific set of permissions for each role. (See the Roles page to create a role). Two important roles to consider are Authenticated Users and Administrators. Any permissions granted to the Authenticated Users role will be given to any user who can log into your site. You can make any role the Administrator role for the site, meaning this will be granted all new permissions automatically. You can do this on the User Settings page. You should be careful to ensure that only trusted users are given this access and level of control of your site.

Hide descriptions

PERMISSION	ANONYMOUS USER	AUTHENTICATED USER	ADMINISTRATOR
Block			
Administer blocks	☐	☐	☑
Comment			
Administer comments and comment settings	☐	☐	☑
View comments	☑	☑	☑

Figure 5-11. Permissions for all roles are configured by navigating to **People** and selecting the **PERMISSIONS** tab.

A module usually adds one or more permissions to this page. For example, the comment module adds five permissions: administer comments and comment settings, view comments, post comments with approval, post comments without approval, and edit own comments. When enabling a module, you will want to visit this page to check whether permissions need to be assigned to a role.

Every user is automatically assigned to the authenticated user role. Additional roles are manually assigned and removed either by editing a user's individual account or by clicking **People** in the administration toolbar using the mass update option.

IP address blocking

Drupal provides you with a mechanism to block IP addresses. IP addresses are blocked from the site before modules are loaded, which means users do not see any site content or graphics (see Figure 5-12). Blocked IP addresses are managed by navigating to **Configuration and Modules ➤ IP address blocking.** Drupal will not let you ban your own IP address.

Sorry, 96.245.132.65 has been banned.

Figure 5-12. Users from banned IP addresses are presented with a simple message.

Blocking IP addresses may or may not have the desired effect. Internet service providers (ISPs) frequently use proxy servers so that all users on their network appear to come from a single IP address. In an attempt to block a single spammer from accessing your site, you could inadvertently block hundreds or even thousands of people. Additionally, spammers usually mask their IP address and frequently change it. I do not recommend blocking IP addresses to stop spammers from accessing your site. Drupal.org has a number of contributed modules to protect against spam, such as the captcha and mollom modules.

Summary

This chapter reviewed the fundamental concepts of people, roles, and permissions in Drupal. People are added to a Drupal site, either by an administrator or by the people themselves, and are assigned to a role that has a number of permissions. These permissions control how people interact with the site, allowing them to do things such as post comments or create web pages. Drupal has three roles by default, to which more can be added: anonymous, authenticated, and administrator. Roles allow you to assign a certain subset of permissions to a user, such as the ability for one user to host a blog and another user to moderate forums. Administrators are given all permissions, unless disabled, allowing them full access to the site. The person who creates the site is a special user who always has full access to the site.

We reviewed the many different sections and screens for configuring people, roles, and permissions, including the add user page, account settings page, permissions page, and IP address blocking page. We discussed how to change system-generated e-mails, how to add roles, how to change who can register for an account, what happens when people cancel their account, and more.

Chapter 6

Enabling and Configuring Core Modules

Drupal comes with a number of core modules automatically included with Drupal 7.x. Many of these modules were automatically enabled when you installed Drupal if you selected the standard Drupal installation profile (which you probably did, if you followed the instructions in Chapter 2). As such, many of these modules have already been covered in depth in previous chapters; the block and comment modules are two such examples. But what happens if you need to enable and configure another module not previously covered or enabled by default?

The goal of this chapter is to cover the process of enabling and configuring core modules included with Drupal but not enabled by the standard Drupal installation. I go through the entire list of modules, explaining how the module works, where to configure the module, and what types of settings you will need to update. Some of the modules I cover include blog, book, contact, forum, locale, and more. Before you start this chapter, you should be familiar with Drupal's administrative section and how content types and nodes work.

Enabling a module

Enabling a module is fantastically easy. Click the **Modules** link in the administration toolbar to view the list of modules, as shown in Figure 6-1. As a note, if you've installed any contrib modules, they will appear on this page as well. Select the check box next to the module you need to enable, scroll to the bottom of the screen, click **Save configuration**, and you're done! After a module is enabled, a system message appears at the top of the screen that says **The configuration options have been saved,** and several links (**help**, **permission**, and **configure**) appear next to the module.

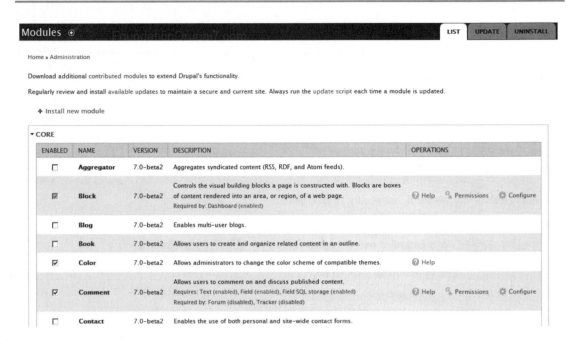

Figure 6-1. Enable modules by clicking the **Modules** link in the administration toolbar.

Knowing when to enable modules is the difficult part, and there is no right or wrong answer. Some people prefer to enable modules all at once, while others (like me) tend to enable modules as they're needed. The general consensus is that it's best not to enable a module if you don't need it. For example, if you enable the forum module and don't use it, users can still access the forum if they have permission. Additionally, modules usually add CSS files, hook calls, and templates, all of which may reduce system performance. My recommendation is to always go through the module list and disable modules you do not use; this is covered in depth in Chapter 10.

Modules frequently provide blocks after they are enabled; navigate to **Structure ➤ Blocks** to organize and configure the various blocks. Chapter 3 discussed the block administration form in detail.

Most modules require you to give permission to users to view or use the module or related functionality. If you are logged in as the superadmin (user #1), by default you have access to all modules, which means the pages you can access may not be accessible by anonymous or authenticated users. My recommendation is to use the devel module (http://drupal.org/project/devel). The devel module is a development and theming tool that I highly recommend enabling when building a site. One of the tools it provides is a **Switch user** block, which allows you to log in as any registered user by clicking their name, as shown in Figure 6-2. This allows you to view the site as an anonymous or authenticated user and can often help when configuring modules. If you can see a page, block, or feature while logged in as the superadmin but not as other users, there's a significant chance the problem lies with module permissions.

Figure 6-2. The devel module provides a **Switch user** block to quickly log in and interact with the site as other users with their role and permissions. Rock on!

Aggregator

The feed aggregator module pulls RSS, RDF, and Atom feeds from other web sites and displays feed content on either a full-page or block view. You will probably use this module if you want to add a **Recent news** block to your site that pulls news from another site. Drupal creates both multiple full-page views and blocks for each feed; you can also categorize and display multiple feeds on a full-page or block. Drupal filters feeds for HTML tags you specify, so for example you could strip all <a> links from RSS feeds and theme as you want.

The aggregator module is configured by navigating to **Configuration ➤ Feed aggregator**. This page displays all feeds, feed categories, and links to each. Start first at the **SETTINGS** tab to adjust settings that apply across all feeds, as shown in Figure 6-3 (you can also access this same page by clicking the **Configure** link next to the module name after the module has been enabled).

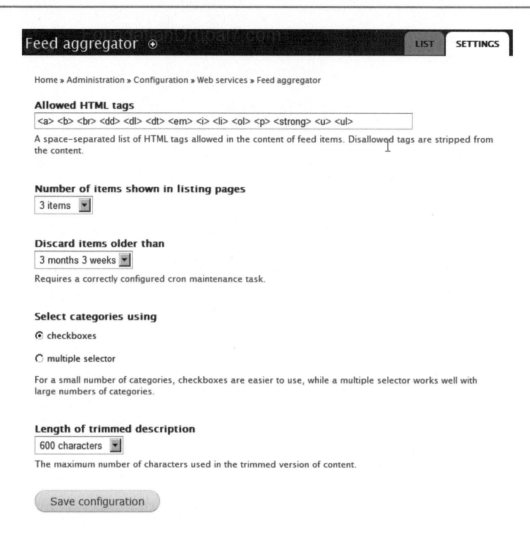

Figure 6-3. Configure the aggregator module by navigating to **Configuration ➤ Feed aggregator ➤ SETTINGS**.

Number of items show in listing pages controls the number of feed items on the `http://example.com/aggregator/sources` and `http://example.com/aggregator/categories` pages. If cron is properly configured, you can use **Discard items older than** to automatically delete feed items older than a certain time. The **Select categories using** option determines how you sort feeds on a category page. If a category page displays feeds from multiple sources, users can select which feeds they want displayed. The **checkboxes** option allows users to select or deselect the displayed feeds and is good for a small number of feeds. The **multiple selector** option allows users to type in the names of feeds, which causes the text box to automatically prefill with available lists of feeds.

After you have added adjusted settings, you can now add a feed or a feed category, if required, as shown in Figure 6-4. Navigate to **Configuration ➤ Feed aggregator**, and select **Add feed**, as shown in Figure 6-5.

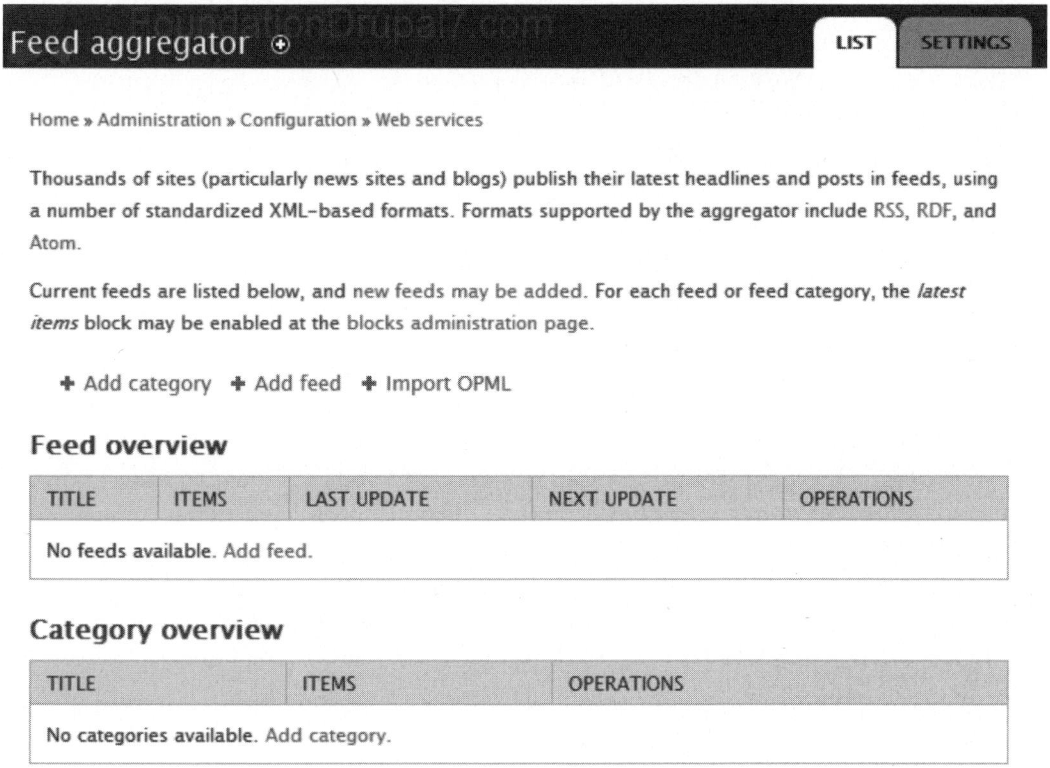

Feed aggregator ⊕

LIST   SETTINGS

Home » Administration » Configuration » Web services

Thousands of sites (particularly news sites and blogs) publish their latest headlines and posts in feeds, using a number of standardized XML–based formats. Formats supported by the aggregator include RSS, RDF, and Atom.

Current feeds are listed below, and new feeds may be added. For each feed or feed category, the *latest items* block may be enabled at the blocks administration page.

✛ Add category   ✛ Add feed   ✛ Import OPML

Feed overview

TITLE	ITEMS	LAST UPDATE	NEXT UPDATE	OPERATIONS
No feeds available. Add feed.				

Category overview

TITLE	ITEMS	OPERATIONS
No categories available. Add category.		

Figure 6-4. Create new feeds or feed categories by navigating to **Configuration ➤ Feed aggregator**.

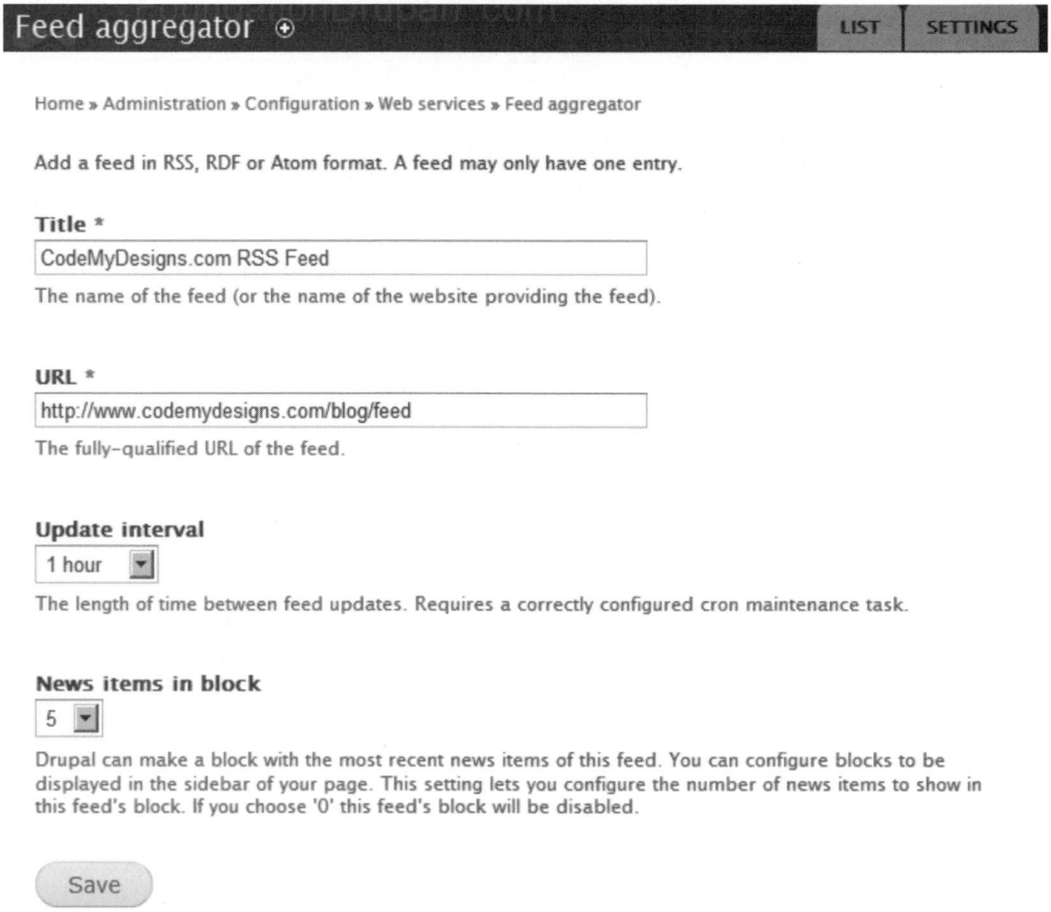

Feed aggregator ⊕   LIST   SETTINGS

Home » Administration » Configuration » Web services » Feed aggregator

Add a feed in RSS, RDF or Atom format. A feed may only have one entry.

Title *

CodeMyDesigns.com RSS Feed

The name of the feed (or the name of the website providing the feed).

URL *

http://www.codemydesigns.com/blog/feed

The fully-qualified URL of the feed.

Update interval

1 hour ▾

The length of time between feed updates. Requires a correctly configured cron maintenance task.

News items in block

5 ▾

Drupal can make a block with the most recent news items of this feed. You can configure blocks to be displayed in the sidebar of your page. This setting lets you configure the number of news items to show in this feed's block. If you choose '0' this feed's block will be disabled.

Save

Figure 6-5. View the **Add feed** form is accessed by navigating to **Configuration ➤ Feed aggregator** and selecting **Add feed**.

The title of the feed appears at the top of the full-page feed view along with the URL and the last time the feed was updated. The URL must be the complete URL for the feed, prefixed with **http://**. Drupal currently allows for three feed types: RSS, RDF, or Atom. If cron is properly configured, the newsfeed will update as configured by the update interval. **News items in block** configures the number of feed items in the block; a block is created for each feed, and you can configure the number for each block. Note that if **Discard items older than is greater than** the newest post on the feed (for example, **Discard...** is at one week and the newest item is two weeks old), then no **ITEMS** will appear in the feed.

Drupal provides a number of full-page views and blocks after feeds are saved. The http://example.com/aggregator page provides a view of all feed items with teaser text, regardless of category. The http://example.com/aggregator/sources and http://example.com/aggregator/categories pages display lists of feed item titles grouped by feed name or category. And of course, you can navigate to `http://example.com/aggregator/sources/ID`, where `ID` is the number of the newsfeed to view feed items from a single feed (see Figure 6-6).

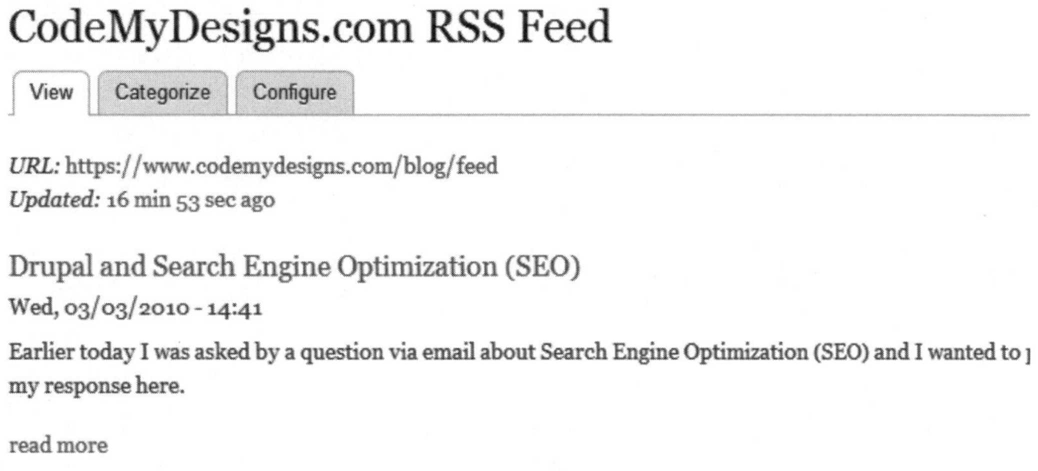

CodeMyDesigns.com RSS Feed

| View | Categorize | Configure |

URL: https://www.codemydesigns.com/blog/feed
Updated: 16 min 53 sec ago

Drupal and Search Engine Optimization (SEO)

Wed, 03/03/2010 - 14:41

Earlier today I was asked by a question via email about Search Engine Optimization (SEO) and I wanted to p my response here.

read more

Figure 6-6. Navigate to `http://example.com/aggregator/sources/ID` to view a newsfeed.

Blog

The Drupal blog module is designed for multiple users. The module allows any user with permission to create a blog. The blog is a content type with a system-generated page and one block (you can create many more using the view module, discussed in Chapter 7). Users are given permission to post content to their own blog, available at `http://example.com/blog/UID`, where `UID` is the user's ID. All blog posts are displayed in a list at `http://example.com/blog`.

The blog is a content type and does not have many configurable options; additional options and features must be added through other modules. Edit the blog content type at **Structure ➤ Content types ➤ Blog ➤ EDIT**, as shown in Figure 6-7. The vertical tab menu contains the same configuration settings as a regular content type; see Chapter 4 for instructions on how to configure a content type.

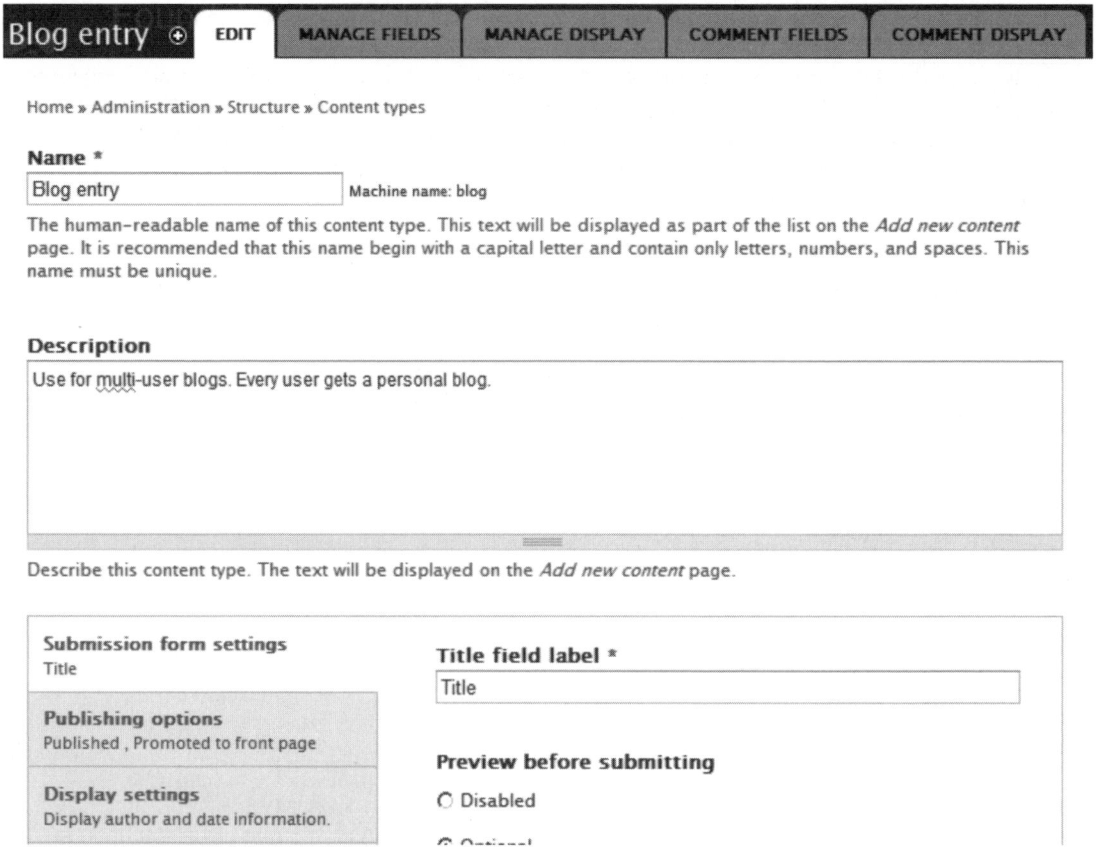

Figure 6-7. The blog's display settings are configured on the content type page at **Structure ➤ Content types ➤ Blog ➤ EDIT**.

You may also want to change comment settings, which affects the way comments display on `http://example.com/blog` and `http://example.com/blog/UID`. Comments have a number of options that can be configured at the content type level. Comments can be displayed either as a straight list or as threaded. A threaded list groups comments according to replies; if a user posts a comment and three people reply to that comment, those four posts are considered a thread and grouped together.

When displaying comments, Drupal automatically includes a pager (that is, links to page 1, page 2, and so on) to view additional comments when the number of comments per page is exceeded. The **Allow comment title** check box adds a comment title field in the comment form that allows users to create a custom title for their comment. If the check box is deselected, Drupal creates a title for the comment based on the first 29 characters of the comment.

It is important to note that the **Default comment settings for new posts** setting applies only to new content; changing this setting to **Closed** (or vice versa) will not affect previously created nodes.

The comment form can appear either on the same page as the node or on a separate page, as shown in Figure 6-8. Deselecting the **Show reply form on the same page as comments** check box displays an **Add new comment** link at the bottom of a node directing users to a second page to add comments. Optionally, users can preview a comment before it is published if **Preview comment** has been set to **Optional** or **Required**. When previewing a comment is **Optional**, both a **Submit** and **Preview** button are available at the bottom of the page; the **Disabled** setting removes the **Preview** button, while the **Required** setting removes the **Submit** button.

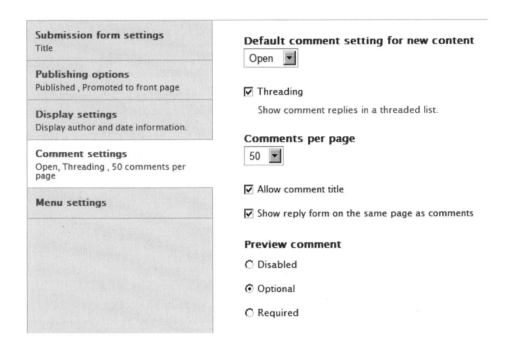

Figure 6-8. The blog's display settings are configured on the content type page at **Structure ➤ Content type ➤ Blog ➤ EDIT**.

After you have made any required changes, you can navigate to **Add content ➤ Blog** to add a blog, as shown in Figure 6-9. The only required field is the title, but you will probably add full text as well. The **Edit summary** link allows you to write your own teaser rather than using the trimmed version of the full text.

Create Blog entry ⊕

Home » Add content

Title *

Body (Edit summary)

Figure 6-9. Create a blog by navigating to **Add content ➤ Blog**.

The blog will be added to the author's blog. If you are the superadmin (that is, user #1), it is recommended either you log in as another user to create content or you change the **Authored by** to another user's name at the bottom of the blog creation form. See Figure 6-10.

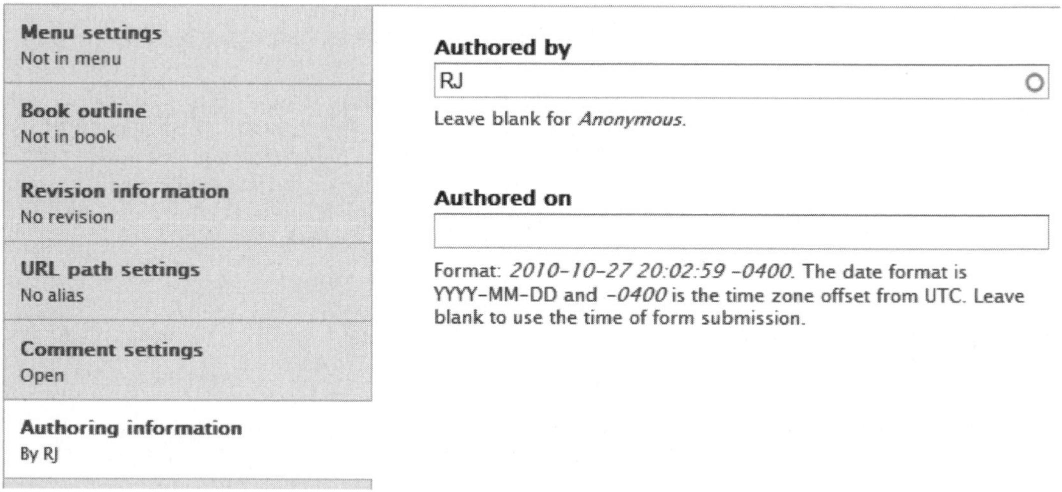

Menu settings
Not in menu

Book outline
Not in book

Revision information
No revision

URL path settings
No alias

Comment settings
Open

Authoring information
By RJ

Authored by

RJ

Leave blank for *Anonymous*.

Authored on

Format: *2010–10–27 20:02:59 –0400*. The date format is YYYY-MM-DD and *–0400* is the time zone offset from UTC. Leave blank to use the time of form submission.

Figure 6-10. Change the **Authored by** field to a user other than the superadmin when creating nodes.

You can increase the functionality of the blog section in several ways. One such way is to add tags so that bloggers can tag content and users can browse all blogs with specific tags. This was covered in Chapter 4 but is a simple process of adding a vocabulary term (**Structure ➤ Taxonomy ➤ Add vocabulary**) and adding that taxonomy term field type to the content type (**Structure ➤ Content type ➤ Blog ➤ MANAGE FIELDS**). You can also add an image field for users to upload images displayed at the beginning of the post.

As previously mentioned, a **Recent blog posts** block is available; refer to Chapter 3 to review how blocks are configured. Several ideas are covered in the appendixes on adding additional blocks and functionality for a blog; see Appendix C and D for ideas.

Book

The book module allows users to write and organize content and is ideal for handbooks or training manuals. You can easily structure content into multiple books, chapters, and pages using a custom navigation menu. A book is a content type with a system-generated page at `http://example.com/book` that displays links to all books, as shown in Figure 6-11.

Books

- Code Snippets
- CodeMyDesigns.com Online Help
- Foundation Drupal

Figure 6-11. The `http://example.com/book` page displays links to all books.

Clicking a book title takes you to the book page. Book pages are nested within book pages; the book's top-level page will have nodes nested under it (for example, **Chapter 1**, **Chapter 2**, and so on), and each of those pages can have nested nodes as well, as shown in Figure 6-12. Drupal provides a number of links to navigate through book pages along with links to add child pages and view printer-friendly pages. If configured, users can comment on each page.

Foundation Drupal

| View | Edit | Outline | Track |

published by RJ on Wed, 10/27/2010 - 20:19

- Chapter 1
- Chapter 2
- Chapter 3

Chapter 1 ›

Add child page   Printer-friendly version   **Add new comment**

Figure 6-12. First page of a book. Chapters 1–3 are nested within the Foundation Drupal top-level book page, and the **Chapter 1** link at the bottom of the page links to the first page of the book.

A block is also created with a menu containing links to all books and pages called **Book navigation**. Configure the module by navigating to **Structure ➤ Blocks**, and select the **Configure** link next to the **Book navigation** block. The module adds one additional configuration setting to the **Book navigation** block called **Book navigation block display**. This allows you to configure whether the block shows on all pages or only on book pages.

Navigate to **content ➤ BOOKS ➤ Settings** to configure the book module, as shown in Figure 6-13. There are two basic settings. You can use the book module on one or more content types through the **Content types Allowed in book outlines** setting. If you have more than one content type selected, you need to select the default content type of the **add child page** link on book pages.

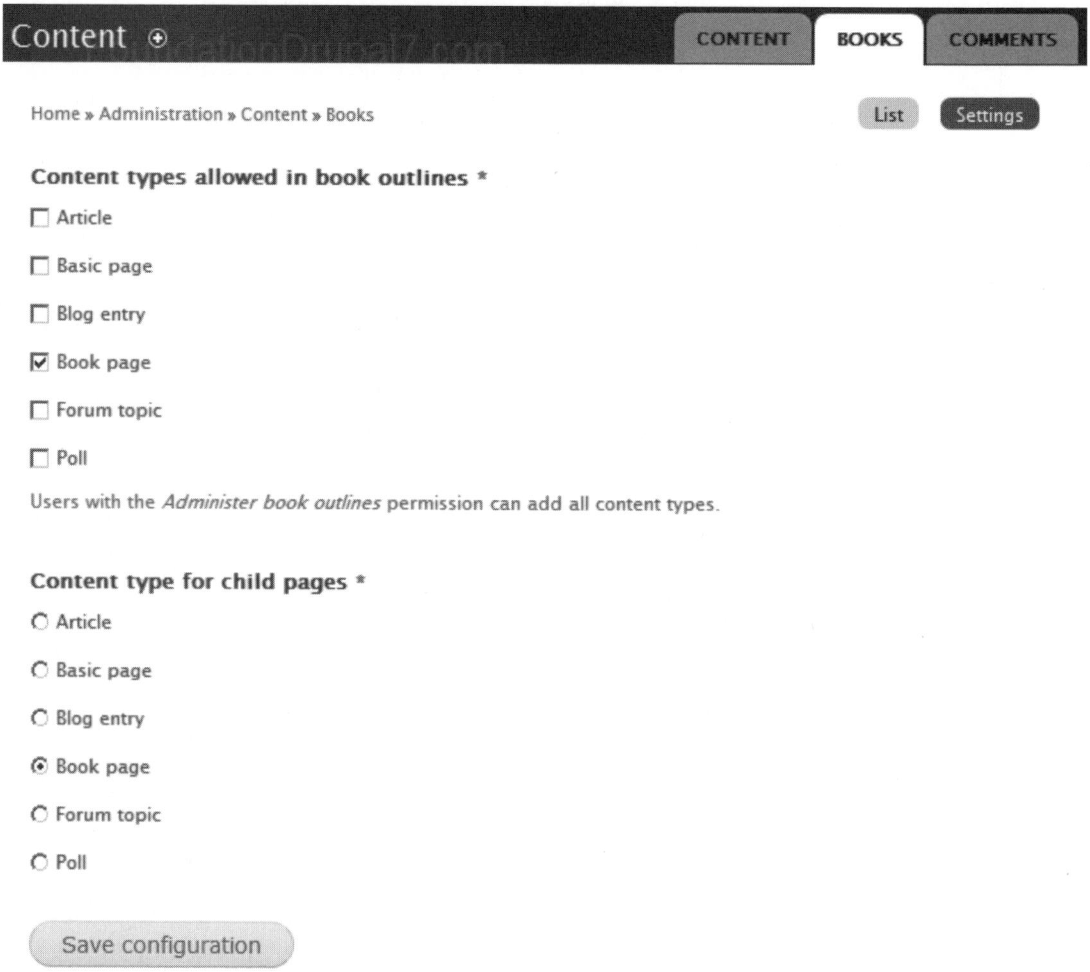

Figure 6-13. Navigate to **Content ➤ BOOKS ➤ Settings** to configure the book module.

Navigate to **Add content ➤ Book page** to create and nest a book page, as shown in Figure 6-14. Alternatively, you can click **add child page** when viewing a book page, which automatically nests a page within that page. The only difference between adding an article or page and a book page is a link in the vertical tabs titled **book outline**. A book page must be part of a book; otherwise, the page will not appear in the book section. To create a new book, select **<Create a new book>** in the book drop-down. The node title will become the name of the new book, so title capitalization is important. Select a book under **parent item** to nest a page. Fill in the remaining information, and click **Save**. Chapter 4 covers many of these settings in detail.

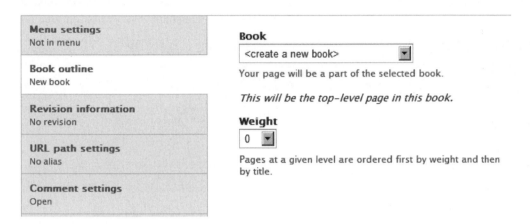

Figure 6-14. The **Book outline** tab on the book creation page allows you to assign a page to a book and nest the page under another page.

Navigate to **Content**, and select the **BOOKS** tab to view links to the book's main page. Select **edit order and titles** to edit and arrange book pages, as shown in Figure 6-15. Use this form to drag and drop the order of book pages and to change the name of book page titles. You will need to select the **edit** link if you need to move a book page to another book.

Show row weights

TITLE		OPERATIONS		
⊕ Chapter 1		view	edit	delete
⊕ How Drupal works		view	edit	delete
⊕ Navigating the administrative interface		view	edit	delete
⊕ Chapter 2		view	edit	delete

Figure 6-15. Edit and arrange book page titles by navigating to **Content ➤ BOOKS ➤ edit order and titles**.

Comments

The comment module allows users to post comments that are associated with a single node; one node can have multiple comments, but a comment cannot be associated with multiple nodes. A comment is not a node. As previously mentioned, the ability to comment can be turned on or off at the individual node level, while the node's content type controls the remaining comment settings.

Comments are managed by selecting **Content ➤ COMMENTS**, as shown in Figure 6-16. A comment is either published and in the **Published comments** section or unpublished and located in the **Unapproved comments approval queue**. Comments can also be deleted, but they are permanently removed from the site.

Figure 6-16. The comment management page allows you to manage published and unpublished comments.

Depending on the permissions assigned to a role, a comment can be either immediately published to the site or sent to the approval queue. The default Drupal installation only allows authenticated users to view and post comments, which means an anonymous user (that is, those not logged in) will not see the form to post new comments. Changing permissions is discussed in depth in Chapter 5.

Comments are displayed and managed in much the same way as content. Although Drupal does not offer a mechanism to filter comments, you can sort the comment list by a number of fields by clicking the column header. Updating a comment's status to unpublished causes it to appear in the **Unapproved comments** queue.

Contact

The contact module adds a contact page at `http://example.com/contact`, as shown in Figure 6-17. The module allows users to send e-mails to one or more people by using a drop-down filled with values you enter. Several fields are automatically added and required, including for the name, e-mail address, subject title, category, and message. Users can select a check box to send an e-mail to themselves and, if logged in, will have the name and e-mail address fields automatically prefilled.

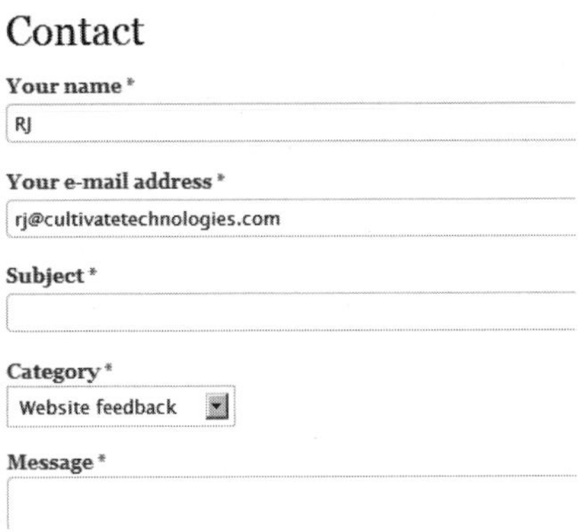

Contact

Your name *

RJ

Your e-mail address *

rj@cultivatetechnologies.com

Subject *

Category *

Website feedback

Message *

Figure 6-17. The contact form is located at `http://example.com/contact`.

The contact module is configured by navigating to **Structure ➤ Contact form**, as shown in Figure 6-18. By default the contact form sends an e-mail to one person, the site administrator. Select the **edit** link for **website feedback** to change this. If an additional category is added, then a **category** drop-down appears on the contact page, allowing a user to route an e-mail to a specific person or department.

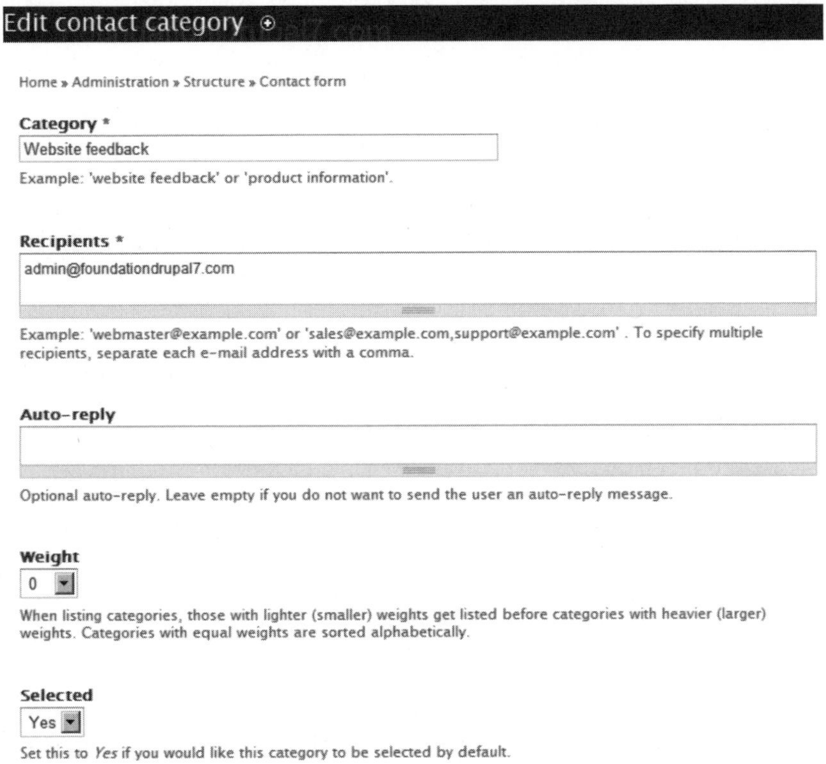

Edit contact category ⊙

Home » Administration » Structure » Contact form

Category *

Website feedback

Example: 'website feedback' or 'product information'.

Recipients *

admin@foundationdrupal7.com

Example: 'webmaster@example.com' or 'sales@example.com,support@example.com' . To specify multiple recipients, separate each e-mail address with a comma.

Auto-reply

Optional auto-reply. Leave empty if you do not want to send the user an auto-reply message.

Weight

0

When listing categories, those with lighter (smaller) weights get listed before categories with heavier (larger) weights. Categories with equal weights are sorted alphabetically.

Selected

Yes

Set this to *Yes* if you would like this category to be selected by default.

Figure 6-18. Navigate to **Structure ➤ Contact form**, and select the **edit** link for **Website feedback** to configure the default e-mail address for the contact form.

The name of the category is listed in the contact page drop-down, so capitalization matters. One or more e-mail addresses can receive form submissions by entering multiple e-mail addresses separated by a comma. The **Auto-reply** field is automatically e-mailed to the person (or spam-bot) that submitted the form; leave this empty to turn off e-mail responses. **Weight** controls the height of the title in the category drop-down on the contact form. If **Selected** is set to **Yes**, then the category will be automatically selected in the category drop-down. Setting this to **Yes** automatically sets other categories to **No**.

Unfortunately, the contact form does not provide a block but only a full-page view. The webform module, which provides a content type to create forms, is a quick and easy solution to fix this. It allows you to create a node with a number of fields, such as for a name, e-mail, and message. The form provides a full-page view and can be configured (through yet another module) to display forms in a block. Because the webform module provides both full-page and block views, you do not need to use the contact module if you are using the webform module. The webform module is covered in depth in Chapter 7.

Forum

The forum module provides forums to which users can post and interact at `http://example.com/forum`. Forums are categorized into containers, forums, and forum topics. Forum topics are posted within forums, and forums are placed within containers; users can only place topics within forums, not containers. Users discuss forum posts using comments. Individual forums and containers can be viewed by navigating to `http://example.com/forum/ID`, where ID is the ID of the forum; see Figure 6-19.

Forums

✦ Add new Forum topic

Forum	Topics	Posts	Last post
Discussion Post your general topic discussions here.			
What's up! Tell us about yourself!	0	0	n/a
Your work! Show us your portfolio	0	0	n/a

Figure 6-19. Forums are accessed at `http://example.com/forum`.

The forum module provides a content type that can be configured at **Structure ➤ Content types** and by selecting the **edit** link next to a forum topic. The only settings you will probably configure from this page are the **Comment settings**. See Chapter 4 for details on configuring a content type.

Navigate to **Structure ➤ Forums**, and click the **SETTINGS** tab to configure display settings for forums and forum topics, as shown in Figure 6-20. **Hot topic threshold** determines the number of comments required before Drupal displays the word *hot* next to a topic. The number of topics per page can range between 10 and 100; if there are more than this number, Drupal provides a pager at the bottom of the page to view additional topics. The default order of topics can be by date or number of comments.

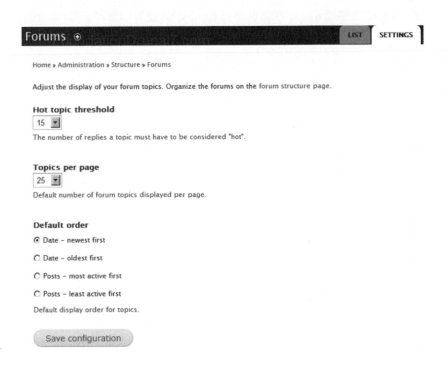

Figure 6-20. Navigate to **Structure ➤ Forums**, and click the **SETTINGS** tab to configure forums.

Containers and forums are added and organized by navigating to **Structure ➤ Forums**, as shown in Figure 6-21. Select the link **Add container** or **Add forum**; remember that forums go in containers, and users can only post topics to forums. The forum or container name is displayed in the forums, so capitalization is important. The description appears under the forum or container name; I recommend keeping it to a few sentences. The parent determines how containers and forums are nested. Usually, containers are placed at the <root> level, while forums are nested within containers, but this is not required. The **Weight** field controls the order in which forums or containers are listed.

Figure 6-21. Navigate to **Structure ➤ Forums**, and click **Add container** or **Add forum** to create containers and forums.

After you have created forums and containers, you can navigate to **Structure ➤ Forums** to view and change their order, as shown in Figure 6-22.

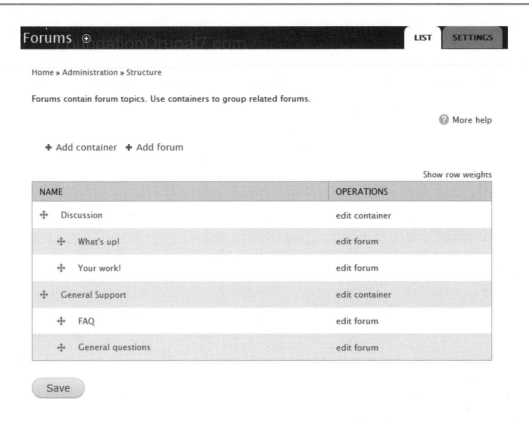

Figure 6-22. Navigate to **Structure ➤ Forums** to edit and change the order of forums and containers.

In some cases, you may require two or more forums with full-page views. For example, you may want two forums, one for designers and one for developers, located on two separate pages. This is easily accomplished by placing containers within containers, as shown in Figure 6-23. Within each container, additional containers and forums have been added. There are now separate pages for forums: one for designers and one for developers.

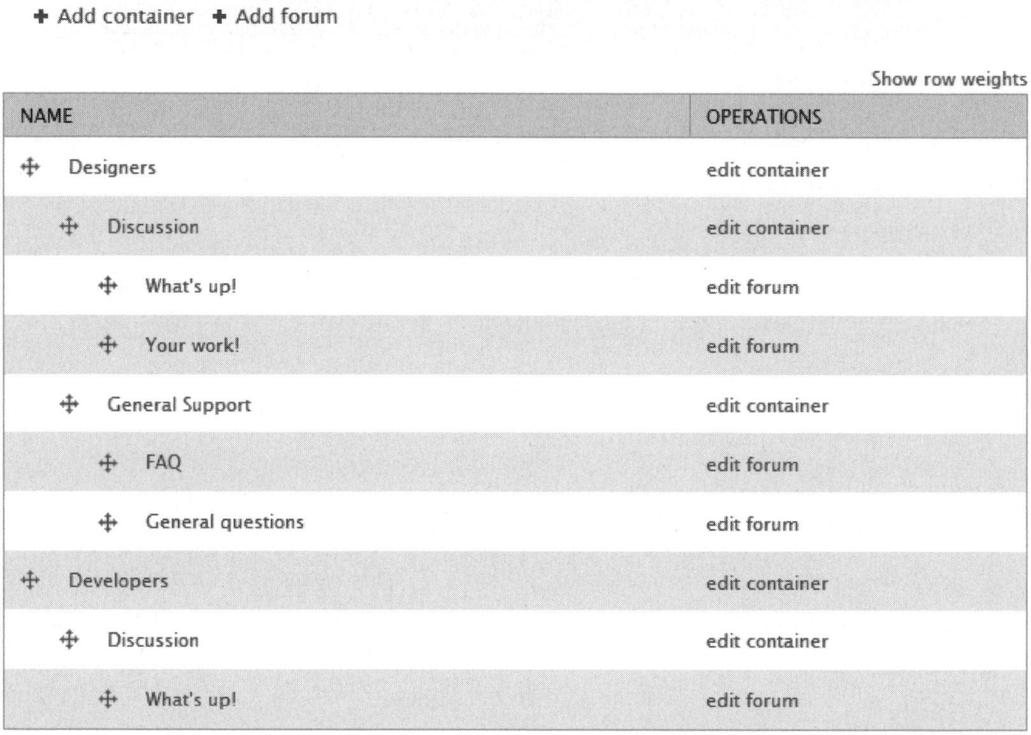

✛ Add container   ✛ Add forum

Show row weights

NAME	OPERATIONS
✛ Designers	edit container
✛ Discussion	edit container
✛ What's up!	edit forum
✛ Your work!	edit forum
✛ General Support	edit container
✛ FAQ	edit forum
✛ General questions	edit forum
✛ Developers	edit container
✛ Discussion	edit container
✛ What's up!	edit forum

Figure 6-23. The forum module configured to display two full-page forums, one for designers and one for developers.

The module also includes a block containing active forum topics. Navigate to **Structure ➤ Blocks** to configure the block. The number of topics displayed in the block can contain between 2 and 20 topics (see Figure 6-24).

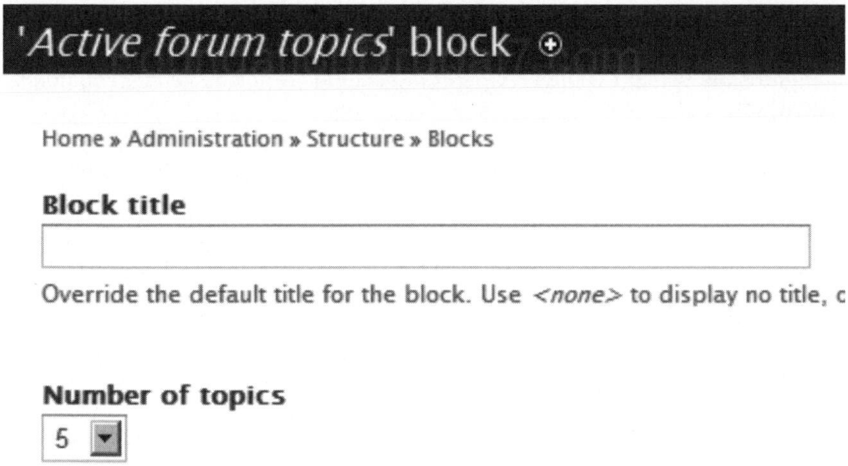

'Active forum topics' block ⊕

Home » Administration » Structure » Blocks

Block title

Override the default title for the block. Use *<none>* to display no title, c

Number of topics

5 ▼

Figure 6-24. The active forum topics block can be configured to display between 2 and 20 topics.

The advanced forum module (`http://drupal.org/project/advanced_forum`) increases the functionality of forums comparable to some stand-alone forum software. Added functionality includes statistics (number of topics, online users, comments, and so on), highlighting unread messages, extra icons, and more.

Language translations, including locale and content translation

Drupal supports content translation through two modules, content translation and locale. The locale module is responsible for translating built-in system text (that is, text strings in the administrative section, system messages, and so on), while content translation provides a user interface for translating user-supplied content (that is, pages, articles, and so on). Many language translations for system text are available at `http://drupal.org/project/translations`; you simply upload the translation to the root Drupal folder and add the language (I'll provide step-by-step setup instructions in a moment).

Locale manages language translation files, which are technically GNU gettext Portable Object files (`.po` for short). Think of a `.po` file as a spreadsheet with two columns; one column contains the original text, and the second column contains the translated version (this is not how the file is structured). Drupal recognizes every link, field, and piece of system content as a string that fills the original text column. Language translation files contain all of Drupal's strings in English with corresponding translations. When a translation is uploaded to the server, Drupal fills a table in the database with language translation values used when the site is displayed in a non-English language. The benefit of this approach is the ease with which you can change translated system content; simply navigate to the translate interface and update the string.

The content translation module provides a UI so that users can translate a node into multiple languages. Drupal does not automatically translate content. User-supplied content is translated on a per-node basis; that is, you must translate content yourself. One of the benefits of this is you can customize each node for a specific language.

Languages can be configured through locale to display through a number of mechanisms.

- A URL, such as `http://uk.example.com/node/1`
- A session parameter such as `http://example.com/node/1?language=uk`
- A language preference from a user's account
- Browser language settings

Setup instructions for the locale module

To set up the locale module, follow these steps:

1. Enable the locale module at **Modules**.

2. Upload the language translation folder to the root Drupal folder (Figure 6-25). All translation files now live in the Drupal directory.

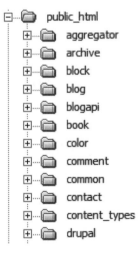

Figure 6-25. Upload the language translation folder to the root Drupal folder.

3. Navigate to **Configuration ➤ Languages**, and select **Add language**.

4. Select the predefined language from the drop-down list, and click **Add language** (Figure 6-26). Drupal will automatically import language translation files into the system if they were correctly uploaded.

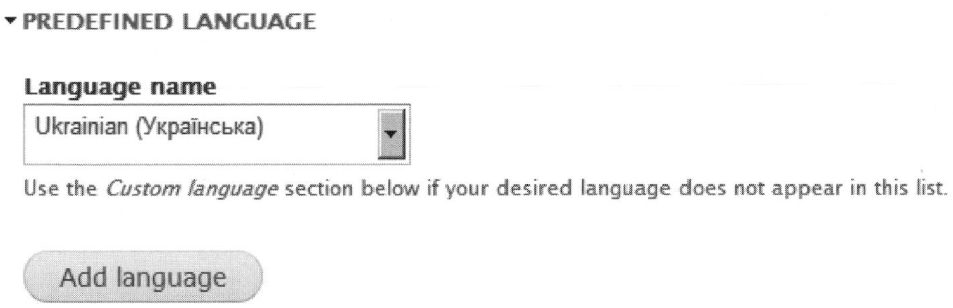

▼ PREDEFINED LANGUAGE

Language name

Ukrainian (Українська) ▼

Use the *Custom language* section below if your desired language does not appear in this list.

Add language

Figure 6-26. Select the predefined language from the drop-down list, and click **Add language**.

5. Configure how languages will be detected and displayed (Figure 6-27). Should languages display differently depending on URL, the user's selection, or another? You need to select at least one check box from **DETECTION METHOD** and click the **ENABLED** checkbox. Make sure the configure it after saving if applicable!

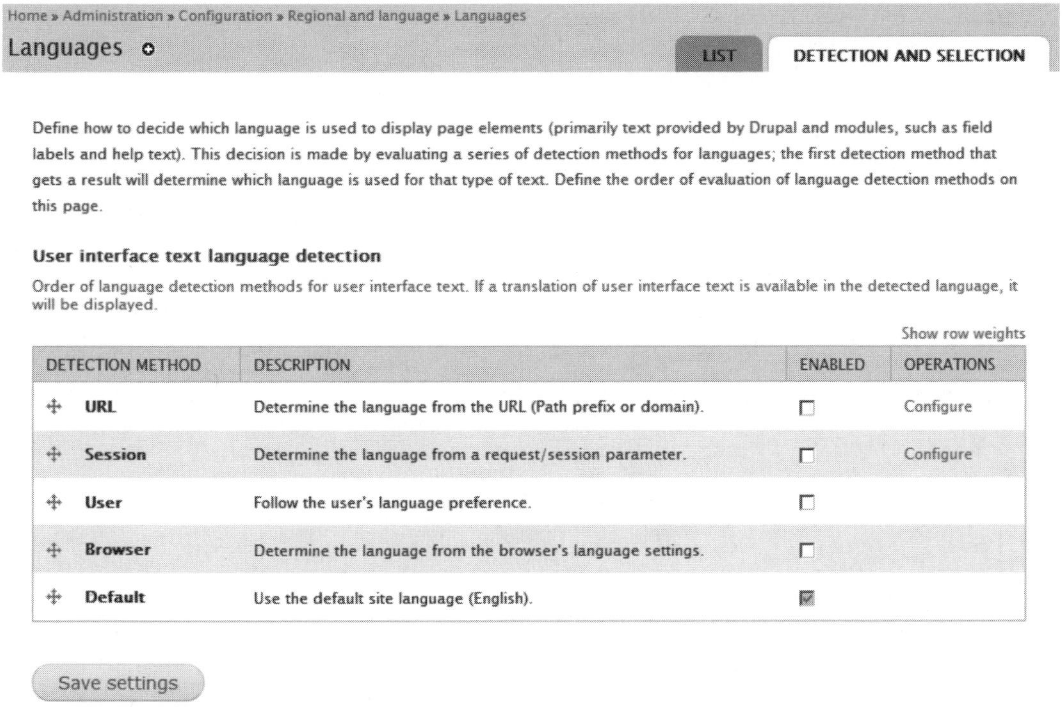

Home » Administration » Configuration » Regional and language » Languages

Languages ○   LIST   DETECTION AND SELECTION

Define how to decide which language is used to display page elements (primarily text provided by Drupal and modules, such as field labels and help text). This decision is made by evaluating a series of detection methods for languages; the first detection method that gets a result will determine which language is used for that type of text. Define the order of evaluation of language detection methods on this page.

User interface text language detection

Order of language detection methods for user interface text. If a translation of user interface text is available in the detected language, it will be displayed.

Show row weights

DETECTION METHOD	DESCRIPTION	ENABLED	OPERATIONS
✛ **URL**	Determine the language from the URL (Path prefix or domain).	☐	Configure
✛ **Session**	Determine the language from a request/session parameter.	☐	Configure
✛ **User**	Follow the user's language preference.	☐	
✛ **Browser**	Determine the language from the browser's language settings.	☐	
✛ **Default**	Use the default site language (English).	☑	

Save settings

Figure 6-27. Navigate to Configuration ➤ Languages and select DETECTION AND SELECTION to configure how languages will be detected and displayed. NOTE: Configuration, Languages, and DETECTION AND SELECTION should be screen text style.

6. Navigate to **Configuration ➤ Translation interface** to see how many strings were translated (Figure 6-28).

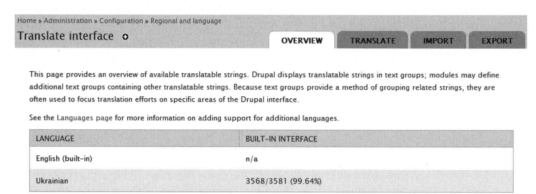

Figure 6-28. Navigate to **Configuration ➤ Translation interface** to see how many strings were translated.

7. Click the **TRANSLATE** tab, and search in the results by **Only untranslated strings** to see all untranslated strings. Click **edit** to quickly update a string. In Figure 6-29, the string **An AJAX HTTP error occurred** does not have a Ukrainian translation.

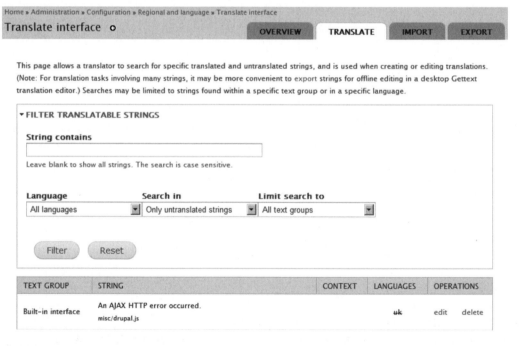

Figure 6-29. Click the **TRANSLATE** tab, and search in the results by **Only untranslated strings** to see all untranslated strings. The string **An AJAX HTTP error occurred** does not have a Ukrainian translation.

8. If there are a number of strings that require translation, it is easier to download the language translation file and edit it with a gettext translation editor such as poedit (`http://poedit.net`). Click the **EXPORT** tab, and select the translation to export under **EXPORT TRANSLATION** (Figure 6-30).

Figure 6-30. Click the **EXPORT** tab and select the translation to export under **EXPORT TRANSLATION** to edit the translation file.

Navigate to **Structure ➤ Blocks**, and place the **language switcher (interface)** block in the appropriate region. This block allows a user to switch between the different language translations via links.

Setup instructions for the content translation module

As previously mentioned, the translation module provides a UI to translate a node into other languages. To set up the content translation module, follow these steps:

1. Enable the content translation module at **Modules**.

2. Navigate to **Structure ➤ Content types**, and edit the content type that requires translation.

3. Select **Publishing options**, and select **Enabled** under **Multilingual support** to allow one translation per node (that is, a node can exist only as English or Ukrainian) or **Enabled, with translation** for multiple translations (which allows both English and Ukrainian per node), as shown in Figure 6-31. This is set to **Disabled** by default.

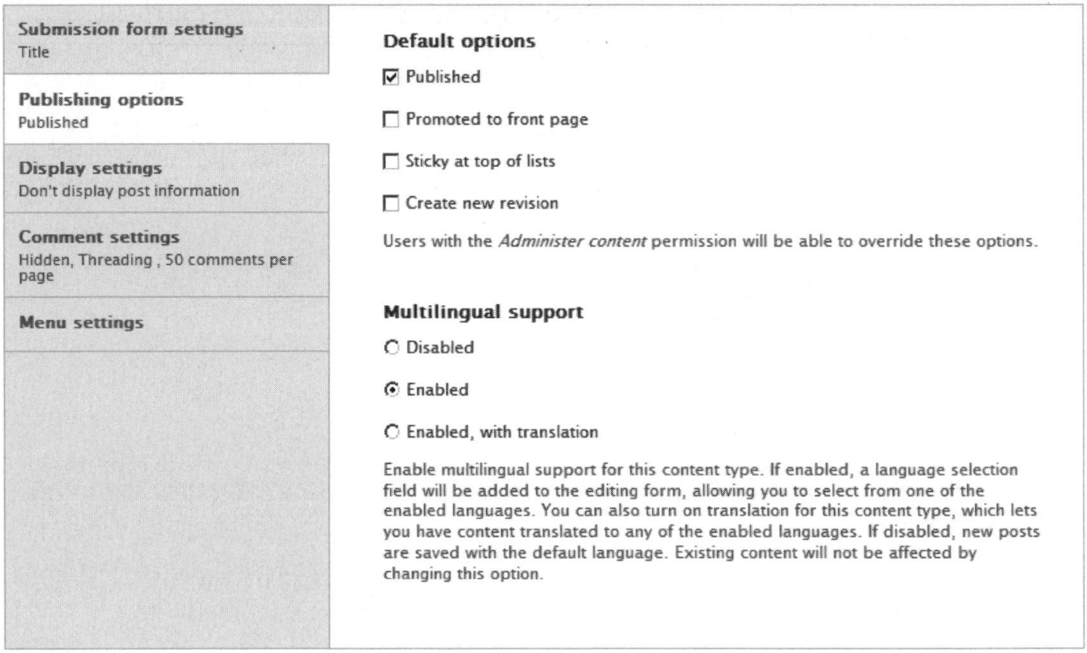

Submission form settings
Title

Publishing options
Published

Display settings
Don't display post information

Comment settings
Hidden, Threading , 50 comments per page

Menu settings

Default options

☑ Published

☐ Promoted to front page

☐ Sticky at top of lists

☐ Create new revision

Users with the *Administer content* permission will be able to override these options.

Multilingual support

○ Disabled

⦿ Enabled

○ Enabled, with translation

Enable multilingual support for this content type. If enabled, a language selection field will be added to the editing form, allowing you to select from one of the enabled languages. You can also turn on translation for this content type, which lets you have content translated to any of the enabled languages. If disabled, new posts are saved with the default language. Existing content will not be affected by changing this option.

Figure 6-31. Edit the content type that requires translation.

After **Multilingual support** is enabled, a **Language** drop-down will appear with all installed languages on the create content form, as shown in Figure 6-32. Note that a **Language neutral** node cannot have multiple translations.

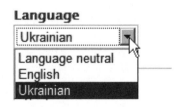

Figure 6-32. After **Multilingual support** is enabled, a **Language** drop-down will appear with all installed languages on the create content form.

If **Enabled, with translation** was selected in the previous step 3, a **TRANSLATE** tab now appears when viewing a node. To translate a node to another language, click the **TRANSLATE** tab and **add translation** for the required node (Figure 6-33).

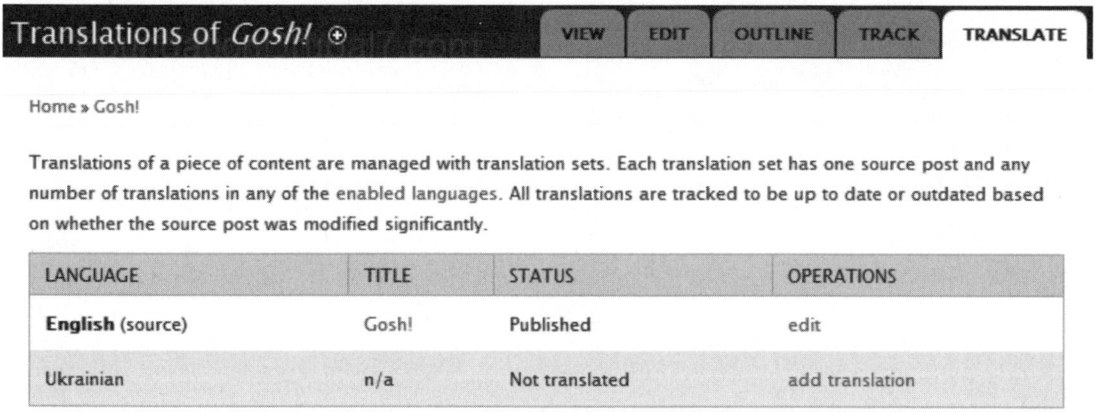

Translations of *Gosh!* ⊕   VIEW   EDIT   OUTLINE   TRACK   **TRANSLATE**

Home » Gosh!

Translations of a piece of content are managed with translation sets. Each translation set has one source post and any number of translations in any of the enabled languages. All translations are tracked to be up to date or outdated based on whether the source post was modified significantly.

LANGUAGE	TITLE	STATUS	OPERATIONS
English (source)	Gosh!	Published	edit
Ukrainian	n/a	Not translated	add translation

Figure 6-33. To translate a node to another language, click the **TRANSLATE** tab when viewing a node and **add translation**.

After a translation has been created, you can now check whether the node requires updated or not. When editing a translated node (that is, not the source node, with the original language) and the translation is not complete, select **This translation needs to be updated** in the translation settings (Figure 6-34).

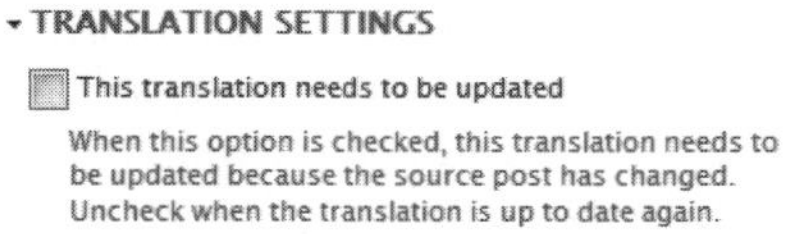

▾ TRANSLATION SETTINGS

☐ This translation needs to be updated

When this option is checked, this translation needs to be updated because the source post has changed. Uncheck when the translation is up to date again.

Figure 6-34. After a translation has been created, you can now check whether the node requires updating.

When updating a source node, you can select **Flag translations as outdated** if translated nodes should be flagged as requiring an update (Figure 6-35).

▾ TRANSLATION SETTINGS

☐ Flag translations as outdated

If you made a significant change, which means translations should be updated, you can flag all translations of this post as outdated. This will not change any other property of those posts, like whether they are published or not.

Figure 6-35. When updating a source node, you can select **Flag translations as outdated** if translated nodes should be flagged as requiring an update.

The local and translation module both add options to the **Content** list screen. Navigate to the **Content** list screen and filter results by **Status ➤ Outdated translation** to view all outdated content (Figure 6-36).

Figure 6-36. Navigate to the **Content** list screen and filter results by **Status ➤ Outdated translation** to view all outdated content.

OpenID

OpenID is an Internet standard that allows users to log in to different services and web sites using the same identity. There are many popular web services that support OpenID, including Google, Yahoo!, MySpace, and more. The OpenID module allows users to log in to a Drupal site using an OpenID. When logging in to your web site, users select the **Log in using OpenID** link and enter their OpenID user name (usually the same user name as the OpenID provider, such as `youremail@gmail.com`), as shown in Figure 6-37. The user is taken to a screen where the OpenID provider requests a password and is returned to your site after successfully logging in. This is great for site administrators if you manage multiple sites; you no longer need to have multiple passwords but can manage your password through your OpenID provider.

Figure 6-37. Enabling the OpenID module creates a **Log in using OpenID** link on the user login block.

To be able to log in to a site using OpenID, users must add an OpenID identity to their account by selecting the **OpenID identities** tab from their user account, as shown in Figure 6-38. Select your user name in the user menu, and click **OpenID identities** to enable OpenID with your account. Enter your OpenID user ID (for example, **youremail@gmail.com**), and you are forwarded to the OpenID provider's site to authenticate your account. After authentication, you are returned to the edit user page with the OpenID server address added.

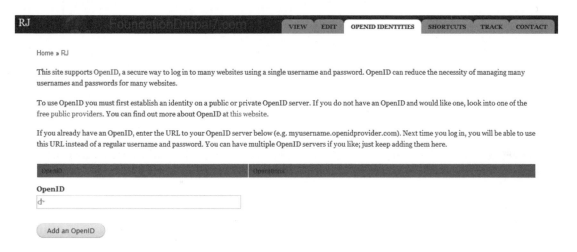

Figure 6-38. Select your user name in the user menu, and click **OpenID identities** to enable OpenID with your account.

Poll

The poll module creates a content type allowing you to ask a question with choices users can select. The module saves all votes (including the user who voted), calculates responses, and has several fine-grain permissions, including the ability to vote on a poll, cancel your own vote, and inspect votes. All polls are displayed at `http://example.com/poll`, or the most recent poll can be displayed through a block. To create a poll, navigate to **Add content ➤ Poll**, as shown in Figure 6-39.

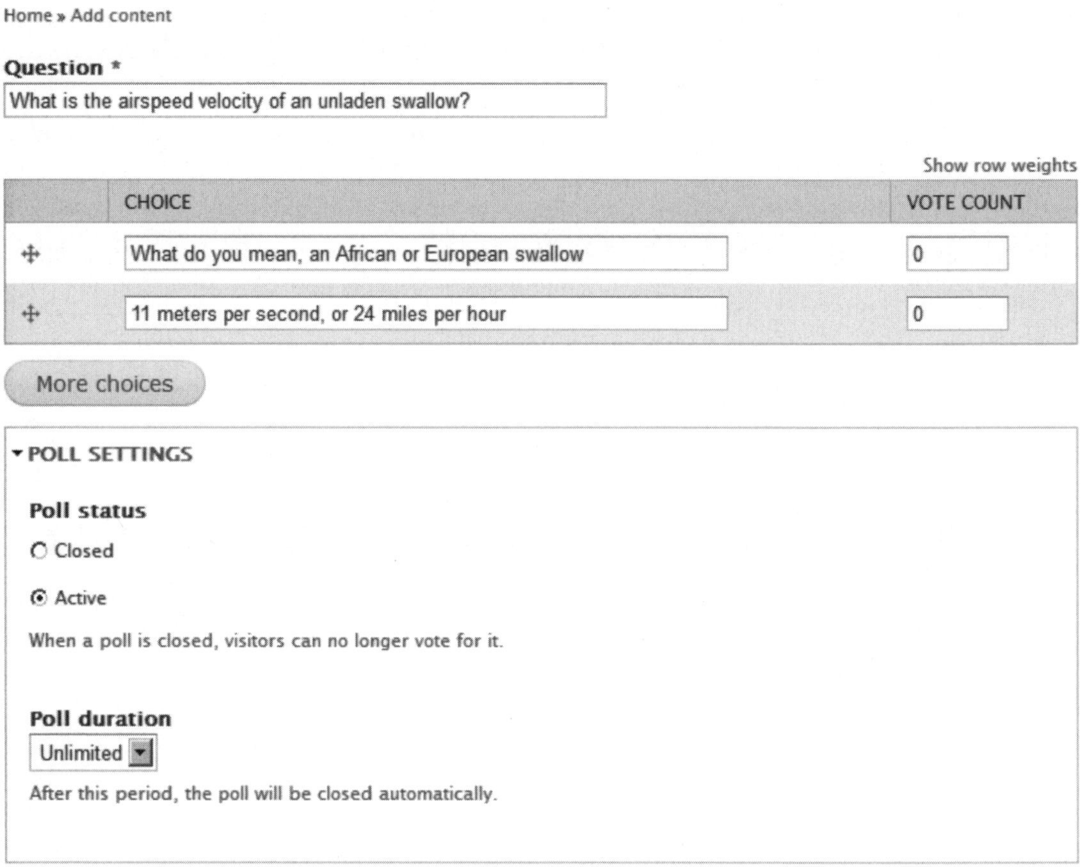

Home » Add content

Question *

What is the airspeed velocity of an unladen swallow?

Show row weights

	CHOICE	VOTE COUNT
✛	What do you mean, an African or European swallow	0
✛	11 meters per second, or 24 miles per hour	0

(More choices)

▼ POLL SETTINGS

Poll status

○ Closed

◉ Active

When a poll is closed, visitors can no longer vote for it.

Poll duration

Unlimited ▼

After this period, the poll will be closed automatically.

Figure 6-39. Navigate to **Add content ➤ Poll** to create a poll.

The **Question** field is the node title and will appear at the top of the poll, as shown in Figure 6-40 for a full-page view of an individual poll. Two choices are included by default, and more can be added by selecting **More choices**. Choices are displayed in the poll using a radio button, which means users can select only one choice. Try the decisions module (`htttp://drupal.org/project/decisions`) if you need more advanced options such as multiple select. **Vote Count** contains the number of times the choice has been selected; when creating a poll, you can insert any number. The **Poll status** setting can be changed at any time to close a poll, or the **Poll duration** can be configured to automatically close it. Closed polls still appear on `http://example.com/poll`; you will need to unpublish or delete a poll to remove it from the page.

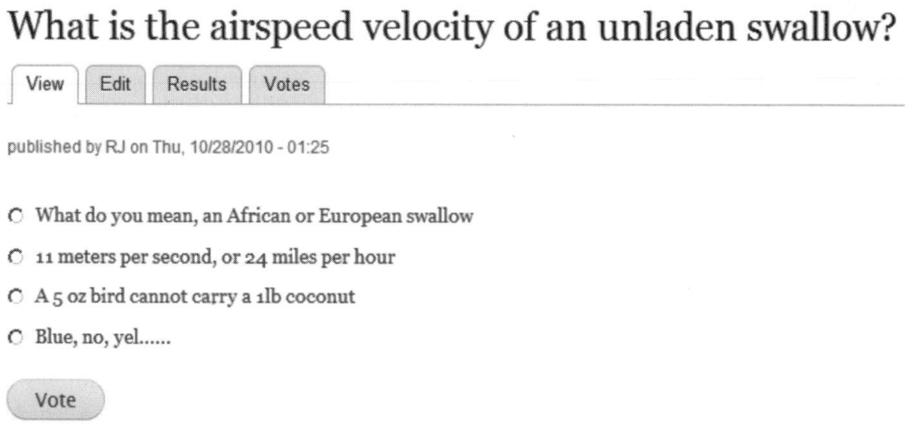

What is the airspeed velocity of an unladen swallow?
View
Edit
Results
Votes
published by RJ on Thu, 10/28/2010 - 01:25
What do you mean, an African or European swallow
11 meters per second, or 24 miles per hour
A 5 oz bird cannot carry a 1lb coconut
Blue, no, yel......
Vote

Figure 6-40. Full-page view of an individual poll

The full-page view of an individual poll contains two important tabs: results and votes. The results tab displays the total number of votes for each choice, as shown in Figure 6-41. If users do not have permission to vote on polls, they will only see poll results. If a user has voted on a poll, the results tab disappears, the poll is replaced with poll results, and a **Cancel your vote** button appears for users with proper permissions. This also happens on the poll block; if a user has voted, the block will contain poll results.

What is the airspeed velocity of an unladen swallow?
View
Edit
Votes
published by RJ on Thu, 10/28/2010 - 01:25
What do you mean, an African or European swallow
24% (7 votes)
11 meters per second, or 24 miles per hour
45% (13 votes)
A 5 oz bird cannot carry a 1lb coconut
24% (7 votes)
Blue, no, yel......
7% (2 votes)
Total votes: 29
Cancel your vote

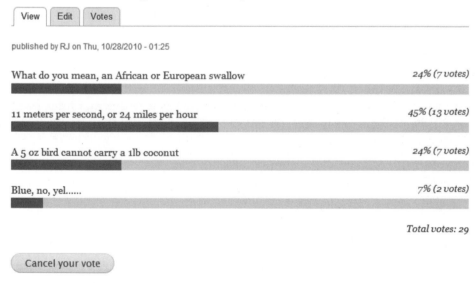

Figure 6-41. Poll results are displayed on the **Results** tab if the user has not voted, or if a user has voted, the **Results** tab disappears, and all results appear on the **View** tab.

The **Votes** tab allows you to inspect individual votes and contains links to submitters' user pages, as shown in Figure 6-42. If anonymous voting is allowed, the IP address of the user will be saved in place of the user name.

What is the airspeed velocity of an unladen swallow?

| View | Edit | Votes |

This table lists all the recorded votes for this poll. If anonymous users are allowed to vote, they will be identified by the IP address of the computer they used when they voted.

Visitor	Vote	Timestamp ▼
RJ	A 5 oz bird cannot carry a 1lb coconut	Thu, 10/28/2010 - 01:27

Figure 6-42. Users with permission can inspect individual votes.

Tracker

The tracker module creates a page accessed at `http://example.com/tracker` with a list of all recently published posts. It also creates a tab on users' homepages with links to posts they have authored, as shown in Figure 6-43. The module does not have any configuration options; you simply enable the module, and it (ideally) works. You will need to create a view (covered in Chapter 7) if you need to change the layout of the page or add permissions.

RJ

| View | Edit | Shortcuts | Track |

Type	Title	Author	Replies	Last updated
Basic page	Hello World	RJ	0	6 sec ago
Poll	What is the airspeed velocity of an unladen swallow?	RJ	0	2 min 37 sec ago

Figure 6-43. The tracker module displays links to all posts authored by a user.

Summary

We reviewed a number of core modules automatically included with Drupal 7.*x*. My goal was to cover the process of enabling and configuring core modules included with Drupal but not enabled by the standard Drupal installation, as covered in Chapter 2. The modules I covered included the following:

- Aggregator, allowing you to import content from other web sites via RSS, RDF, and atom feeds
- Blog, allowing multiple users to manage and post to a sitewide blog
- Book, allowing for content to be organized into a book including chapters and pages
- Comment, allowing for users to comment on a specific node
- Contact, creating a sitewide contact form with multiple categories allowing for e-mails to be routed to specific users or departments
- Forum, creating a forum to which users can post content and reply to others' posts
- Locale and content translation, allowing for translation of content into multiple languages
- OpenID, allowing for users to log in with an OpenID account
- Poll, allowing you to post questions and possible answers to which users can vote; includes simple reporting on responses
- Tracker, allowing users to track content they have posted on the site

Each one of these modules has a number of contributed modules available at Drupal.org that increase available functionality and features. Check out Appendix B to learn more about these modules.

Chapter 7

Essential Contributed Modules

In this chapter I discuss in-depth seven absolutely essential modules to every project I work on. These are modules that will help take your Drupal site to the next level. I cover everything from creating URL path patterns with Pathauto and using views to query and display data to entering content with WYSIWYG HTML editors. This chapter will help you sharpen your Drupal skills while learning about the modules that will set your site apart.

Adding and enabling a contributed module

Contributed modules are located in either the `sites/all/modules` directory or a site-specific directory, as discussed in Chapter 2. I generally categorize modules into one of two groups; either it's a module I will use on all future sites or it's a module that will be used on only one site. If I plan to use a contrib module on future sites moving forward, such as a What-You-See-Is-What-You-Get (WYSIWYG) HTML editor that will be used on every site I develop, then I add the module to `sites/all/modules`. However, if it's a site-specific module, such as one custom developed for a single site, then I always add it to the site-specific directory. After you have installed the module, it will appear on the **modules** page. Select the check box next to the module you need to enable, scroll to the bottom of the screen, and click **Save Configuration**—you're done! After a module is enabled, a system message appears at the top of the screen that says **the configuration options have been saved**, and several links, **help**, **permission**, and **configure**, appear next to the module.

Defining URL path patterns with Pathauto

Pathauto allows you to automatically create customized URLs for nodes, taxonomy terms, and user pages based on user-supplied or system-generated variables (called **replacement patterns** in Drupal, but we'll get into that shortly). This means you can create system-generated URLs pointing to specific web pages, and whenever a node, term, or user is created, it is automatically given a URL. For example, you may want all blogs accessed by navigating to `example.com/blog/[user:name]/[node:title]`, where `user:name` is the user's name and `node:title` is the title given to the blog node. Pathauto makes this very easy by automating the process; you simply create a URL pattern for the content type, and Drupal creates the URL for each page. Cool! This has many applications and is especially relevant for search engine optimization (also known as SEO, which is covered in Appendix A). All URLs added by Pathauto are displayed by navigating to **Configuration ➤ URL aliases** and clicking the **LIST** tab, as shown in Figure 7-1.

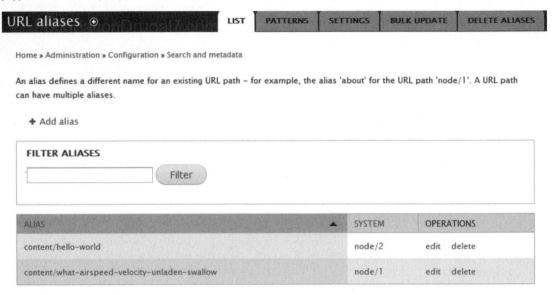

Figure 7-1. Navigate to **Configuration ➤ URL aliases**, and select the **LIST** tab to view all URL aliases generated by Pathauto.

Node, taxonomy term, and user path settings

I'll start with the **PATTERNS** tab because there are several topics I need to cover first before moving to general and punctuation **SETTINGS**. Click the **NODE PATHS** link to view URL replacement patterns for all content types, as shown in Figure 7-2. You can set both the **Default path pattern** and the content-type specific pattern from this fieldset. All system content types are listed on this page and are blank by default; if a content type does not have a pattern, then it displays the **Default path pattern**. Click the **REPLACEMENT PATTERNS** link to view a list of tokens that automatically generate values depending on the node. These are placed into the fields above (such as **Default path pattern**) and include a number of values, such as the node's ID, content type, taxonomy term, created date, and more. The **Internal feed alias text** setting is used to generate aliases to specific nodes' RSS feeds.

When building and managing a site, there are times when you create nodes before configuring Pathauto. Selecting **BULK UPDATE** tab to automatically create URLs for each node without an alias upon save. There are also times when you make configuration changes to Pathauto and you want to update all old URLs to the new path pattern. The easiest way to do this is to click the **DELETE ALIASES** tab, delete all the **content** aliases, and then go back and **Select the types of un-aliased paths for which to generate URL aliases** from the **BULK UPDATE** tab. I do not recommend doing this on production sites, because Drupal does not save the aliases after they are deleted, and if users or search engines try to access a page, they will receive a 404 not found error. If you need to change aliases after a site is in production, I recommend using the path_redirect module (`http://drupal.org/project/path_redirect`), also discussed in the appendix.

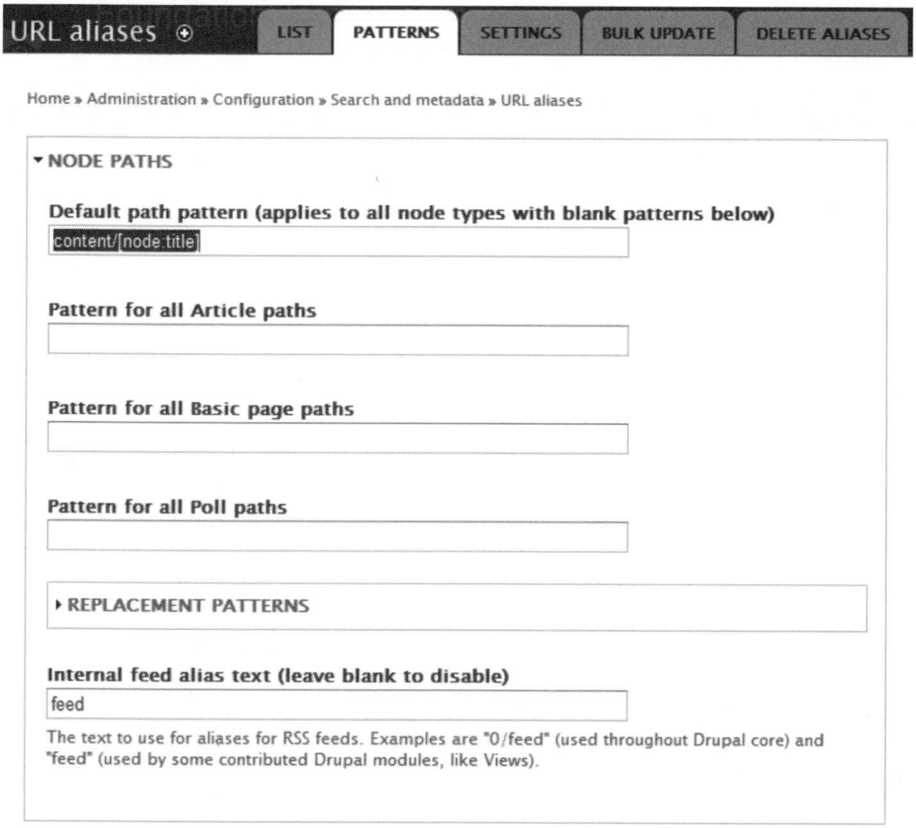

Figure 7-2. Click the **PATTERNS** tab to view configuration settings.

General and punctuation settings

There are a number of settings under general settings; click the **SETTINGS** tab to view all of them. The **Verbose** check box determines whether a message will be displayed when saving a node, taxonomy term, or user and when the URL is changed, as shown in Figure 7-3. This usually happens when, for example, a path pattern is based on the node title (for example, `http://example.com/gallery/[node:title]`) and the title is changed during a save. The **Separator** setting is the Unicode character placed between words in titles, including both spaces and punctuation such as colons or apostrophes. Generally speaking, I tend to use a hyphen so I can optimize my site for Google. This requires a bit of an explanation. When doing a search on Google for *hello world* (with a space), Google returns sites with both spaces and hyphens in the domain and page title. However, do a search for *hello_world* (with an underscore), and Google returns sites with the underscore; it does not return any sites with dashes or spaces. If you want people to find your page on the Internet by searching Google using *hello world*, then it's best to use a hyphen. However, there are times when it's important for an underscore to appear in search results, such as when people search specifically for *hello_world*. By default, Pathauto removes any underscores from the URL. If underscores are important to you, I recommend clicking the **PUNCTUATION** link at the bottom of the page and selecting **No action (do not replace)** for **Underscore _**.

Character case determines whether Drupal changes a replacement pattern to lowercase or keeps it as the same.

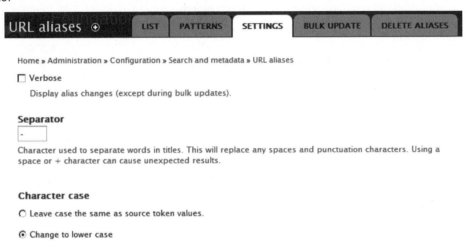

Figure 7-3. Click the **SETTINGS** tab to view configuration settings.

Figure 7-4 shows the next two configuration settings. **Maximum alias length** is the maximum length of a generated URL, which is capped at 255. The **Maximum component length** setting is the maximum length of any replacement pattern, such as the **[node:nid]**. I usually leave these at their default settings.

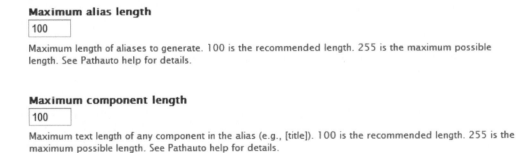

Figure 7-4. Click the **SETTINGS** tab to view configuration settings.

Figure 7-5 shows the final group of general settings. **Update action** determines what happens when a node is saved and a replacement pattern is changed, such as the **[node:title]**. By default, Pathauto is set to create a new alias and delete the old. As explained in the previous section, I do not recommend changing URL paths after a site has gone into production. You could change this to create a new alias and leave the existing alias functioning, basically creating two URLs to access the same node. The issue with this is that a search engine may penalize your search rankings if it finds "duplicate" content on your site.

My recommendation is to use the path_redirect module, which when enabled gives you an additional setting under **Update action** to create a new alias and redirect old alias to new alias.

The **Reduce strings to letters and numbers** setting simply removes all Unicode characters. Alternatively, you can use the transliteration module (http://drupal.org/project/ transliteration), which provides a **Transliterate prior to creating alias** check box, which in combination with Pathauto removes Unicode text and transliterates it to the US-ASCII alphabet.

Strings to Remove refers to all the character strings Pathauto will remove from replacement patterns. For example, if the **[node:title]** contains "Hello to the World" and the strings **to** and **the** are listed in **Strings to Remove**, then only "Hello World" will be in the URL.

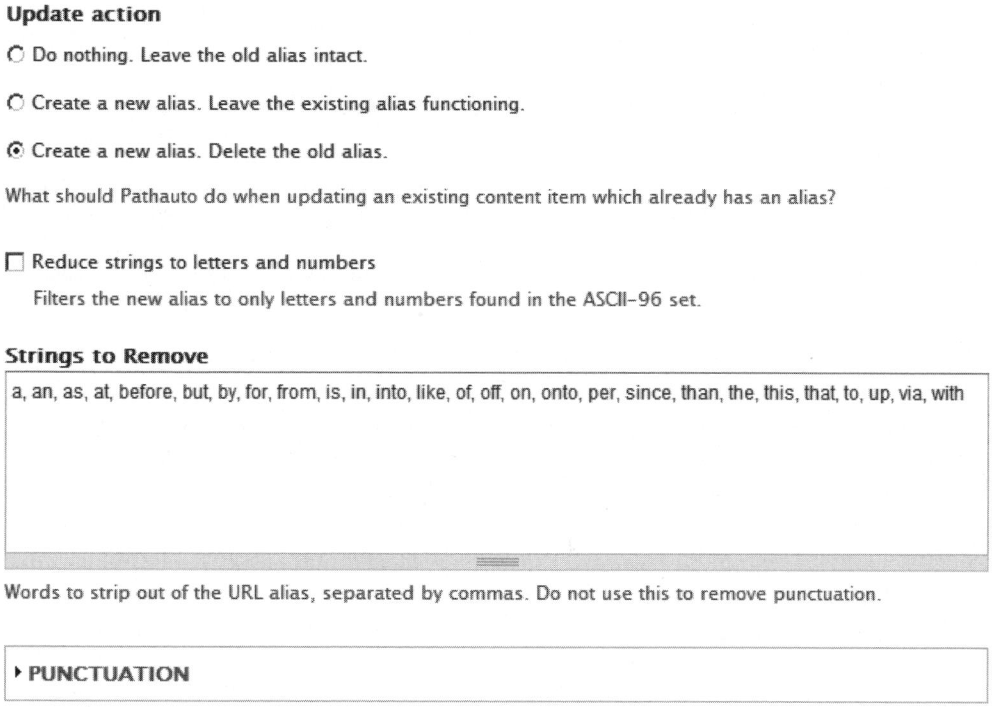

Update action

○ Do nothing. Leave the old alias intact.

○ Create a new alias. Leave the existing alias functioning.

⊙ Create a new alias. Delete the old alias.

What should Pathauto do when updating an existing content item which already has an alias?

☐ Reduce strings to letters and numbers

  Filters the new alias to only letters and numbers found in the ASCII-96 set.

Strings to Remove

a, an, as, at, before, but, by, for, from, is, in, into, like, of, off, on, onto, per, since, than, the, this, that, to, up, via, with

Words to strip out of the URL alias, separated by commas. Do not use this to remove punctuation.

▸ **PUNCTUATION**

Figure 7-5. Click the **SETTINGS** tab to view configuration settings.

Punctuation settings allow you to configure how Pathauto works with characters such as quotes, commas, periods, and more, as shown in Figure 7-6. Pathauto can remove the character, replace it with the separator, or take no action and insert it into the URL. The only change I recommend making is changing the **Underscore** setting to **No action**, as described in the previous section.

Figure 7-6. Click the **SETTINGS** tab to view configuration settings.

Using views to query and display data

The views module allows you to control how content in Drupal is presented. It's a tool allowing you to build database queries that pull nodes, node revisions, taxonomy terms, comments, files, users, fields, and more, plus any related data such as fields, into a web page, block, or RSS feed. Output is easily configurable and themeable. It can be used to display images, lists of content, summaries of content, and more. I almost always use the views module on every project, using it to create things such as the following:

- A right sidebar block that displays a list of the most recent blog items, with each item linking to the node's full-page view
- A list of images in a grid format that open a Lightbox2 view of the image when clicked
- A customized homepage that displays a single node depending on an "active date" field
- A sortable catalog with drop-down boxes, check boxes, and search boxes so a user can sort and limit content displayed by the view
- A list of the most recently purchased items on a user's account page
- A jQuery slideshow of images attached to a specific content type
- A full-page monthly calendar with event titles that link to the full-page event view, plus an accompanying mini-calendar that can fit in a sidebar

My goal for this section is to explain the basic workflow of the views module and to demonstrate how to create a custom view for the front page. For more specific examples, such as how to create the views listed previously, check out Appendix B.

The views administration UI

You access the views interface by navigating to **Structure ➤ Views**, as shown in Figure 7-7. Two tabs are available, **LIST** (default) and **TOOLS**. The default **LIST** page lists all views currently on the site, along with several drop-downs to sort and restrict the list. Individual views can be either enabled or disabled; the views module provides a number of default views available to override system-generated pages. Once enabled, a default view can be edited, exported for use on another Drupal installation, cloned, or disabled; only created views can be deleted. Note the system message about installing and enabling the advanced_help module (`http://drupal.org/project/advanced_help`); this can be a great resource when creating a view.

I'll discuss a couple of the drop-down selectors on this page just to give you an idea of how views works. **Storage** refers to how a view is saved and can be either **normal**, **default**, or **overridden**. A default view is either a view provided by views or a contrib module that is unaltered, such as the **archive** or **frontpage** view. Once a default view has been changed, it is then saved by views and becomes overridden; you can also revert it to the default view. This brings up a good point: many modules hook into the views API, adding their own views that you can go in and override. A normal view is a view that has been added to the site through either the **Add new view** or **Import view from code** link.

Type refers to the type of data the view is pulling, including **Comment**, **Node**, **File**, **Node revision**, **Term**, **User**, and more. Think of it as what you want to query; do you want to query nodes, files, or comments? This value is entered when creating a view and cannot be changed afterward. It also changes many of the default settings available when creating a view; see the next two sections for details.

Displays is how the view is being displayed in the site, which can be through a **Block**, a **Page,** and/or an RSS **Feed**. Note that all views are displayed through one of these three.

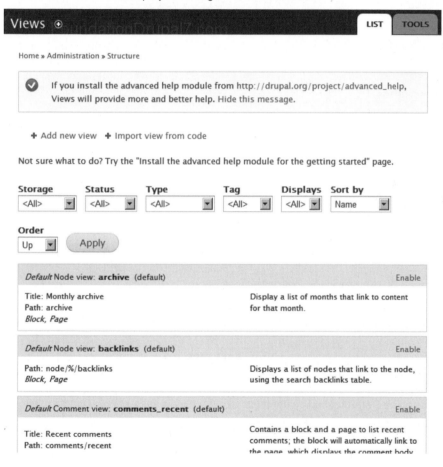

Figure 7-7. The Views homepage is accessed by navigating to **Structure ➤ Views**.

Adding a view

To add a view, navigate to **Structure ➤ Views**, and click the **Add new view** link at the top of the page, as shown in Figure 7-8. The **View name** setting is the machine-readable name, used when theming the site. The **View description** setting is a short description that appears on the views administration UI. The **View tag** is also used on the administration UI to sort views; any value entered here will appear in the **Tag** drop-down, as shown in Figure 7-7. **View type** was discussed in the previous section; your selection here determines the fields available on the next page; click **Next** to continue.

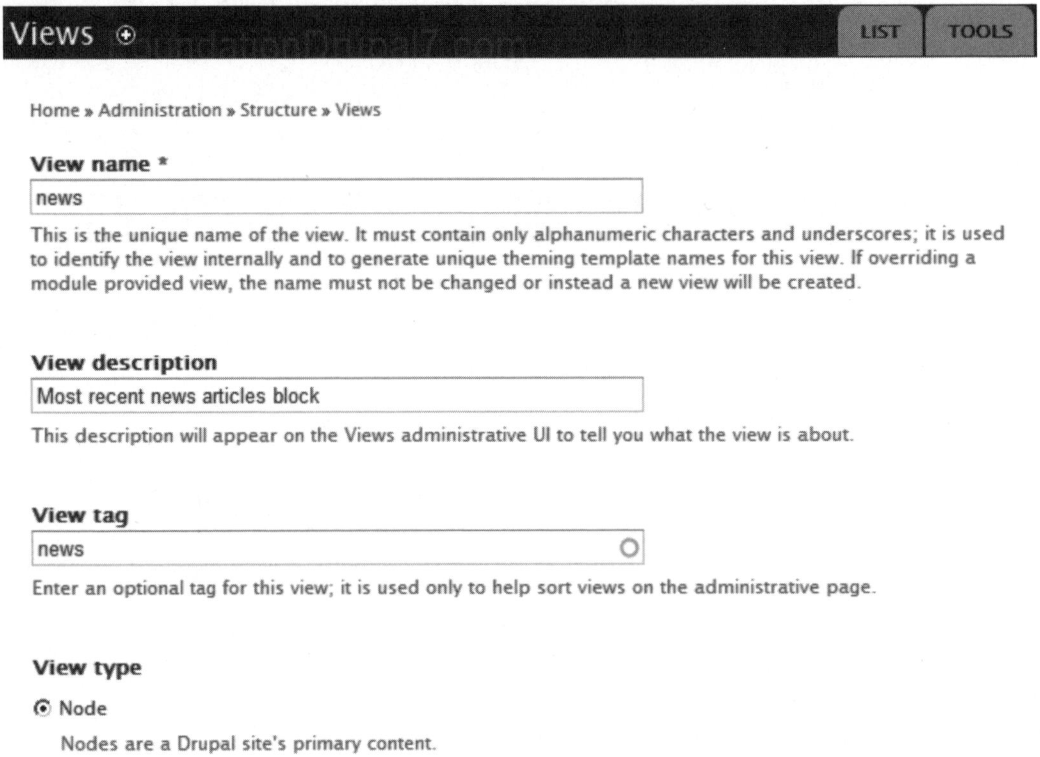

Figure 7-8. Navigate to **Structure ➤ Views**, and click the **Add new view** link at the top of the page to add a view.

See Figure 7-9 for the edit view screen; you are sent to this page after you add a view or when you edit a view. This is the page you will visit most frequently when editing a view, and it's a page with which you should become familiar. There are four columns; the left column lists one or more displays, including the **Defaults** display. The **Defaults** display contains all default view values; if you add additional displays to the view, such as a block, feed, or page display, these additional displays inherit default values. Each display has three columns with display-specific settings. This means you can have multiple views listed in the left column, all based on default values but with settings overridden at the individual view level. Note that the view is not saved until you click the **Save** button at the bottom of the page.

Figure 7-9. Users are sent to this page after they add a view or when they edit a view.

When creating a view, I tend to think of the default display as the starter view; you first set default values across all related views, such as the header, footer, and fields, and then add individual views that display associated data through blocks, feeds, or pages. The display can either use the default values or override them. This means, for example, you can have multiple views all related to a set of default values. This commonly happens when you have a block containing information that contains a **more** link to a full-page view. In this case, you would have a defaults tab, a page display, and a block display, as shown in Figure 7-10. Each display can override default values; this is not to be confused with overriding a default view given by views or a contributed module, as discussed earlier. If a page, block, or feed display has display-specific settings (for example, in Figure 7-10, the **Machine Name** and **Name**), then the label font is black and nonitalicized, but if the display is sharing values with the view (that is, **Title**, **Use pager**, **More link**, and so on), the labels are light gray and italicized.

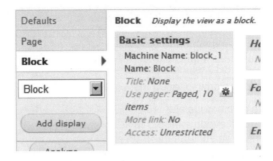

Figure 7-10. This view has both a page view and a block view that share default values.

Please note that if you make any changes to settings within a page, block, or feed display, you must click the **Override** button if you want changes to be reflected for that specific display, as shown in Figure 7-11. If you do not click the **Override** button, then any changes made will be changed to the default display. This actually happens quite a bit for both beginners and experienced users of this module; I can't tell you how many times I've thrown my hands in the air and exclaimed "Gosh!" when I realized I completely changed a view because I forgot to use the **Override** function. One workaround to this problem you may want to try is to export the view before you start making any changes. Exporting a view gives you a complete backup of the view; if you make any mistakes, such as forgetting to override one or more fields, you can simply delete the view and import the backup.

Figure 7-11. You must click the **Override** button when making changes to a view if you want the settings to be specific to a page, block, or feed display; otherwise, you will change only the default display values.

Each individual display has three columns of information, with each column containing a number of categorized settings for the individual view. Each settings category has several pieces of information; all have links, and some have gear icons. Clicking a link or an icon opens an additional form at the bottom of the screen to which you can make configuration changes. If there is an icon, the link is used to select the main setting (that is, plug-in, pager type, and so on), and the icon is used to configure settings within each main setting. Referring to Figure 7-9, selecting the **Unformatted** link next to **Style** in the **Style settings** category opens the dialog box shown in Figure 7-12 underneath the main view area. After you have selected the style plug-in and clicked **Update**, the icon is used to configure the selected plug-in's settings.

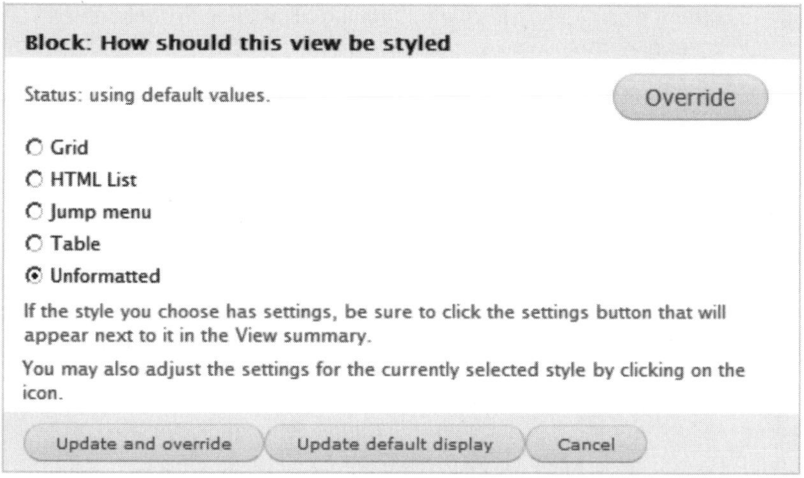

Block: How should this view be styled

Status: using default values.

Override

○ Grid
○ HTML List
○ Jump menu
○ Table
◉ Unformatted

If the style you choose has settings, be sure to click the settings button that will appear next to it in the View summary.

You may also adjust the settings for the currently selected style by clicking on the icon.

Update and override   Update default display   Cancel

Figure 7-12. Clicking the link next to the **Style** label in the **Style settings** category opens a form to select a style plug-in.

I broadly categorize each column as settings, display, and logics, separated (mostly) by the left, center, and right columns. I'm going to divide the rest of this chapter into separate sections accordingly, with the goal of explaining how to add a view.

Settings

In the left column, you see category settings for the display, including **View settings** (available only on **Defaults** display) **Basic settings**, **Advanced settings**, and **Style settings**, plus a category for **exposed form**. If you're looking at a page, block, or feed display, a corresponding **settings** category will appear underneath **Exposed form**, and the **View settings** category will disappear.

View settings are global settings for the view, including **Description/Tag**, which appears on the view module's administrative UI. This is the only category that is specific to the **Defaults** display; the remaining categories (**Basic**, **Advanced**, **Style**) appear on and can be overridden at the **Page**, **Block**, and **Feed** display levels.

The **Basic settings** category has a number of settings. You may need to change the display **Name** if you have a number of views; this is also the name that appears in the left display column. The **Title** appears at the top of the view where the page, block, or feed title is output by the theme. **Use pager** determines the number of items in a list and whether a pager is used to scroll through the list; click the gear icon to adjust the number of items per page. A block display may also have a **More link** that points to a specific page view; this is used when you want to link a block view to a specific page view. **Access** options allow you to restrict who can access the view by either **role** (for example, **anonymous**, **authenticated**, and so on) or by a **permission** granted on the **People ➤ permissions** page.

Advanced settings are a catchall group of configuration settings. If **Yes** is selected, **Use AJAX** will display a block or page using Ajax for paging (**Use pager** under **Basic settings** must be enabled), table sorting (the **Style** setting under **Style settings** must be set to **Table** and configured properly), and exposed filters (if configured properly in the **Exposed form** category, discussed in the next section). This is not recommended if the view is used as the main content (that is, a full-page display), because it will prevent linking to content displayed by the view. **Caching** allows you to cache the results of the views query, allowing you to boost performance on a production site.

Query settings allow you to configure advanced MySQL settings, which are beyond the scope of this book. If you are interested in learning more, check out `http://dev.mysql.com/doc/refman/5.0/en/distinct-optimization.html` to learn about the `distinct` command, and check out `http://api.drupal.org/api/function/hook_db_rewrite_sql/6` to learn about disabling SQL rewriting.

Style settings allow you to configure and customize how the view is styled when output. By default, the views module comes with five styles: **Unformatted**, **Grid**, **HTML List**, **Jump menu**, and **table**. Many other modules add additional style plug-ins, including calendars, slideshows, pop-ups, and more. Many of these are discussed in Appendix B. **Row style** allows you to change how data is output; by default, rows can be output as either fields or nodes. If **fields** is selected, you will need to add fields to display, as discussed in the next section. **CSS class** allows you to add a class to the individual view, used primarily for theming. **Theme: information** presents a list of theme templates available to override the views module's theme templates and is covered in the next chapter.

When building the logic behind a view (covered in a later section), one setting category is called **Filters**, which allows you to restrict the list of results based on a number of values, such as the time a node was created or the number of comments. When creating filters, you can also expose them to end users so they can limit results manually. An example of an exposed form would be the drop-down select boxes in Figure 7-7, which give you the ability to sort and restrict the list of views. The **Exposed form** category provides a number of settings for exposed filters, such as **Exposed form in block** and **Exposed form style**.

Each display has a number of settings. A page display must have the **Path** set; otherwise, you would not be able to access the view. This is similar to creating a path for a node. **Menu** links can also be created and added to any system menu. The **Block settings** category, available on all **Block** displays, allows you to assign a title to the block view, as shown on the block administration page. You can also enable caching for the block. The **Feed settings** category requires you to enter a **Path** for the feed, plus you must also attach it to a display, from which it pulls data and creates an RSS feed.

Display

The next set of configuration settings impacts the way the content is output in the page, block, or feed display. Note that in this section, in order to override the default display, you must click the category header (that is, **Header**, **Footer**, **Empty text**, or **Fields**), as shown in Figure 7-13.

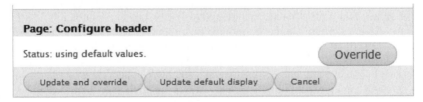

Figure 7-13. Click the category header to override the default view settings.

You'll also notice that each category has a plus icon and an icon with arrows pointing up and down. Clicking the plus icons opens a form underneath the main view so that you can add one or more customized fields. If there is more than one customized field in a category, the arrow icon allows you to adjust the relative height of each customized field.

The **Header** and **Footer** categories allow you to place text and/or fields in the header or footer of the display, that is, above or below the view on a page, block, or feed. Click the plus icon to view the list of available fields. The **Empty text** section allows you to customize the content displayed on a view that returns no results. This is similar to the **Header** and **Footer**, except that the **Header** and **Footer** appear whether a view has results or not.

The **Fields** category allows you to select fields to output in each row of your results; see Figure 7-14 for a partial list of all the fields available to choose from after clicking the plus icon. There is a large list of fields! The fields you select will depend on what you want the view to display and how you've configured the site. For example, if you are creating a slideshow, you will most likely select the node title and an image field as the fields to output. This means you have two fields in the category; use the arrow icon to adjust the order in which the fields are output. After you add your fields, you will next create the logic behind which fields are presented.

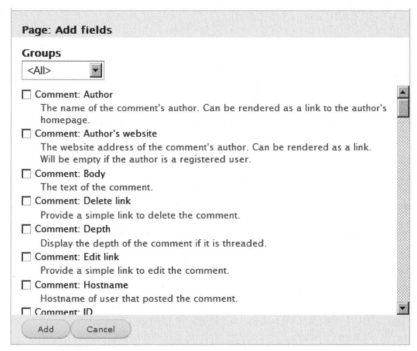

Figure 7-14. The **Fields** category allows you to select fields to output in each row of your results.

Logic

When you initially create a view, you select the type of content you want to query, such as nodes, comments, node revisions, and so on. The **Relationships**, **Arguments**, **Sort criteria**, and **Filters** categories allow you to configure exactly which content should be displayed. If your view is querying nodes and you do not change anything in these four categories, then all nodes in the system will be displayed in the list of results. **Filters** allows you to restrict the list of results by any number of values, such as the node's author, the node's creation time, the number of comments a node has, whether a node has been promoted to the front page, and more. For example, you may want to create a block that displays a list of the most recent blog posts. You would select one filter: **Node: Type**, which you would set to the blog content type (remember to click the plus icon to see the list of available filters). I always recommend adding either the **Node: Published** filter or the **Node: Published or admin** filter; otherwise, content that is not published will appear in the list.

You may also want to sort the list using the sort criteria category. For example, you may want to sort the list by post date so that the most recent blog posts show first. Simply add **Node: Post date** to **Sort criteria**, configured to sort by **Descending**, as shown in Figure 7-15. You can also add the field **Node: Sticky** if you want to enable the **promote to top of list** check box when creating a node. Referring to Figure 7-15, you'll notice that I changed the order of the **sort criteria** setting so that **Node: Sticky** is above the **Node: Post** date. Sort order is preserved in a view so that the list is searched first by the first field, then the second field, and so on.

Figure 7-15. The **Filters** category allows you to restrict the list of results, while **Sort criteria** sorts the list.

When you add filters or sort criteria, you have the opportunity to expose each field, as discussed earlier in the chapter. This allows users to manually sort and filter the list of results. When a field is exposed, the word **Exposed** is displayed to the right of the field title.

Arguments allow you to filter a view based on a value in the URL path, such as a number, a word, or a date, that is related to the node. For example, you may want a view that displays all nodes of a certain taxonomy term, which frequently happens when you're creating a blog or a catalog. Using Pathauto, you would first create a URL pattern so that a node's primary taxonomy term is the last word in the URL. Then you would add an argument so that the view uses the URL path to get the term name, which it uses as a filter. See Appendix B for examples of how to use arguments.

Relationships allow you to connect a node with a secondary node (or user) so that only secondary nodes or users that are related to the starting node are queried; these fields are then available in the **Fields** category to insert into your view (covered in the previous section). For example, you may want to relate a node to the person who created it so that you can then pull information related to that specific user, such as their signature. This is usually used in tandem with the node_reference module or user_reference module, both of which are located in the cck module (`http://drupal.org/project/cck`).

Previewing and saving a view

Click the **Preview** button at the bottom of the screen to preview the view. If you have an argument in the view, such as a term, enter it in the **Arguments** field. Once you are satisfied with the view, click the **Save** button. When creating a view, don't forget to click the **Save** button; otherwise, you will lose all your work. It's easy to forget. Once you hit **Save**, the views module will check your view and let you know whether anything is missing, such as a path for a page or feed display. You can successfully save after you fix all the error messages.

Enabling and updating the front-page view

Views provides a default node view that simulates the default front page; this is perfect if you want to use a view as a homepage, which I highly recommend. This is a straightforward process of enabling the view and pointing your default front page to the view front page. Let's do it:

1. First, go to the views homepage by navigating to **Structure ➤ Views**.

2. Click the **Enable** button in the **frontpage** box; afterward, the box will look like Figure 7-16.

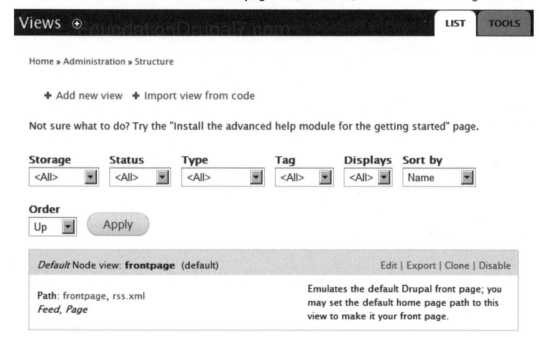

Figure 7-16. The **frontpage** view has been enabled.

3. Next, navigate to **Configuration ➤ Site information**.

4. Change the default front page to **frontpage**, as shown in Figure 7-17.

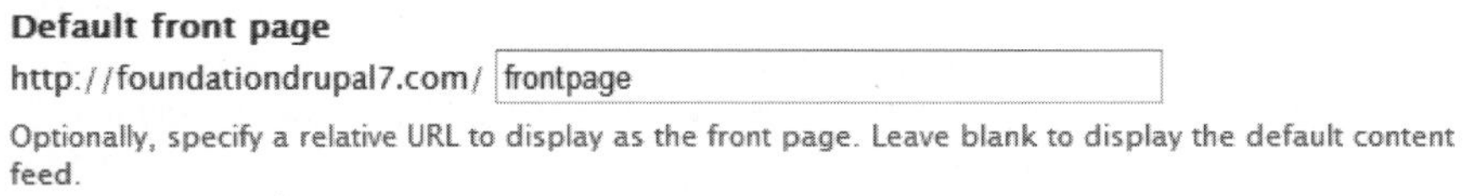

Default front page

http://foundationdrupal7.com/ | frontpage

Optionally, specify a relative URL to display as the front page. Leave blank to display the default content feed.

Figure 7-17. Update the Default front page to point to the new view.

Now you're ready to edit the view!

Entering content with WYSIWYG HTML editors

A WYSIWYG editor allows people to create web-friendly text in a browser. It allows you to write text and apply HTML markup to the text you write, such as changing the font size and font color, displaying icons, and more. You most likely use an HTML editor when you write e-mails if you use a web-based service for e-mail, such as Gmail, Hotmail/Live, or Yahoo! The best module to use to install a WYSIWYG editor is the (drumroll, please) Wysiwyg module (`http://drupal.org/project/wysiwyg`). This module allows you to install any of a number of WYSIWYG editors, including TinyMCE, CKEditor, YUI (Yahoo!), and more.

WYSIWYG editors also allow you to embed images and videos from third-party sources such as Flickr and YouTube. If you want to upload images and videos to your own server using a WYSIWYG editor, I recommend using the IMCE module (`http://drupal.org/project/imce`) along with the IMCE Wysiwyg bridge (`http://drupal.org/project/imce_wysiwyg`). These two modules allow you to upload files directly to the server through a WYSIWYG editor, including the ability to resize images and saving to multiple directories. Unfortunately, a limited number of WYSIWYG editors are supported using this method, including CKEditor, FCKeditor, and TinyMCE. Another alternative to insert images and files into your WYSIWYG content area is to use the Insert module (`drupal.org/project/insert`). This module allows you to upload files using Drupal's built-in Field API and then insert those files into the content area. My recommendation is to play around with both modules and see which one is the best fit for your work style and preferences.

Installing the WYSIWYG module and configuring Drupal involves a number of steps:

1. After installing and enabling the module, navigate to **Configuration ➤ Wysiwyg profiles**; the list of supported WYSIWYG editors is listed on this page. Click the download link to download an editor.

2. Install the appropriate editor in a directory called **libraries** located in the **sites/all** directory, as shown in Figure 7-18. You may need to create this directory; refer to Chapter 2.

Figure 7-18. Install the appropriate editor in a directory called **libraries**, which is located in the **sites/all** directory.

3. Although not required, I recommend configuring an input format specifically for the WYSIWYG editor. Navigate to **Configuration ➤ Text formats** to add a format, as shown in Figure 7-19. This allows you to easily assign permissions to roles so that one role can access a limited version editor while another role can access a full version.

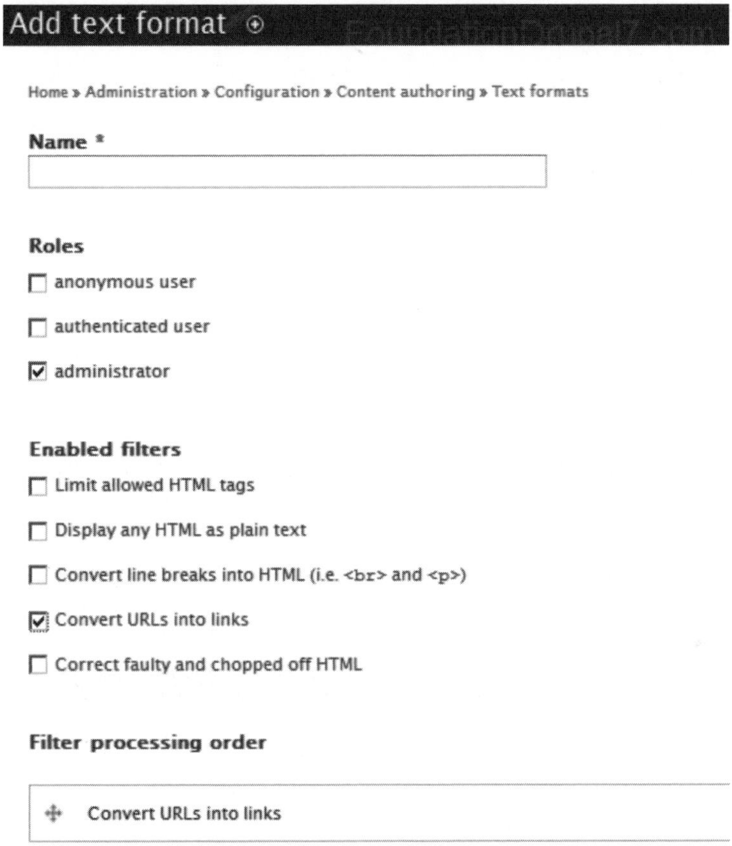

Figure 7-19. Navigate to **Configuration ➤ Text formats** to add a format.

Note that one of the benefits of the WYSIWYG module is that the editor is tied to a specific filter, which you cannot do with standalone editors. This means you can have different filter settings per editor, so that a user with an administrator role can have different filters than an anonymous user. This is ideal when you want to limit the functionality of an anonymous user's WYSIWYG editor but give administrators full functionality.

4. Return to the **Configuration ➤ Wysiwyg profiles** page, which has now changed. If you added an **INPUT FORMAT**, it will also appear in the list, as shown in Figure 7-20.

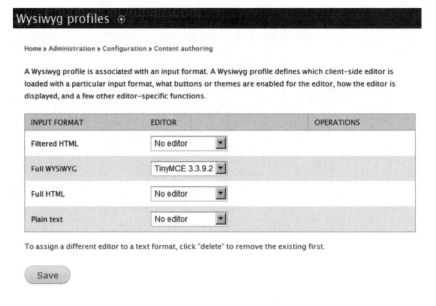

Figure 7-20. If you added an INPUT FORMAT, it appears on the Wysiwyg profiles page.

5. By default, no editors are assigned to an input format. If you added a text format (aka **INPUT FORMAT**), select the editor you just installed to be used, and save; this editor will be used when the format is selected during content creation, as shown in Figure 7-21.

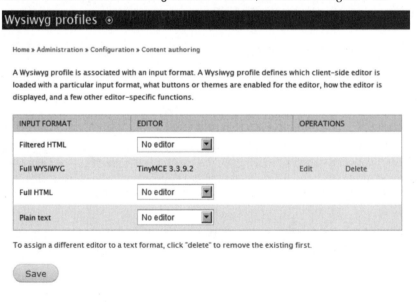

Figure 7-21. Select the editor you just installed to be used and save.

6. Click the **Edit** button next to the installed WYSIWYG editor; this allows you to customize the editor for that specific **INPUT FORMAT**, as shown in Figure 7-22.

Note: There are a number of options to upload and insert images through the WYSIWYG editor. I have had good luck with IMCE (http://drupal.org/project/imce) and Insert (http://drupal.org/project/insert). If you enable one of these modules, you will need to click **Buttons and Plugins** *and select the appropriate check boxes.*

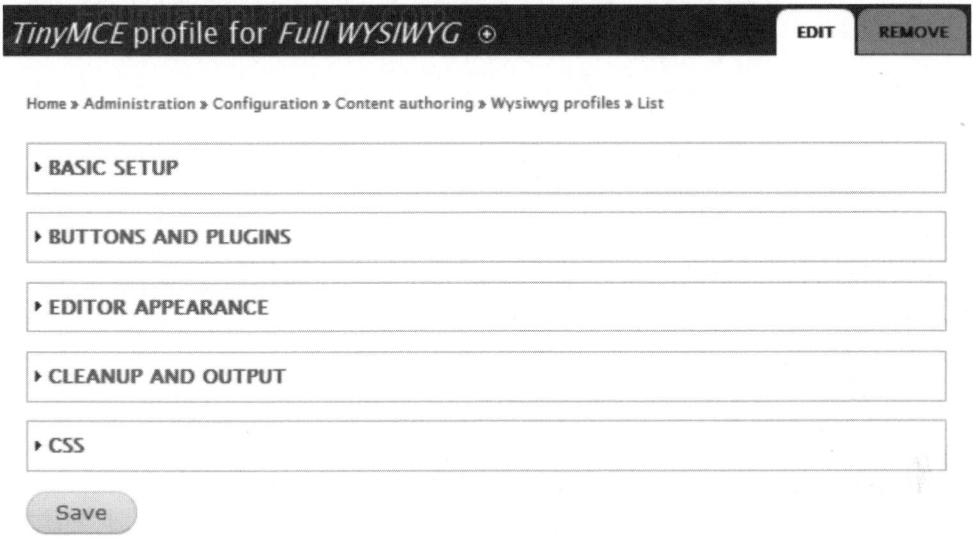

TinyMCE profile for *Full WYSIWYG* ⊕ EDIT REMOVE

Home » Administration » Configuration » Content authoring » Wysiwyg profiles » List

▸ BASIC SETUP

▸ BUTTONS AND PLUGINS

▸ EDITOR APPEARANCE

▸ CLEANUP AND OUTPUT

▸ CSS

Save

Figure 7-22. Click the Edit button to customize the editor for that specific INPUT FORMAT.

7. Don't forget to add permissions so that a specific role can view the format! Navigate to **People,** select the **PERMISSIONS** tab, and scroll down to the **Filter** category, as shown in Figure 7-23; see Chapter 5 for details.

Filter

Administer text formats and filters *Warning: Give to trusted roles only; this permission has security implications.*	☐	☐	☑
Use the Filtered HTML **text format** *Warning: This permission may have security implications depending on how the text format is configured.*	☑	☑	☑
Use the Full WYSIWYG **text format** *Warning: This permission may have security implications depending on how the text format is configured.*	☐	☐	☑
Use the Full HTML **text format**			

Figure 7-23. Navigate to **People**, select the **PERMISSIONS** tab, and scroll down to the **Filter** category to assign permissions.

8. To test whether it works, select **Add content ➤ Basic page**, and change the text format to the text format you configured earlier, as shown in Figure 7-24.

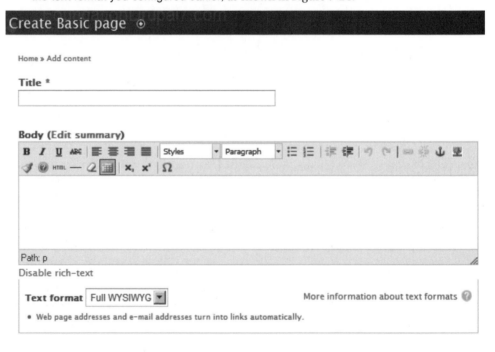

Figure 7-24. Select **Add content ➤ Basic page**, and change the **Text format** to the text format you configured earlier.

JavaScript menus with DHTML Menu

The DHTML Menu module (`http://drupal.org/project/dhtml_menu`) allows you to quickly add JavaScript animation to vertical drop-down menus, such as the core management or navigation menus that appear in the left sidebar, as shown in Figure 7-25. When enabled, you simply click a link, and all the menu items nested underneath the original link open without requiring a page refresh. Note that this module works only for horizontal menu links, not vertical links, and it does not cause menu links to pop out or drop down like you see on many popular sites. This module simply removes the need to refresh the screen when clicking a menu item with child links. All menus are automatically enabled, which means you need to manually disable each menu if you don't want the JavaScript drop-down to work. The module also adds a **DHTML Menu** link to the administrative toolbar with a number of configuration settings. I generally just turn this module on and forget about it; I find that default settings are fine unless a client requests otherwise.

Navigation

- ▸ *Add content*
  - ◦ Article
  - ◦ Basic page
  - ◦ Poll
- ◦ Recent content

Figure 7-25. The management menu with DHTML Menu enabled allows for JavaScript drop-down links.

Creating forms with webform

The webform module allows you to create an individualized form per node. That is, you can create a form to collect e-mail addresses, uploaded files, radio buttons, check boxes, and so on, where each node has a different set of fields to collect data. Furthermore, each form has a number of included features, such as reporting and data export.

There are a number of differences between the webform module and other methods used to collect data in Drupal. One of the main differences is that web form submissions are not saved as nodes. If you create a content type and add fields to the content type to collect user-submitted data, all submissions are saved as a node and can be accessed at /node/[nid] by users with the proper permissions. This is not so with web forms; data is saved in a table and can be accessed only by using the webform module. This has its pros and cons; webform makes it very easy to collect, store, and retrieve data. However, data is not nodes and does not have the functionality associated with nodes, such as commenting, workflows, and ease of integration with other Drupal modules.

When do you use the webform module instead of creating a content type? Here are a few rules of thumb I tend to follow:

- The webform module is preferred when you need to save data and plan to export data to Excel or another third-party application.
- The core contact module is preferred over the webform module if you require a single contact form that can be directed to more than one person.
- The core poll module is preferred over the webform module if you want to give users the ability to see voting statistics immediately after they vote.
- Content types are preferred when you want each submission to be accessible by navigating to /node/[nid].
- Content types are preferred when you want to do something with data, such as displaying it in a view or sending it to a user for review.
- Content types are preferred when you want the flexibility of using Drupal's core fields or contributed field modules.

Content types can also be webform-enabled, allowing you to attach a unique web form to every node of a specific content type. This can be beneficial if, for example, you want to create a customized "Contact Us" form for each node of a specific content type. For example, you may have an automobile content type and, at the bottom of each automobile node, want to include a form that salespeople can customize.

Configuring the webform module

Navigate to the **Configuration** page and select **Webform settings** under the **CONTENT AUTHORING** header. Your first set of configuration settings are **Webform-enabled content types**, as shown in Figure 7-26. By default, the module creates and enables a content type called **Webform**.

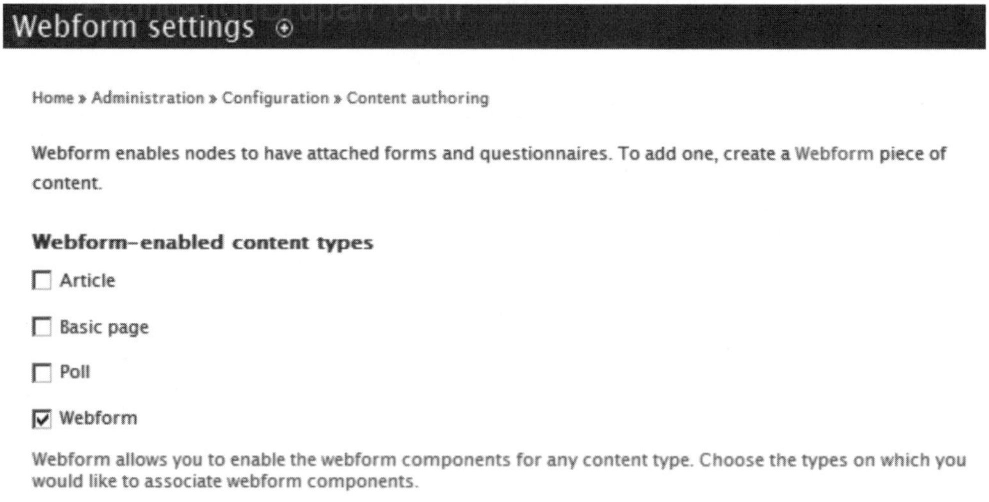

Webform settings ⊙

Home » Administration » Configuration » Content authoring

Webform enables nodes to have attached forms and questionnaires. To add one, create a Webform piece of content.

Webform–enabled content types

☐ Article

☐ Basic page

☐ Poll

☑ Webform

Webform allows you to enable the webform components for any content type. Choose the types on which you would like to associate webform components.

Figure 7-26. By default, the webform module creates and enables a content type called **Webform**.

The webform module includes a number of available data-entry fields, as shown in Figure 7-27. If all fields are selected, then all fields will be available to be added to a web form.

Webform allows you to enable the webform components for any content type. Choose the types on which you would like to associate webform components.

NAME	DESCRIPTION	ENABLED
Date	Presents month, day, and year fields.	☑
E-mail	A special textfield that accepts e-mail addresses.	☑
Fieldset	Fieldsets allow you to organize multiple fields into groups.	☑
File	Allow users to upload files of configurable types.	☑
Grid	Allows creation of grid questions, denoted by radio buttons.	☑
Hidden	A field which is not visible to the user, but is recorded with the submission.	☑
Markup	Displays text as HTML in the form; does not render a field.	☑
Page break	Organize forms into multiple pages.	☑
Select options	Allows creation of checkboxes, radio buttons, or select menus.	☑
Textarea	A large text area that allows for multiple lines of input.	☑
Textfield	Basic textfield type.	☑
Time	Presents the user with hour and minute fields. Optional am/pm fields.	☑

Figure 7-27. The list of fields available for a web form

When a web form is submitted, an e-mail is automatically sent to a user. **DEFAULT E-MAIL VALUES** sets a default e-mail address that can be overridden at the individual node level, as shown in Figure 7-28.

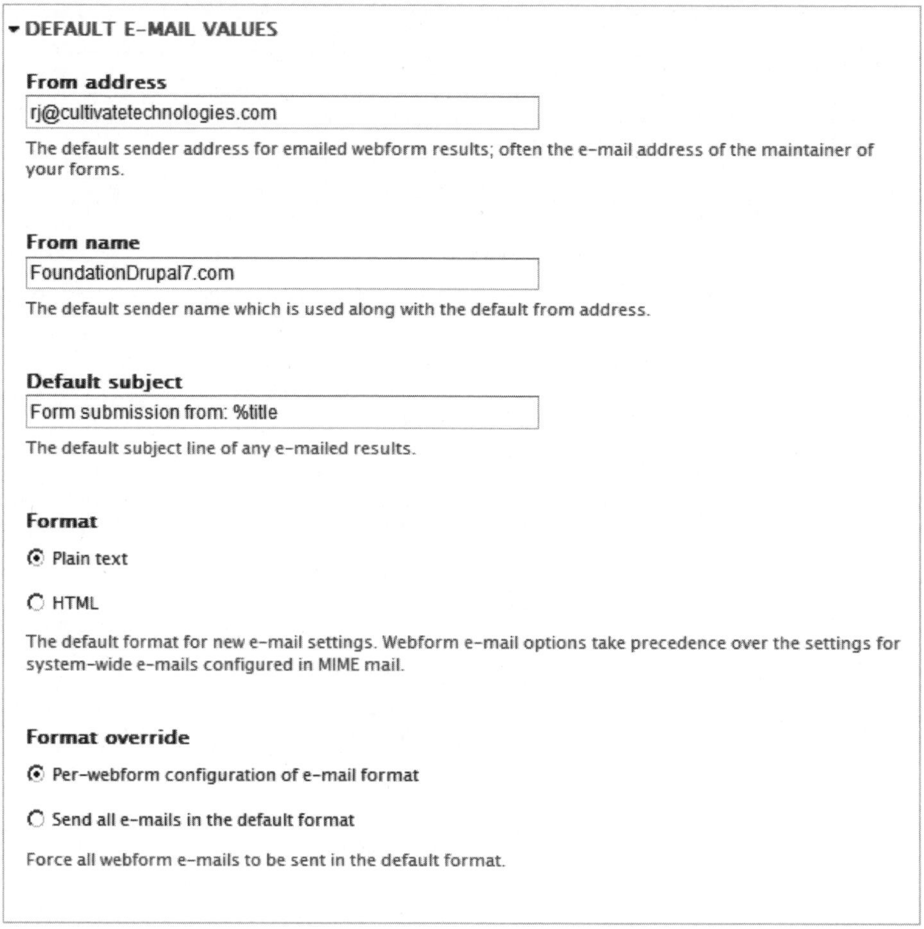

Figure 7-28. Default e-mail settings are used across all web forms; these can be overridden at the individual node level.

There are also a number of advanced configuration options, as shown in Figure 7-29. The **Allow cookies for tracking submissions** check box allows you to place a cookie on a user's machine to help prevent against a user repeatedly submitting a form. Note that this feature is not necessary, because the webform module also uses IP addresses and user names to prevent repeated submissions. I generally leave this deselected unless I start to have problems with obnoxious users, at which point I enable it. You can also configure the From address on generated e-mails, which I usually set to **Long format** unless the server has problems with e-mails.

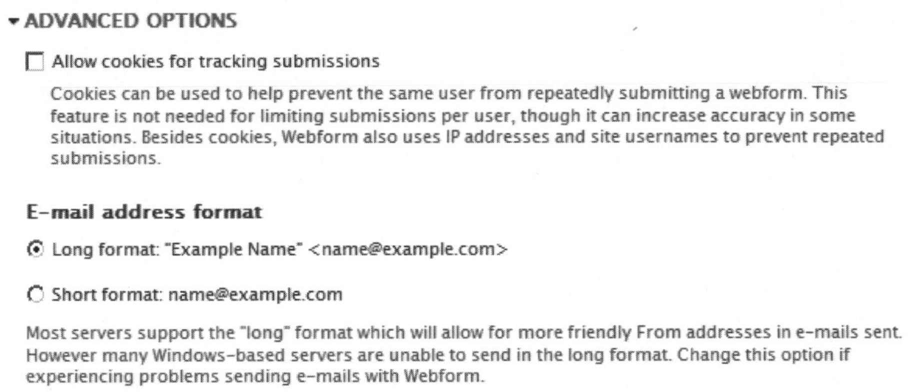

▼ ADVANCED OPTIONS

☐ Allow cookies for tracking submissions

Cookies can be used to help prevent the same user from repeatedly submitting a webform. This feature is not needed for limiting submissions per user, though it can increase accuracy in some situations. Besides cookies, Webform also uses IP addresses and site usernames to prevent repeated submissions.

E-mail address format

◉ Long format: "Example Name" <name@example.com>

◯ Short format: name@example.com

Most servers support the "long" format which will allow for more friendly From addresses in e-mails sent. However many Windows-based servers are unable to send in the long format. Change this option if experiencing problems sending e-mails with Webform.

Figure 7-29. Advanced web form options, including cookie and e-mail address configuration settings

You can also configure **Default export format** and **Default export delimeter**, as shown in Figure 7-30. A delimiter is the character used to separate data values in the exported text file and is required only when **Default export format** is set to **Delimited text**.

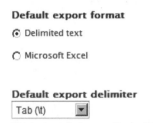

Default export format

◉ Delimited text

◯ Microsoft Excel

Default export delimiter

[Tab (\t)   ▼]

This is the delimiter used in the CSV/TSV file when downloading Webform results. Using tabs in the export is the most reliable method for preserving non-latin characters. You may want to change this to another character depending on the program with which you anticipate importing results.

Figure 7-30. Default export format and delimiter options

The final advanced option is **Submission access control**, as shown in Figure 7-31. When creating a web form, you have the option to choose which role(s) may submit the form. In some cases, you may have set permission to view the content type through the **People ➤ PERMISSIONS** page or through a content access module; in this case, you can safely select **Disable webform submission access control**. Otherwise, you will want to select the **select the user roles that may submit each individual webform** option, giving you very precise control over who can submit forms, such as anonymous or authenticated users.

Submission access control

◉ Select the user roles that may submit each individual webform

○ Disable Webform submission access control

By default, the configuration form for each webform allows the administrator to choose which roles may submit the form. You may want to allow users to always submit the form if you are using a separate node access module to control access to webform nodes themselves.

Figure 7-31. Submission access control.

Creating a web form

In this example, I will show how to create a very simple contact form using the webform module:

1. Navigate to the **Add content** page, and select **Webform**.

2. Enter the node title, and click **Save**, as shown in Figure 7-32. Note that the default **Webform** content type does not include a body field.

Figure 7-32. Navigate to the **Add content** page, and select **Webform.**

3. After you click **Save**, you will need to begin adding fields that appear on the web form (see Figure 7-33); click the **Add** button to progress to the next screen.

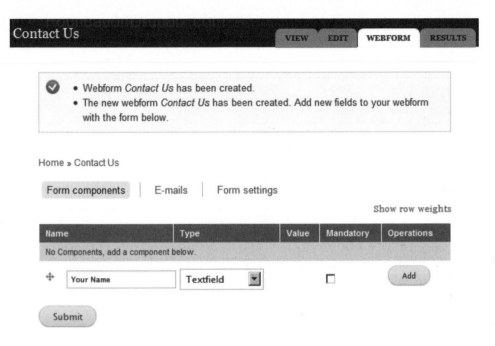

Figure 7-33. Begin adding fields that appear on the web form.

4. Fill out the form components, such as **Label**, **Field Key**, and more; the options vary depending on the field type selected in the previous step. Make sure to click **submit** at the bottom of the page after you're finished configuring the field.

5. Follow steps 3 and 4 to create additional fields.

6. You can also add e-mail responses to forms by clicking the **E-mails** link immediately above the list of fields, as shown in Figure 7-34. If an e-mail address field was created as a form component, it will appear in this list, allowing the form to send an e-mail to the user who submitted the form. Enter or select the correct e-mail address, and click **Add**.

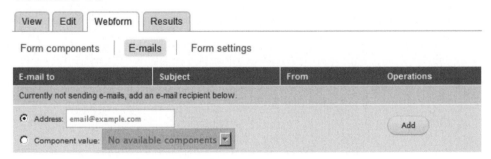

Figure 7-34. Add e-mail responses to forms by clicking the **E-mails** link.

7. Select the **Form settings** link to configure settings such as the confirmation message, redirect URL, submission limit, roles that can submit the form, and advanced settings, as shown in Figure 7-35.

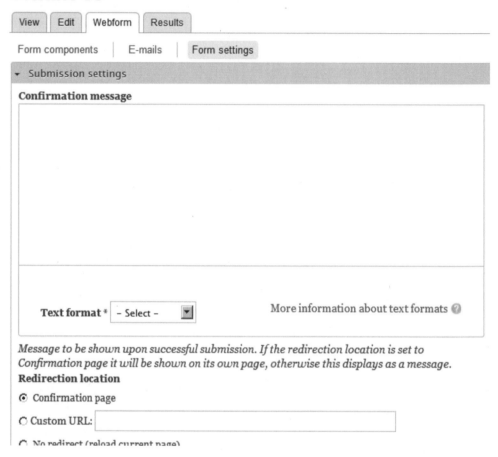

Figure 7-35. Select the **Form settings** link to configure settings such as the confirmation message, redirect URL, and more.

8. Navigate to the full-page node view to see the form; note that the **Edit** tab allows you to edit node settings (see Figure 7-36). The **Webform** tab is for editing form components, e-mails, and form settings, and the **Results** tab is for viewing submissions and exporting data.

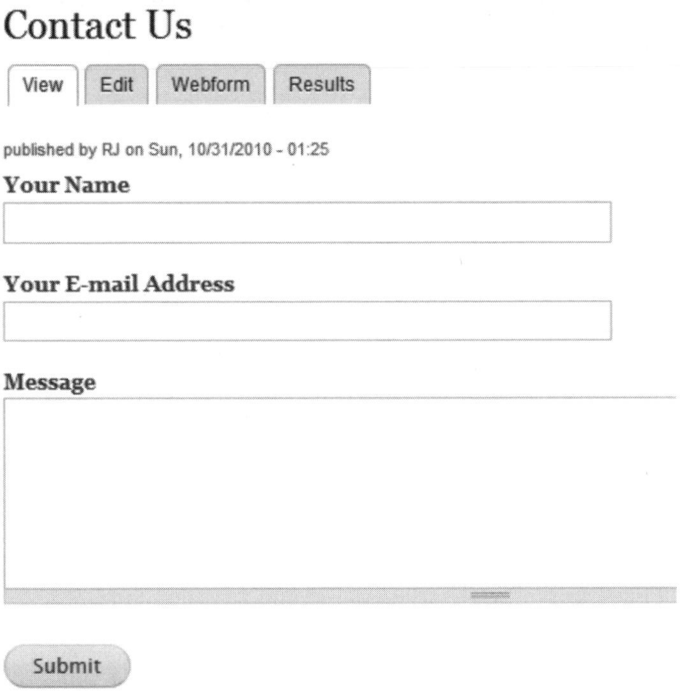

Contact Us

View | Edit | Webform | Results

published by RJ on Sun, 10/31/2010 - 01:25

Your Name

Your E-mail Address

Message

Submit

Figure 7-36. Navigate to the full-page node view to see the form.

Spam control with Mollom

Whether we like it or not, we all have to deal with the problem of spam. After your site has been on the Internet for a few months, bots begin to find it and submit forms, including comment, user, and node creation forms. A captcha is used to require users to submit an answer in response to a question, such as a math problem or disfigured letters. I recommend using the Mollom module to control spam; one of the main benefits of Mollom is that it doesn't present a captcha to the user the first time they submit the form, but only if a form response fits the profile of a spam submission. In this way, users aren't burdened with having to enter captcha responses every time they submit a form.

1. Enable the module.

2. Go to http://mollom.com to create an account and obtain your API access keys.

3. After you have your public and private keys, navigate to **Configuration ➤ Mollom**, and click the **SETTINGS** tab to add keys and configure the module (see Figure 7-37).

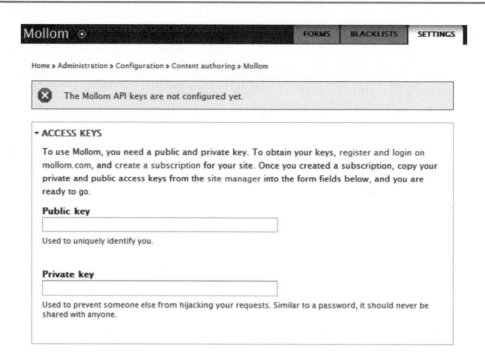

Figure 7-37. Navigate to **Configuration ➤ Mollom** and click the **SETTINGS** tab to add keys and configure the module.

4. Click the **FORMS** tab, click the **Add form** link, and select the forms you want Mollom to protect (see Figure 7-38).

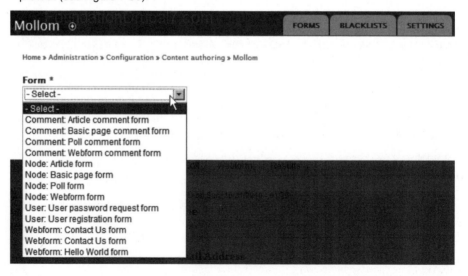

Figure 7-38. Click the **FORMS** tab, click the **Add form** link, and select the forms you want Mollom to protect.

5.	Next, select the fields to analyze, and configure Mollom on a form-by-form basis (see Figure 7-39).

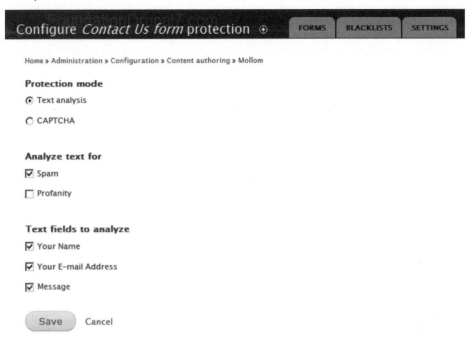

Figure 7-39. Submission access control

Your form is now protected (see Figure 7-40)!

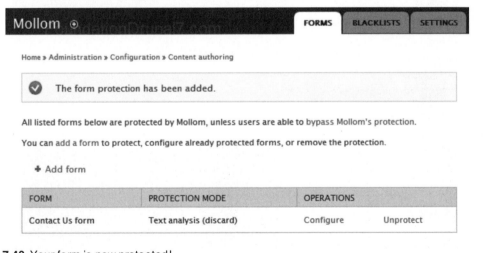

Figure 7-40. Your form is now protected!

Site statistics with Google Analytics

Google Analytics (`http://google.com/analytics`) is a powerful tool for analyzing site traffic and visitor usage patterns. Google Analytics can be added to any Drupal site by using the Google Analytics module (`http://drupal.org/project/google_analytics`). This module allows you to automatically insert the required JavaScript from Google in the footer of your site, plus a number of role, page, and user-specific information.

1. Enable the module.

2. Navigate to **Configuration ➤ Google Analytics** to configure the module; you must enter a Google Analytics account number for the module to work (see Figure 7-41).

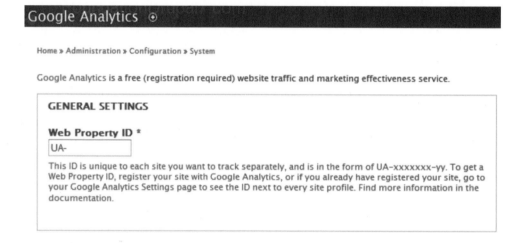

Figure 7-41. Navigate to **Configuration ➤ Google Analytics** to configure the module.

3. If you are using the IMCE module, it is recommended you remove tracking from all **imce*** pages (see Figure 7-42).

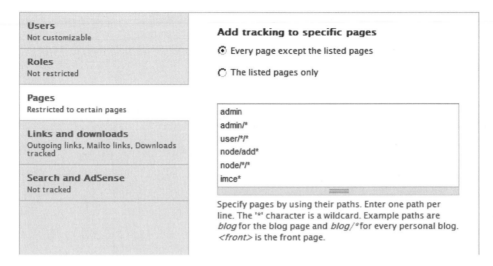

Figure 7-42. If you are using the IMCE module, it is recommended you remove tracking from all **imce***
pages.

4. Adjust other settings as required, and click **save**. To test, navigate to the front page (or any page), and open Firebug. The JavaScript for Google Analytics should print immediately after the footer.

```
⊞ <script src="/sites/all/modules/google_analytics/googleanalytics.js" type="text/javascript">
⊞ <script type="text/javascript">
⊞ <script type="text/javascript" src="http://www.google-analytics.com/ga.js">
⊞ <script type="text/javascript">
```

Summary

I covered several modules in this chapter that will help you take your Drupal site to the next level. I started by discussing Pathauto and how you can create URL path patterns using replacement patterns based on node values. I then talked about the views module, which is a way to query and present data in lists around your site. I then walked you step-by-step through the process of enabling a WYSIWYG editor and JavaScript drop-down menus. Then I moved into the webform module and talked about how easy it is to create web forms that capture information from users and segued into how to control spam from web forms with the Mollom module. I closed the chapter by discussing the Google Analytics module to analyze web site usage statistics.

Chapter 8

Theming a Drupal Website

This chapter was contributed by Stephanie Pakrul.

In this chapter, we will cover how to create a theme for your Drupal site. Theming in Drupal is very powerful; it's not just a matter of creating a "skin" for your website. You have precise control over the User Interface (UI) and where your data fields are placed. The Fusion theme, discussed in this chapter, is a point-and-click solution for managing the theme in your site. Fusion also helps with one of the most challenging things when you're first working with Drupal: understanding the dividing lines between content, configuration, and theming. We'll walk through some specific examples from start to finish and leave you with the tools you need to find more information about various theming topics.

Build first, then theme

A Drupal site without content is kind of like an uninflated balloon. Once you have a bit of content to play with, then you can place it into regions to make the layout come to life, create views to list data in different ways, and create new sections or pages to link to from your menus.

If you're working on a brand new site, before you continue with configuring your layout and styles, step away from the theme for a bit and think about the content that's going to be on your site. Maybe you're going to have some news items on your front page, so you'd first want to add some Article nodes (even if they're just dummy text for now!). Perhaps you have an "About us" page or contact form that needs to be added to your Primary links menu. Maybe you know you're going to have some text blocks listing your product's top features, or your company address, or showing the latest comments on the site. Or maybe something requiring additional Drupal modules, like an image gallery or video blog.

Tip: Often you need to build a Drupal site without having real content ready to go. There are tools to help! Visit lipsum.com to generate dummy text content and dummyimage.com to create dummy images. The Devel module (http://drupal.org/project/devel) also comes with a Devel Generate sub-module that can automatically create dummy content for your site.

Whatever it is that your site will be, the next steps will go much more smoothly (and be a lot more fun!) if you get this functionality and some content in place first *before* you start theming.

Using a Drupal theming framework: Fusion

In this chapter we will be using Fusion, one of the most popular base themes for Drupal. Other popular Drupal base themes you may run into include Zen, Framework, and Basic. Each has its own approach, and you may want to check them out once you get a handle on how theming works in Drupal. We'll create a subtheme of Fusion, which inherits all the features and base code from Fusion itself. Fusion also includes a commented starter theme that we'll edit to create the custom look and feel for this theme.

Installing Fusion core

Download Fusion core from http://drupal.org/project/fusion and place it in your themes folder (usually sites/all/themes – you may need to create this folder). Alternatively, you can install Fusion through Drupal's UI, similar to modules. Go to **Appearance** and click the **Install new theme** and follow the steps on screen. Refer to the first section of Chapter 7: Essential Contributed Modules for instructions on how to install a theme/module.

Similar to core and contributed modules, Drupal themes can have a primary and sub-theme, including Fusion. A primary theme can often be used as a core theme, so that multiple sub-themes can inherit various templates and theme settings from the primary theme. This is ideal if you want to build sites using a starter theme, so that all sub-themes can share properties and you don't have to spend time re-writing the same code. You'll need the core theme installed, such as Fusion Core, for the sub-theme to work.

Installing a Fusion sub-theme

We'll be using the Vibe theme (Figure 8-1) as our example throughout this chapter. The Vibe theme is a sub-theme of Fusion and is perfect to show how Fusion works. It can be downloaded free at http://drupal.org/project/vibe.

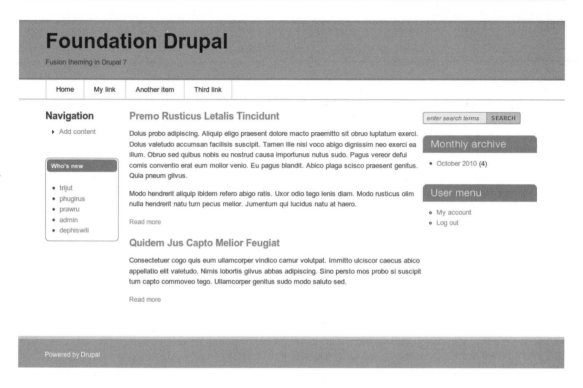

Figure 8-1. Vibe sub-theme screenshot.

We're using this theme because it is a good, simple example of a Drupal theme. There are quite a few free Fusion themes available on drupal.org, so you will have many to choose from if Vibe doesn't strike your fancy!

Install Skinr

The Skinr module is used to provide an interface for much of Fusion's settings. It is not required for our first steps, but we'll be using it shortly. It allows you to apply graphic "skins" to certain parts of your site, such as blocks or regions. Usually a site's design will have different visual styles for different parts of the site, so you can use Skinr to set these styles through Drupal's interface rather than hard-coding (ie. editing CSS files) them to parts of the site within the theme.

Skinr is available for download at http://drupal.org/project/skinr. Refer to Chapter 6 for instructions on how to install a module.

Creating your layout

First we'll plan the layout of our theme. It's important to figure out what kind of content goes where, so we know how to build the structure of our theme in Drupal. Then we will configure the basic layout settings, position our content, and start theming – through clicking and code!

Planning your theme

Some elements of the page in Figure 8-1 above are pretty obvious to pick out – there's a logo, menu, and a search box. But when you get down to blocks and regions, things can get a little more confusing.

One of the most important things to understand when setting up your theme's layout is how blocks and regions work. Regions are containers, and blocks are content that go inside regions. In this case, we have two sidebars, with a wider middle column for our main site content. The sidebars and content columns are regions, and there can be multiple blocks inside those regions. If you don't put any blocks inside any of these regions, the region will not be displayed.

There are also elements here that aren't blocks, like the logo, which are configured and displayed through the theme. In the next steps, we'll configure the basic theme settings and then adjust the layout of the sidebars and blocks.

Theme settings

Visit the theme settings page for your theme to enable or disable basic settings, such as your site's name, logo, and slogan. You can access this settings page by clicking **Appearance** in the toolbar, and then click the **Settings** link next to your current theme.

Thinking about the design you will be turning into a Drupal theme, enable the theme settings that make sense for your site. Will you be displaying a graphical logo or other header image in the theme? If so, you probably want to check the "logo" option for your theme. Similarly, check the other options you want to use, like a text-based site name, slogan, or a shortcut icon ("favicon").

Working with the grid layout

Fusion is a grid theme. You may have heard of CSS grids, such as 960gs or YUI. They're a great way to give your design a professional and tidy look, and they eliminate a lot of decision making and hand tweaking by giving you a standard set of layout choices. Grids also take care of common cross-browser issues when dealing with layout, especially in older web browsers like Internet Explorer 6 and 7. Fusion is based on these grid systems, and allows you to lay out your theme very easily from Drupal's UI, or even to create custom grid definitions. (http://fusiondrupalthemes.com/support/theme-developers/grid-concepts)

Grids can be any size or number of columns, but widths such as 960 and 980 pixels are common, because they are nicely divisible and fit on the still-common 1024px wide screen resolution. This is where the 960gs Grid System gets its name. It most frequently uses a 12 or 16 column grid, but 24 columns is also popular. We don't need to get too far into the technical details, but another term to be familiar with is "gutters" – the margin of space in between columns. Fusion's gutters are 20px by default, but you can override these in your subtheme if necessary.

Figure 8-2 shows an example of a web site with a translucent pink overlay showing where the grid columns fall. A similar overlay is available as a setting you can toggle on in any Fusion theme.

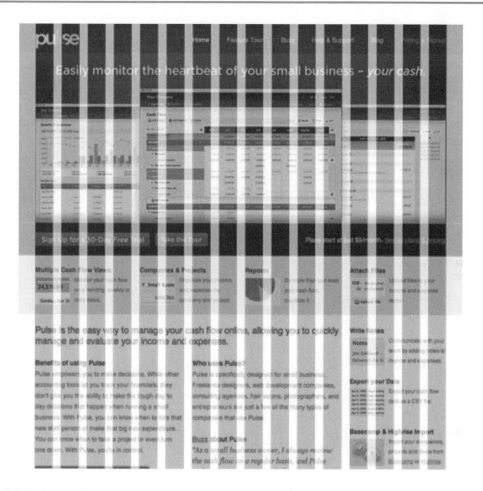

Figure 8-2. Web site with overlay showing the CSS grid (from 960.gs)

Theme widths

Fusion themes are switchable between fluid width and fixed width versions with just a few clicks. This controls whether the page width should be at a set pixel dimension (fixed) or stretch and contract to match the visitor's screen size (liquid).

To adjust the settings:

1. Visit the **Appearance** section of your site, then click the **Settings** link next to your theme to go to that theme's configuration page.

2. Scroll down to **FUSION THEME SETTINGS** and select the **GENERAL SETTINGS** fieldset (Figure 8-3).

3. Click **LAYOUT** to expose the section labeled **Select a grid layout for your theme**.

4.   Select either **960px 12 column grid** or **Fluid 12 column grid**, then scroll to the bottom of the screen and click **Save configuration**.

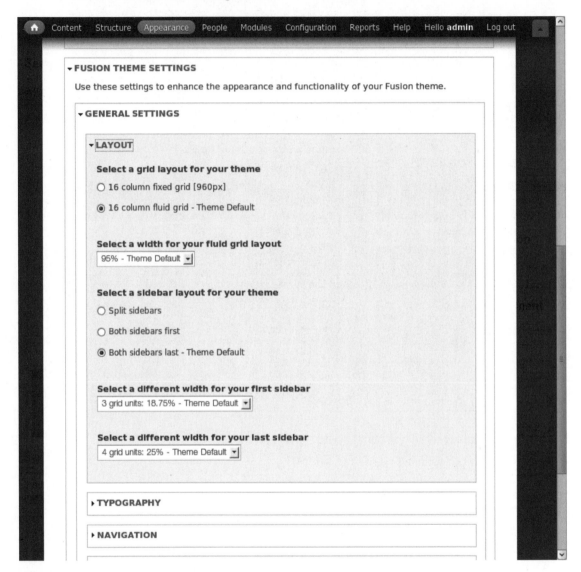

Figure 8-3. Changing **LAYOUT** settings in Fusion.

Changing the sidebars

You can change the width and position of the sidebars through settings, and the content area will shrink in response.

1. Visit the **Appearance** section, then click **Settings** next to your Fusion sub-theme to go to that theme's configuration page.

2. Scroll down to **FUSION THEME SETTINGS** and click the **GENERAL SETTINGS** fieldset, as seen in Figure 8-3.

3. Click **LAYOUT** to expose the sidebar controls.

4. Use the pop-up menus labeled **Select a different width...** to control how wide the sidebars will be, then scroll to the bottom of the screen and click **Save configuration**.

The widths for sidebars and blocks are expressed in **units**, which is a reference to the grid columns used in Fusion.

Get content in the right places on the page

Beyond just selecting the page and sidebar widths, Drupal's blocks allow you to create hundreds of layout options for different types of content. Go to your block configuration page at **Structure ➤ Blocks** and click the **Demonstrate block regions** link to see all the available regions in the theme, see Figure 8-4. The block configuration page is covered in depth in Chapter 3.

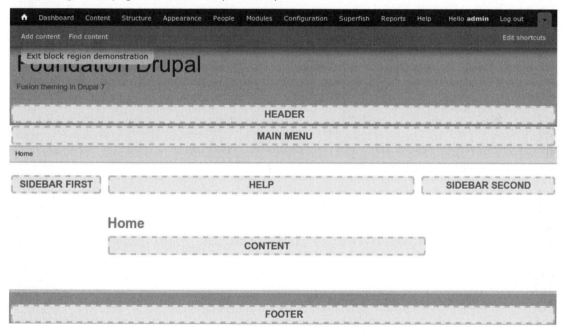

Figure 8-4. Vibe's regions, displayed using the **Demonstrate block regions** link on the block configuration page.

Each of these regions can hold one or more blocks. Blocks can be in any number of columns or rows. These regions are collapsible, meaning that they are not rendered if there is no content in a region.

Go ahead and drag some blocks into the section with the name of the regions you'd like them to appear in. When you're done, save the page and visit your site's home page to get an accurate look at your new content layout. You might be thinking, *but I want to have a special home page layout*, or *I need different content appearing on different pages*. Through Drupal's block visibility, you can show and hide different blocks on different pages. Visit Chapter 3: Configuring a Basic Drupal Website to review block configuration settings.

Adjust block widths and alignment

Blocks in a Fusion theme are automatically aligned (floated, in CSS terms) to the left, and sized to divide the widths equally between each block in a region. If you'd like to adjust this and make certain blocks a different width, or change the positioning, you can do this by editing the block's skin. A "skin" is a collection of CSS or other code that defines the way a certain piece of content should appear. Just like Fusion comes with settings for page width and sidebars, it also comes with skins that can control widths and positioning of blocks.

If you haven't already enabled the Skinr module, do this now. Once enabled, you'll notice that clicking on the gear icon in the top right corner of the block provides an option to **Edit skin**. Click on this and you will be presented with Fusion's options for widths, positions, and other helpful styles.

Let's try this out with a block in the header. Place the **User** menu block in the Header region, as covered in the previous section. By default, it will display below the site name, see Figure 8-5; not a very attractive spot! But we can change its position with just a few clicks.

Figure 8-5. Default position and size of **User** menu block in the Header region.

Click the **Edit skin** link and apply the styles for **Width: 3 units wide**, **Content alignment: Right align content within its container**, and **Block position: Float block to the right**, see Figure 8-6. Click **Save**.

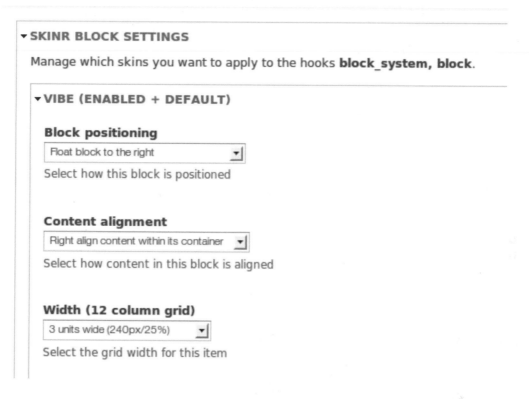

Figure 8-6. In the Skinr settings screen to edit block width and position

Remember, Fusion uses a grid, which is where the "units" comes from – 3 units wide on a 12 column grid means the block will be 1/4th the total width.

The menu block now appears right aligned in the header, see Figure 8-7!

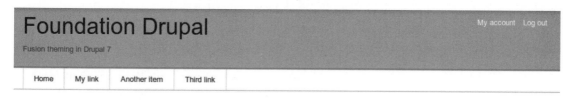

Figure 8-7. User menublock in the Header region with the **3 units wide** and **Float block to the right** skins applied.

Styling your site

Now that we've got a handle on our site's layout through Fusion's grid and positioning settings, let's start making things a bit prettier using the skins included with the Vibe theme, plus doing our own CSS overrides.

Styling your site with Skinr

Skins can come from one of three places:

1. Included with a theme (or module) you've downloaded, usually in a sub-folder such as /skins

2. Downloaded separately from your theme

3. Skins you write yourself

Vibe includes a few skins that you can apply to blocks on your site. Out of the box, blocks in the sidebars aren't much to look at (Figure 8-8).

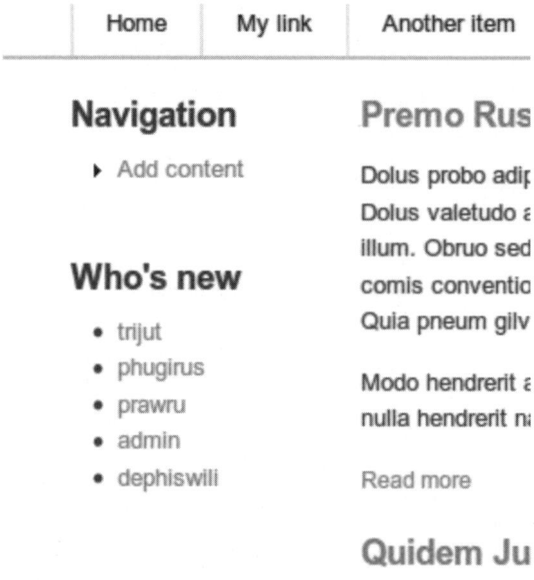

Home	My link	Another item

Navigation

▸ Add content

Who's new

- trijut
- phugirus
- prawru
- admin
- dephiswili

Premo Rus

Dolus probo adip
Dolus valetudo a
illum. Obruo sed
comis conventio
Quia pneum gilv

Modo hendrerit a
nulla hendrerit na

Read more

Quidem Ju

Figure 8-8. Sidebar blocks without any skins applied in the Vibe theme.

But we can apply a color skin that has some nice styling on the blocks we choose. Click the gear to edit the skin on this block, see Figure 8-9.

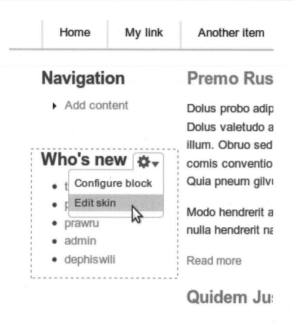

Figure 8-9. Editing a block skin in the Vibe theme

Then select the **Orange Block color skin** in the Skinr settings screen and **Save** this block, see Figure 8-10.

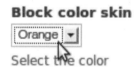

Figure 8-10. Select the **Orange** skin option under **Block color skin.**

Now this sidebar block has the orange skin applied and looks quite different! See Figure 8-11.

Figure 8-11. Who's new block in the sidebar with orange color skin applied.

Skins aren't just for colors and fonts, but can also alter the layout or even the way parts of the site interact. For example, you might apply a skin to a menu to turn it into a dropdown navigation menu, or add JavaScript functionality to a form. We'll also tell you where you can download more of these skins.

Let's apply another skin that comes with the Vibe theme to one of our blocks.

these Figure 8-12 to see the default search block, placed in the sidebar.

Figure 8-12. Default search box with basic form styling

Edit the skin on this block, and under **Form Styles**, apply the **Compact, one-line form** skin, see Figure 8-13.

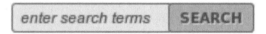

Figure 8-13. The same search box with compact form skin applied.

You can see how using a theme that comes with skins like these can dramatically improve the look of your site! Using Skinr, you can apply skins selectively to different parts of your site to customize it without needing to edit code.

> *Tip: There is a growing community of Drupal users creating and contributing skins to a repository where you can mix-and-match these skins in any theme. Visit http://fusiondrupalthemes.com/snippets to browse free skins for download and drop them into any Fusion theme for instant theme tweaks!*

Styling your site with CSS

Here we'll cover the easiest way to make small tweaks to a theme. If you're downloading an off-the-shelf theme but would like to make a few adjustments, you can keep your changes isolated to a single CSS file so you don't lose the ability to upgrade your theme later.

> *Tip: One of the toughest things to get your head around in Drupal is knowing where to make a change. Drupal core and additional modules can have configuration settings that can dramatically change the look of how your content is displayed. For example, you can select a different image style or field formatter in your content type's Display Fields section, see Chapter 4: Adding content types or fields, or rearrange the order of fields in a view, see Chapter 7: Essential modules. Before you dig into the theme, check out the configuration options available for your content to see if the change you're looking for can be made there.*

Working with the Fusion Vibe theme, let's say you want to change the font for the site name. You could make a custom subtheme, but that would be more effort than needed for just a few lines of CSS. Here we'll show you how to use a special file to do some custom changes to the theme. We'll get into creating your own full subtheme later.

Using local.css

If you're using a Fusion-based theme, it should come with a file called **sample.local.css**. Other themes may also come with a similar file to use for overriding CSS, but you'll have to check the documentation for your theme.

To get started, rename this file to **local.css** and save the file. Now we can go ahead and start putting CSS in this file to change the appearance of the theme.

> *Tip: CSS aggregation is a performance feature of Drupal, but can also cause frustrations when theming. Visit the **Configuration ➤ Development** page, and scroll down to the Bandwidth Optimization section. If the **Aggregate and compress CSS files into one file** option is checked, all your modules' and theme's CSS files will be automatically aggregated into one file. This means if you make any changes to the theme, such as updating a CSS file, the changes won't be seen until you clear the theme cache or disable CSS aggregation. CSS aggregation should only be used when you're ready to launch your site, because otherwise changes made in your theme's CSS files will not be updated. Visit Chapter 10: Going Live for a full list of things to-do before launching your site.*

CSS styling basics

Drupal has a lot of bits and pieces to learn. But much of Drupal theming is simply styling HTML output with CSS. If you already know some CSS, or have worked with theming for another CMS or blogging platform like Wordpress, you're already ahead!

There are lots of great books and tutorials out there about learning CSS, and we won't be going through the basics here beyond what is needed for our examples. W3Schools (http://www.w3schools.com/) is an excellent place to learn about CSS and HTML.

Tools

Firebug is an extension for the Firefox web browser that is extremely valuable even if you're just doing basic CSS edits. You can use it to 'inspect' the code of your site, and make temporary changes, live in your browser. We'll be using it in our next step to determine the CSS needed to style our site name. You can download Firebug at http://getfirebug.com/

The Chrome web browser has a similar feature under **Tools ➤ Developer Tools**.

Example: styling the site name

Perhaps you find the site name bland, and you'd like to make it even bigger and with a more classic serif font. Once you have Firebug installed, open the panel from **Tools ➤ Firebug ➤ Open Firebug** (or hit F12). Click the Inspect **element** button as shown in Figure 8-14.

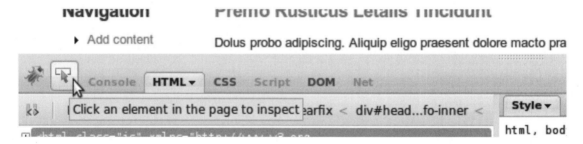

Figure 8-14. Inspect Element option in the Firebug panel.

When this option is activated, you can select an element on the page by double-clicking on it directly, see Figure 8-15.

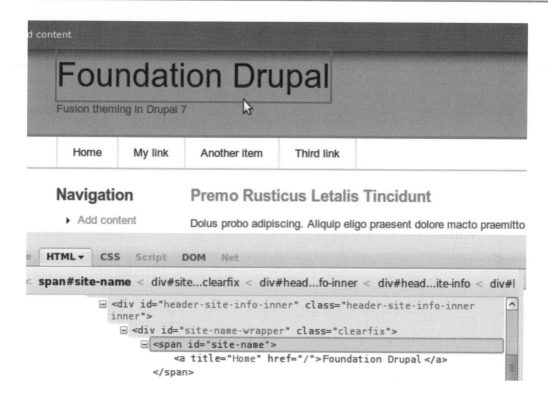

Figure 8-15. Double-click on the site name to get more information about it in Firebug.

We'll target this span tag in our CSS in order to alter the way it appears for our theme. In your newly saved local.css file, add the following lines:

```
#site-name {
  font-family: Georgia, Times New Roman, serif;
  font-size: 400%;
  font-weight: bold;
}
```

Save the file and reload your site. Your site name should now look like the screenshot in Figure 8-16.

Figure 8-16. The updated site name, styled with CSS in the local.css file

Using the **local.css** file like this is great if you have found a theme that's similar to what you're looking for, but need to make a few adjustments. For example, you might want to add in your company's logo as a large header, change the colors to match your branding, or update the font styles.

If you want to create a theme from scratch from a custom design, read on ahead!

Creating your own custom Drupal theme

A Drupal theme consists of several types of files:

- An .info file – this is Drupal's own type of definition file, where you set things like the theme name and certain defaults.
- CSS files – these are style sheet files, which control the visual look and feel of your website.
- PHP files – these are the backbone of a Drupal theme and tell your website what to display where. Also called "template files" when ending in .tpl.php.
- Image files – these will end in .gif, .jpg, or .png, depending on the type of image. These images are specific to the theme and are different than images uploaded when creating a node.
- JS files – these are JavaScript, used to add front end functionality and display effects, like drop down menus.

While most themes will have a mix of all of these file types, only an .info file and CSS file(s) are necessary to create a completely unique theme.

Drupal themes inherit template files and CSS from Drupal core and from any additional modules you may have installed. You then *override* these styles and template files in your own theme if needed.

Figure 8-17 is a diagram showing a page layout in Drupal and the various files it's made up of.

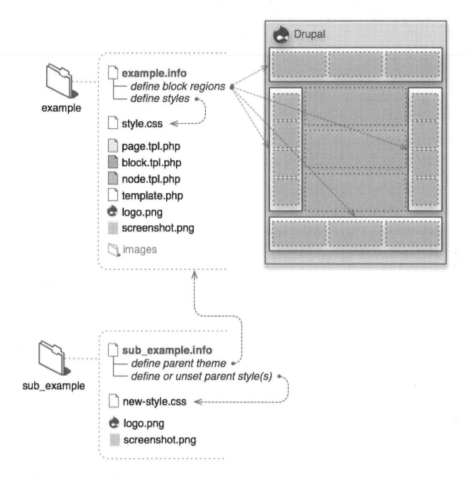

Figure 8-17. A typical page layout in Drupal and the various files it's made up of. Creative Commons via http://drupal.org/node/171194

The vast majority of Drupal sites are themed using a base theme or starter theme. While it's certainly possible to start from scratch, creating a subtheme of a base theme keeps you from reinventing the wheel and usually provides a lot of helpful features when creating your own theme.

Copy and edit Fusion's starter subtheme

Create a copy of the **fusion_starter_lite** folder from the Fusion folder and rename to the name of your choice (eg. **mysite_theme**):

1. Rename the **.info** file to the same name you just gave the folder, e.g. **mysite_theme.info**

2. Open the **.info** file and give your theme a more descriptive name and full description here

3. On this line: `stylesheets[all][] = css/mysite-theme-style.css`, replace the **fusion-starter-lite** part with your theme's name

4. Rename the css file in the **css/** folder to match the name above

5. Upload to your site and enable your new theme in the Appearance section

Adding style to your theme

Assuming you've got the basics of your site's content in place, we'll move onto the biggest part of theming – making your design come to life with CSS!

Even before you start theming, there is a lot of work that's already been done by the template files and CSS provided by Drupal core, modules, and Fusion. This saves you from having to code the basics from the ground up, and provides a functional structure for displaying your Drupal site.

To see where this is coming from, using your browser, view the source of your site (in Firefox, right-click and View Page Source), and find the section of code just under `<style type="text/css" media="all">` within the `<head>` tag.

You'll see a number of CSS files loaded, depending on which modules you have installed. The list should look something like this:

modules/system/system.css

modules/system/system-behavior.css

modules/system/system-menus.css

modules/system/system-messages.css

modules/contextual/contextual.css

modules/node/node.css

modules/user/user.css

sites/all/modules/views/css/views.css

modules/comment/comment.css

modules/filter/filter.css

modules/field/theme/field.css

modules/shortcut/shortcut.css

modules/toolbar/toolbar.css

sites/all/themes/fusion_core/css/style.css

sites/all/themes/fusion_core/css/typography.css

sites/all/themes/mysite_theme/css/mysite-theme-style.css

sites/all/themes/fusion_core/css/grid12-960.css

Most of these come from Drupal core, but by looking at the folder paths, we can also see that there is one from the Views module we've got installed, a couple from the Fusion Core base theme, and our own subtheme's CSS file.

As we mentioned earlier, Firebug is a great tool for understanding what styles are being applied to what sections of your site. In figure 8-18 below, we are inspecting the site name in Firebug, and you can see that the **#site-name** div has CSS properties applied to it in order to increase the font size and line height.

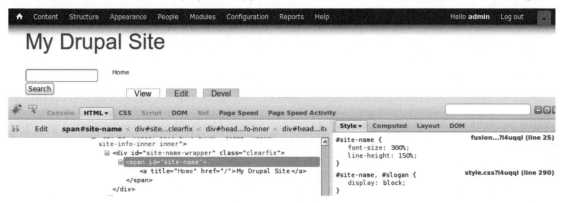

Figure 8-18. Inspecting the site name markup and applied CSS in Firebug

---

Tip: Browser-specific CSS files

If you're already familiar with web development, you are probably well aware that different browsers often don't display web pages the same, particularly IE (Internet Explorer). Many sites need to use some browser-specific CSS, files that are loaded conditionally, depending on the visitor's web browser. Fusion makes this easy and automatic. Just put your IE-specific CSS in a file using the following naming scheme: ie7-fixes.css. This is supported for ie6-fixes.css through ie9-fixes.css.

Writing your own CSS

When starting your Drupal theme, you want to first think about the elements that are consistent across the whole site. This usually includes things like typography and page backgrounds. In our design from the Vibe theme, we have the 12pt Helvetica font in dark gray used throughout the design, with blue links. Also the main page background is white, with a blue header, and gray footer. Let's go ahead and set these basic elements in our theme. Since Fusion is designed for creating your own subtheme, it includes documentation in the form of starter CSS and comments in the main CSS file to help you make changes.

Open up your theme's CSS file (the one you renamed to mysite-theme-style.css) in your text editor and you'll see it starts with the following comment:

```
/* Basic Typography & Colors
```

We can follow along with this helpful 'scaffolding' of CSS selectors and comments to set the basics for typography. Fusion already sets the page background to white and default font to Helvetica/Arial, so we don't need to do anything for this, but we'll set the font color and size, and link colors.

```css
/* Basic Typography & Colors
---------------------------------------------------------------- */
/* Add general site styling here for typography and background */
body {
  color: #333;
  font-size: 75%;
}


/* Default link styles - separate a:visited for a different visited link style */
a,
a:link,
a:visited {
  color: #26A6C5;
}

/* Hover/active link styles. Don't forget :focus for accessibility */
a:hover,
a:focus,
a:active {
  color: #26A6C5;
}
```

> Tip: Fusion uses percentages for fonts rather than pixels because they offer the most backwards-compatible accessibility options for readers who want to increase the text size, and they are a bit easier to understand than 'ems', another popular sizing unit. But if you're more comfortable with ems, or your project requirements mean pixels are ok, then by all means use whichever sizing unit you'd like!

Now let's do the blue background and white text for the header. Remember, you can use Firebug or your browser's inspection tool to see the markup and CSS being applied. We use Firebug in this case to figure out which <div> we need to target with our CSS.

```css
/* Header Region

---------------------------------------------------------------- */
.header-group {
  background-color: #33BEDE;
  border-bottom: 3px solid #1BA0CC;
  color: #FFF;
}
```

```
.header-group a {
  color: #FFF;
}
```

We'll also similarly style the footer, including adding padding at the top of the region so it doesn't bump up against our page content.

Fusion puts a 1.5em margin on the bottom of all blocks, but here we want some additional padding on the inside of the gray region at the top. We'll stick with the 1.5em to keep vertical rhythm consistent.

```
/*  Footer Region
-------------------------------------------------------------- */

.footer {
  background-color: #ACACAC;
  border-top: 5px solid #D6D6D6;
  color: #FFF;
  float: left;
  padding-top: 1.5em;
}

.footer a,
.footer a:visited {
  color: #FFF;
}
```

> *Tip: Right-to-left theming*
>
> *Drupal is a CMS that supports multilingual sites, including those with right-to-left (RTL) languages. You can add "-rtl" to the end of any CSS filename to create RTL-specific overrides. Learn more about RTL theming at http://fusiondrupalthemes.com/support/theme-developers/compatibility-standards*

Content-specific theming

With some basic theming in place, we'll now jump into doing styling that targets more specific content on the page. In order to re-create styles similar to the Vibe theme in our own theme, we'll target blocks in the left and right sidebars separately. If you haven't already, go ahead and place some blocks in your sidebars so we have something to look at while theming.

First, let's give all blocks in the left sidebar the orange border and rounded title.

Add the following CSS to your theme's stylesheet:

```
.region-sidebar-first .block .inner {
  background-color: #fff;
  border: 1px solid #DB610C;
  border-radius: 8px;
  -moz-border-radius: 8px;
  -webkit-border-radius: 8px;
}

.region-sidebar-first h2 {
  background-color: #DB610C;
  border-radius: 6px;
  color: #fff;
  font-size: 90%;
  margin: 2px;
  padding: 2px 8px;
  -moz-border-radius: 6px;
  -webkit-border-radius: 6px;
}

.region-sidebar-first .block .inner .content {
  margin-top: 1.5em;
}
```

Note that we're using some browser-specific properties (-moz and –webkit-border-radius) in order to get rounded corners supported by most browsers. We'll stick with a CSS-only solution for the purposes of this example, but if you need to support Internet Explorer, you'll have to look into using images or a JavaScript-based solution.

Now let's change the style for blocks in the second (right) sidebar so they have the tall rounded blue header, and a custom white font.

Add this CSS to your theme's stylesheet:

```
.region-sidebar-second .block h2 {
  background-color: #1BA0CC;
  border-top-left-radius: 8px;
  border-top-right-radius: 8px;
  color: #fff;
  font-family: 'Helvetica Neue', Helvetica, Arial, sans-serif;
  font-size: 150%;
  font-weight: normal;
  letter-spacing: 1px;
  padding: 7px 15px 5px 15px;
  -webkit-border-top-left-radius: 8px;
  -webkit-border-top-right-radius: 8px;
  -moz-border-radius-topleft: 8px;
  -moz-border-radius-topright: 8px;
}
```

Reload your site and you'll see the new changes to your sidebar blocks! See Figure 8-19.

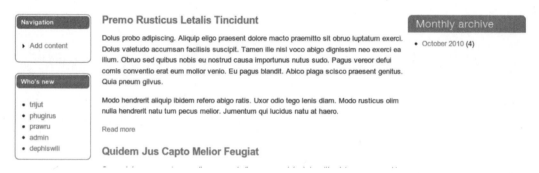

Figure 8-19. Our newly-styled sidebar blocks

Advanced topics

The following topics are more advanced and won't be covered here in detail, but you might be interested in looking up more information to use them in your theme.

Doing more with Skinr

We ended off the previous section by styling blocks to look a certain way in certain regions. This is a great first step when you're theming your site, but the power of Fusion + Skinr is to make these styles available *selectively* and in a way that you or your site editors can control. The next logical step would be to turn these region-specific block styles into *skins*.

Skinr documentation is available at http://drupal.org/node/578574 and is in the process of being updated for Drupal 7. This handbook plus the documentation available on the Fusion website (http://fusiondrupalthemes.com/support/theme-developers) will cover all that you need to know about turning these CSS styles into Skinr skins that you can control through Drupal's UI, including:

- Controlling which form widgets are used for your skins

- Creating skins for more than just blocks – Views, Panels, content types, and more!
- Restrict skins to a certain kind of content
- Conditionally load CSS or JS files along with your skin
- Learning how to stack styles for more flexible, modular CSS
- Creating Skinr styles that apply to the entire page, or whole sections of your site

This is an exciting and rapidly evolving area of Drupal, and this approach is quickly being adopted by many top Drupal themers and theme systems. Take a look at the links above if you'd like to learn more!

Using PHP and template files

Sometimes you need to override a template (tpl.php) file in your theme to add the content or styling you need if it is not a change that can be made in pure CSS. Often this is just to change the markup, such as rearranging fields, or restructuring the <div>s in a template to meet certain layout requirements. This where the more advanced power of Drupal's theming system comes into play, using PHP to access data and Drupal's "hooks" for ultimate control over your site!

Tip: Theme registry

The template files that are being used in your theme are cached by Drupal in something called the theme registry. When you add, remove, or make changes to a tpl.php file, you may need to rebuild the theme registry. You can do this by visiting Configuration > Development > Performance and click Clear all caches. If you are going to be making regular changes and wish to avoid this step, install the Devel module (http://drupal.org/project/devel) and enable the setting to rebuild the theme registry on every page reload.

We won't be walking through this code in detail, because this is just an exercise to show an example of editing a template file. You can find lots of snippets on drupal.org that you can easily copy and paste into a template file to achieve the desired effect. When you're searching for these snippets, make sure you read the comments because often there are updated versions or other tips for when you are working with the code. Also, make sure you are using snippets for Drupal 7, as many snippets may be from Drupal 5 or 6 and may not always work.

As an example of copying and editing a template file, let's add the number of comments next to the title of the comments area so it looks like "4 Comments" rather than just reading "Comments". See Figure 8-20.

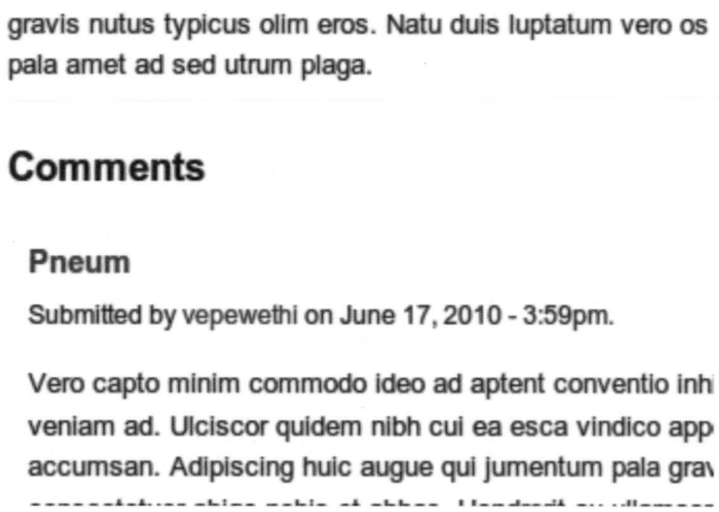

gravis nutus typicus olim eros. Natu duis luptatum vero os
pala amet ad sed utrum plaga.

Comments

Pneum

Submitted by vepewethi on June 17, 2010 - 3:59pm.

Vero capto minim commodo ideo ad aptent conventio inh
veniam ad. Ulciscor quidem nibh cui ea esca vindico app
accumsan. Adipiscing huic augue qui jumentum pala gra\

Figure 8-20. Default output of **comment-wrapper.tpl.php** before we override this template file

In order to do this, we need to override the contents of the **comment-wrapper.tpl.php** file. Copy the original version of it from the Fusion Core theme folder to your subtheme's folder.

Open the newly added **comment-wrapper.tpl.php** file and update the code within it so the file looks like the code below. Note that we have only changed the code on line 4, but the contents of the entire file are shown below.

```php
<div id="comments" class="<?php print $classes; ?>"<?php print $attributes; ?>>

  <?php if ($content['comments'] && $node->type != 'forum'): ?>

    <?php print render($title_prefix); ?>

    <h2 class="title"><?php print format_plural($node->comment_count, '1 Comment',
'@count Comments'); ?></h2>

    <?php print render($title_suffix); ?>

  <?php endif; ?>



  <?php print render($content['comments']); ?>



  <?php if ($content['comment_form']): ?>

    <h2 class="title comment-form"><?php print t('Add new comment'); ?></h2>
```

```
<?php print render($content['comment_form']); ?>

<?php endif; ?>
```

```
</div>
```

What we're doing here is saying: if there are comments, show the value of the comment count variable next to the text **Comments**. So, if there are four comments, the title for the comments are will read **4 Comments** rather than just **Comments**.

We got the code for this value from Drupal's API documentation for the node template file, available at http://api.drupal.org/api/drupal/modules--node--node.tpl.php/7

We're also using the **format_plural** function to properly display the text: http://api.drupal.org/api/function/format_plural/7

This type of theming will start to veer into development, but you can find a lot of pointers if you search drupal.org for the results you're trying to achieve. Chances are good that someone has tried to do the same thing and posted a code snippet in the forums or handbook. Give it a try (back up your site first!) – the best way to learn is through trial and error!

See Figure 8-21 for the end result.

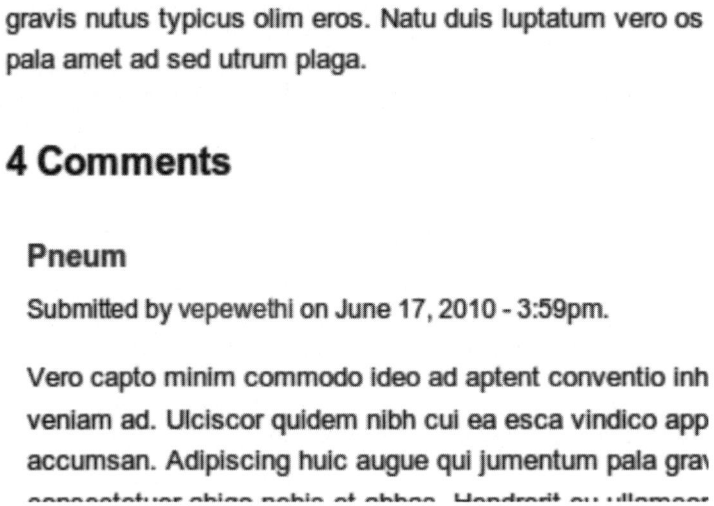

gravis nutus typicus olim eros. Natu duis luptatum vero os pala amet ad sed utrum plaga.

4 Comments

Pneum

Submitted by vepewethi on June 17, 2010 - 3:59pm.

Vero capto minim commodo ideo ad aptent conventio inh veniam ad. Ulciscor quidem nibh cui ea esca vindico app accumsan. Adipiscing huic augue qui jumentum pala grav ~~consectetuer obioe nobio et obbee. Hendrerit eu ullemeer~~

Figure 8-21. Our edited version of comment-wrapper.tpl.php with the comment count

After making changes to an existing *.tpl.php file or adding a new *.tpl.php file, you need to clear the site cache on the Performance page. This reloads the theme's files and loads the changes that have been made.

> *Security Tip: When you start dealing with .php files, you should familiarize yourself with security practices in Drupal. When you're displaying output through PHP that has been generated by a user, you run the risk of security exploits if these values are not properly sanitized. You can learn more about this very important topic at http://drupal.org/writing-secure-code*

Other template files

The same idea applies to changes made to theme files such as the **block.tpl.php**, **node.tpl.php**, and the **page.tpl.php**. Fusion doesn't include all possible template files, so you can add any tpl files from Drupal itself or various modules by copying these from the original folder into your sub theme's folder.

You can learn more about potential template files in Drupal's documentation: http://drupal.org/node/190815.

Using the template.php file

The **template.php** file in your theme is a powerful way to add module-like code to your theme to run advanced functionality. Code snippets you find online or other modules may require you to add code to this file, which is where you'll probably first run into it.

It is best to put any code other than a simple conditional statement in template.php instead of directly in a tpl.php file, which should be used only for markup, not complex logic. This is very important; many of the coding mistakes made by people new to Drupal is to add things like database calls and other functions into tpl.php files. The general rule of thumb to follow is that if the data are not available in the tpl.php file, then add it to **template.php**. To add **template.php** code, simply create a new template.php file in your subtheme and add the necessary code. It will automatically run Fusion's **template.php** file as well.

Summary

In this chapter, we reviewed how to theme a site using the Fusion core theme. Fusion is a powerful theming tool in that you can make most changes through Drupal's UI. We discussed how Fusion uses a grid approach to theming, helping with cross-browser compatibility and making it much easier to adjust the layout of a page. We also reviewed the Skinr module and how to add custom skins to blocks, regions, and other page elements. Finally, we closed with a review of how to create your own Fusion sub-theme and many of the common tpl.php files you may want to include.

Chapter 9

Designing for a Browser

If you're like me, you remember the 1990s and the glory days of Dreamweaver and tables. Then came CSS and a bunch of Dreamweaver extensions I could never quite get to work: menu builders, asset managers, link checkers, and more. Fortunately, Drupal is able to handle the logic behind a web site, so the task of a web designer is no longer focused on designing in Dreamweaver but focused on the design itself.

This chapter discusses best design practices for two popular design programs, Adobe Photoshop and Adobe Illustrator CS5, and how to configure each for web design. Although I try to generalize the concepts as broadly as possible, I recommend you own a copy of one of the programs or at least be familiar with how they work to follow along. I discuss a number of design-centric topics in the first section of the chapter, such as monitor resolution and working with text, and I include a real-life example of how to lay out a Photoshop file for a Drupal template. I close the chapter with step-by-step instructions on how to configure Photoshop and Illustrator for perfect colors and pixel-perfect lines.

The browser as the new canvas

Designing for a browser is different from designing for print in many aspects. When artwork is printed using a press, you have control over the size and color of the final piece and know exactly how it should look after printing. There should be little to no variation between two printed pieces depending on the quality of the press.

A browser is different in that the final piece looks different on every screen in which it is displayed. Monitors come in different sizes, resolutions, and aspect ratios; a web site that looks great on your 24-inch wide-screen monitor with 1920 × 1200 resolution may not fit on the average 1024 × 768 monitor. In addition, the monitor will display colors differently than another monitor depending on calibration, type of monitor (LCD or CRT), age of monitor, type of video card, room lighting, and other factors. Fonts pose a significant problem as well. The result is that a web site must be designed to look great and display correctly on the largest number of computers. As such, there are general guidelines to follow (see the section "Configuring Photoshop and Illustrator for best results" later in this chapter).

One common misconception is that a browser displays images at a lower resolution than print. The argument frequently used is that a screen can display only 72 or 96 dots per inch (dpi), while a printing press can print 600 dpi, 1200 dpi, or higher. This is misleading and not how a video monitor works. Think of it this way: a 6-inch × 4-inch piece of paper printed at 300 dpi means there are 1800 × 1200 pixels on the sheet of paper. If this same image were placed on a monitor with a resolution of 1920 × 1200 pixels, the image would fill up the majority of the screen, regardless of whether the monitor was 21 or 60 inches.

A computer's operating systems uses dpi to calculate text size. This means if users adjust the dpi of their video cards, the size of screen text will change. Users can further adjust text size through the browser, and there is even a Drupal module that allows users to adjust screen size from a block on the web page. This means text size is relative to users' computer settings, which can result in a number of frustrations when designing text for a site:

- Text size on the design file may not be the size on the screen.
- Text may flow out of a container.
- Images may move or disappear.

My recommendation is to create the design file using the ideal font size and allow room around the header text and menu links for a font up to 25 percent larger (see Figure 9-1).

Figure 9-1. Additional space was added to the top, bottom, and sides of the menu links to allow room if a user has large system font settings.

Using a template-driven approach

The word *template* has bad connotations among graphic designers. For many, the term elicits images of once-designed web sites resold to multiple people. They were often sold at a fraction of the price for a custom-designed web site, resulting in the devaluation of a designer's services and hourly wage. Other times, the term *template* refers to a poorly designed web site—bland layout, one text-only content area, three header links, blinking GIFs, and sparkles that follow the mouse pointer.

Templates are not bad when properly used. A template is a way to structure graphics and information so that related content appears consistent across pages. It allows the end user to easily understand the flow of information and directs their eye to important sections of the page. In Drupal, templates are HTML documents into which a template engine renders content, and CSS is used to mark up this content. As shown in Figure 9-2, each page is composed of a number of templates, the most important of which include the following:

- The full-page template (for example, `page.tpl.php`)
- The node's content template (for example, `node.tpl.php`)
- A block's template (for example, `block.tpl.php`)

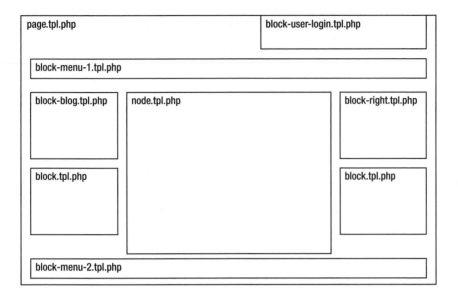

Figure 9-2. Example of node, block, and page templates used to create a page in Drupal

A page can be configured to include or change templates depending upon a number of factors, the most common of which include the following:

- Content type
- URL path alias
- Block type
- Region
- Module outputting content
- Node ID
- Front page

The three templates previously described (page, node, block) and the ability to include or change templates provide a foundation from which to structure images and content within a design file. Your primary goal is to create a single file containing all artwork, organized in a way to quickly create images. I have found it easiest to organize design files into multiple layers categorized by blocks, content types, and background. Name the folder accordingly, and then add images and content subfolders into each folder (see Figure 9-3). The result is that you can quickly turn off any piece of content, block, background, or content type. See Figure 9-4 for a PSD file with all the content and content types turned off.

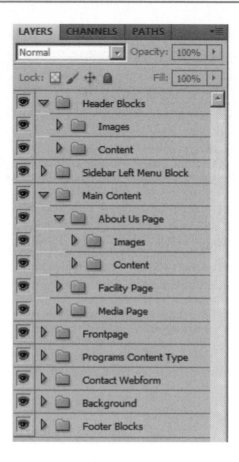

Figure 9-3. In Photoshop, organize design files into multiple layers categorized by blocks, content types, and a background, with images and content in separate folders.

After your files have been formatted, you can configure Photoshop or Illustrator to automatically slice the design file into JPEGs, PNGs, or GIFs. You can even set the name of each image to match your theme's CSS files. See the section "Slicing, optimizing, and saving web site images" later in this chapter for details.

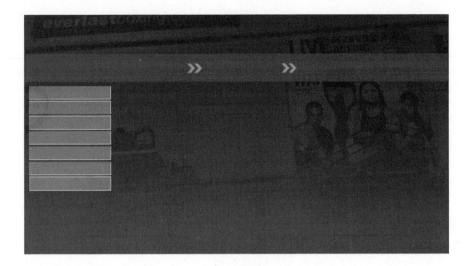

Figure 9-4. Example PSD file with all content and content types turned off

Here are some general guidelines I follow when creating the layer structure for a design file:

- Place site-wide elements on their own layer, including the background, menu links, header, and footer.
- Place each content type in their own layer, including basic pages.
- Within each layer, include two subfolders, one for content and one for images.
- The front page should have its own layer.
- If you have a block that is specific to a content type or page, place the block in the corresponding content type or page layer.
- Use *lorem ipsum* text for all content to be managed by Drupal, including primary and footer menu links.

Working with text

Working with text poses several challenges for graphic designers. Text can be displayed in one of two formats: as system-rendered text or as an image. System-rendered text is the preferred method to display content on the Internet because it reduces the size of web pages and increases search engine rankings (search engines currently cannot index or understand image text). However, browsers rely on fonts installed on end users' machines to display text, which means you are limited to about 10 or 15 fonts if you want text to display correctly across 95 percent of all browsers (there are some advanced methods to overcome this, such as `@font-face` or Microsoft's Web Embedding Fonts Tool; check out `www.craigmod.com/journal/font-face` for a great primer). This presents a challenge for web designers: you want to embed fonts as images so the page looks great, but if you do, you sacrifice search engine rankings. Here are some general questions to ask and guidelines to follow when considering your options:

- How important are search engine rankings? The answer should determine whether menu links or title headers are displayed as images.
- Always use system-rendered text in main page content; do not use an image.
- If you use images for links or headers, consider using the signwriter module, which automatically converts text to images using any font you require.

Configuring Photoshop and Illustrator for best results

Photoshop and Illustrator are two of the most popular programs used to design a web site. Whether you create the design file or someone creates the design file for you, configuring these programs for best results should be the first step when developing a web site.

Color settings

One of the most common problems when using Photoshop or Illustrator to create images for the Web is **color shift**. That is, the color of the image on the screen is different from the color of the image produced by the **Save for Web and Devices** tool. This occurs when color settings and color profiles are incorrectly configured.

Devices that reproduce color, such as printers and monitors, are not capable of reproducing the full range of colors viewable to the human eye. Rather, each device produces a range, or **gamut**, of colors. A monitor, for example, uses red, blue, and green (RBG) to produce colors, while a printing press uses cyan, magenta, yellow, and black (CMYK). Color profiles translate color between devices and ensure the color output by a printer matches the color output by a monitor. Color shift most frequently occurs when the color profile is configured for a device other than the target monitor.

Setting up Photoshop and Illustrator to correctly save and display images for the Web is a relatively easy process. When starting a new project in Photoshop, simply navigate to **File ➤ New** and select **Web** from the **Preset** menu; this configures Photoshop to automatically assign the correct color profile and color settings for web images. The process is the same in Illustrator except that it is called a **new document profile** instead of a preset (see Figure 9-5).

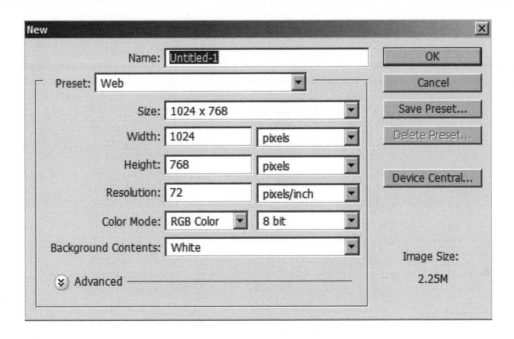

Figure 9-5. In Photoshop, navigate to **File ➤ New** and select **Web** under **Preset** when creating a new file to automatically assign the correct color settings and color profile to web images.

Frequently, someone will give you a file, and you will need to manually adjust color settings and color profiles, instead of using preset settings. As shown in Figure 9-6, you will need to assign the correct color profile by navigating to **Edit ➤ Color Settings** and selecting **sRGB IEC61966-2.1**.

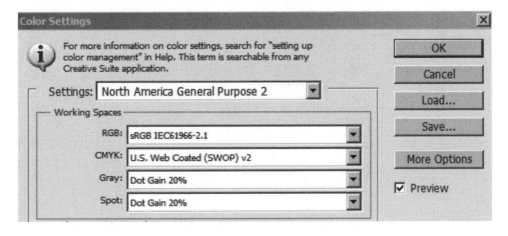

Figure 9-6. Navigate to **Edit ➤ Color Settings** and select **sRGB IEC61966-2.1** to set the color profile.

Next, you will need to set the document color mode to RGB, the colors a monitor uses to reproduce color. In Photoshop, navigate to **Image ➤ Mode** and select both **RGB Color** and **8 Bits/Channel** (see Figure 9-7). In Illustrator, navigate to **File ➤ Document Color Mode**, and select **RGB.**

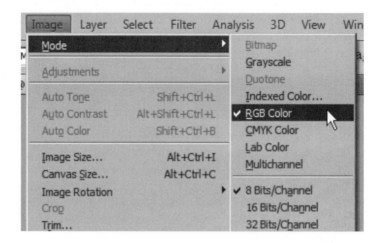

Figure 9-7. In Photoshop, navigate to **Image ➤ Mode** and select both **RGB Color** and **8 Bits/Channel** to set the color mode.

Now that you have set up Photoshop or Illustrator to use the correct colors, you need to configure Photoshop to display the correct colors on your monitor. In either Photoshop or Illustrator, navigate to **View ➤ Proof Setup** and select **Monitor RGB**. This displays the image on your monitor as it would display on the Web on your monitor. Next, select **View ➤ Proof Colors** to enable color proofing (see Figure 9-8).

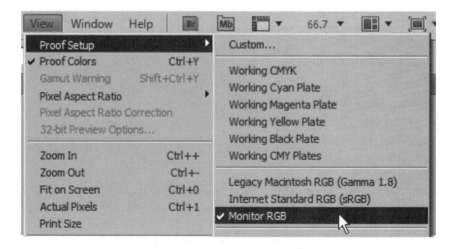

Figure 9-8. In Photoshop or Illustrator, navigate to **View ➤ Proof Setup**, select **Monitor RGB**, and select **View ➤ Proof Colors**.

Creating pixel-perfect lines and shapes

One of the most frustrating experiences I've had when using Photoshop or Illustrator is creating pixel-perfect lines and shapes. If configured for print, Photoshop or Illustrator will output an image at 300 dots per inch, but the **Save for Web** function saves it at 72 dpi. The result is that lines appear fuzzy, as shown in Figure 9-9. I can't tell you how many "bloody hell" experiences I've had trying to create a pixel-perfect line.

Figure 9-9. A pixel-perfect line on the top is contrasted with a fuzzy line on the bottom. Both are 1-pixel lines.

This is especially problematic when using CSS borders around `<div>`s, as you frequently will with Drupal blocks and regions. Many times, you'll find that you place a `border-right` and `border-left` around a block `<div>` and place an image at the top or bottom of the block with borders that connect. If the lines in the top or bottom image are blurry and the CSS lines are perfect, it creates a mismatch.

Photoshop settings

Although this isn't necessary for pixel-perfect lines and shapes, I highly recommend setting **Rulers** and **Type** to **pixels**. Web browsers display images using pixels, so this setting will help during the design process. As shown in Figure 9-10, navigate to **Edit ➤ Preferences ➤ Units & Rulers**, and select **pixels** for both **Rulers** and **Type**.

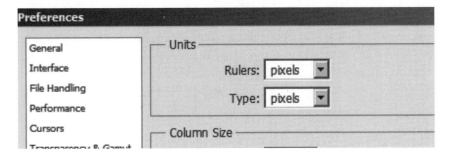

Figure 9-10. Navigate to **Edit ➤ Preferences ➤ Units & Rulers**, and select **pixels** for both **Rulers** and **Type**.

Photoshop only gives you the option to snap rectangles and rounded rectangles to pixels. Select the Rectangle or Rounded Rectangle tool, and then click the rectangle or rounded rectangle icon in the options toolbar. Select the **Snap to Pixels** check box, as shown in Figure 9-11.

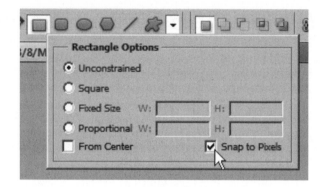

Figure 9-11. Select the **Snap to Pixels** check box in the options toolbar to create pixel-perfect rectangles or rounded rectangles.

There is no option to snap lines to pixels. Rather, you must select **View ➤ Actual Pixels** and then create a line (or select 100 percent in the **Navigator** window). Overall, creating a line when the view is greater or less than 100 percent results in fuzzy lines.

Illustrator settings

You must set a few preferences before you can begin designing a site. Figure 9-12 shows how to navigate to **Edit ➤ Preferences ➤ Units** and set **General**, **Stroke**, and **Type** to **Pixels**.

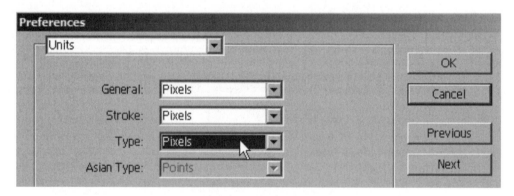

Figure 9-12. Navigate to **Edit ➤ Preferences ➤ Units** , and set **General**, **Stroke**, and **Type** to **Pixels**.

Next, navigate to **Edit ➤ Preferences ➤ General**, and set **Keyboard Increment** to **0.5 px**. You will use this when working with 1-pixel lines (see Figure 9-13).

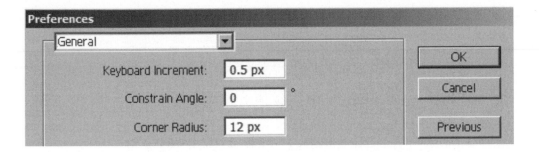

Figure 9-13. Navigate to **Edit ➤ Preferences ➤ General**, and set **Keyboard Increment** to **0.5 px**.

Finally, open the **View** menu, and select **Pixel Preview**. This option displays the artboard as it would appear on the Web. Selecting this option automatically selects the **Snap to Pixel** option, also available in the **View** menu (see Figure 9-14).

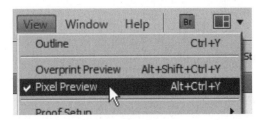

Figure 9-14. Open the **View** menu, and select **Pixel Preview**.

Snap to Pixel must be enabled when creating shapes. There are a few simple steps you must follow to create a pixel-perfect shape:

1. Create the shape, making sure **Snap to Pixel** is enabled.

2. Align the shape's stroke to the inside or outside.

   Note that in earlier versions of Illustrator, you'll need to set the stroke weight to **0.999 px**, as shown in Figure 9-15; otherwise, the top line will come out fuzzy.

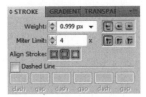

Figure 9-15. In older versions of Illustrator, you may need to set the stroke weight to to **0.999 px**; otherwise, the top line will come out fuzzy.

Creating a line is a similar process:

1. Create the line, making sure **Snap to Pixel** is enabled.

2. If the stroke weight is an even number, you are finished. If it is an odd number, disable **Snap to Pixel**.

3. Use the arrow key to nudge the line in the appropriate direction.

Slicing, optimizing, and saving web site images

The file looks great, and you're ready to save JPEGs, GIFs, and PNGs to the `files` directory in your Zen subtheme. Slicing your file in Photoshop or Illustrator gives you a quick and easy method to name and save all (or just one) required images at once in a single directory. This section takes you through the process of using the Slice tool, optimizing images, and saving images.

Using the Slice and Slice Select tools

The Slice and Slice Select tools, available in both Photoshop and Illustrator, allow you to slice the file into multiple areas to create separate image files when saving for the Web. **Slicing** a file is a simple process of using the Slice tool to draw boxes around page elements, while the Slice Select tool is used to adjust the size of the box. When slicing a file, Photoshop and Illustrator automatically divide the file into multiple slices (see Figure 9-16).

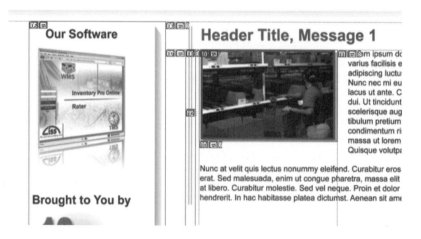

Figure 9-16. The Slice and Slice Select tools slice the file into multiple areas used when saving images for the Web. Image used by permission of Ken Lawrence of KRLCorp.com.

While slicing a file takes experience, there is a general process used to slice a file:

1. Use the Slice tool to draw a box around the header. Photoshop and Illustrator automatically divide the remainder of the file into multiple slices.

2. Draw a box around any other important design elements, using the Slice Select tool to adjust the size of each box.

3. Click **Save for Web & Devices** in the **File** drop-down list.

4. Select the Slice Select tool, and double-click each design element you need to save to the Web.

5. Select **Image** for **Slice Type**, and type the name you want for the saved image file, as shown in Figure 9-17. The remaining options are not used.

Figure 9-17. Select **Image** for **Slice Type**, and type the name you want for the saved image file.

6. After you are finished slicing the file, navigate to **View ➤ Show**, and select **Slices** to hide or display slices.

Optimizing web site images

Navigate to **File ➤ Save for Web & Devices**, and use the **Preset** drop-down to view the different file formats available for optimizing and saving images. There are three basic file types you can save your image as: JPEG, GIF, and PNG. Although there are technical differences between file types, the end user usually doesn't know or care what type is used. Your goal is to select a preset that results in the highest-quality image at the lowest image size. Keep in mind the larger an image, the longer it takes to download, so a web site using several large images will take longer to load.

JPEGs are superior to GIFs for storing full-color or grayscale images such as photographs, while GIFs and PNGs are great for images with a few colors and/or sharp edges, such as logos or text. GIFs and PNGs also allow you to include transparency, which is ideal for blocks and other layered page elements. My recommendation is to try multiple presets and determine which one results in the best image at the smallest size.

Saving images

By default, Photoshop and Illustrator save every slice that has been created. To save a specific slice, select **File ➤ Save for Web & Devices**, select the **Slice Select** tool in the upper-left corner of the box, and select the slice you want to save (hold the Ctrl key to select multiple slices). When you click the **Save** button, a dialog box appears for you to select the folder in which to save your files. At the bottom of the box, select **Selected Slices** in the **Slices** drop-down, as shown in Figure 9-18.

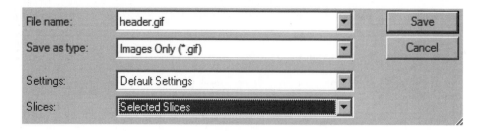

Figure 9-18. Select **Selected Slices** from the **Slices** drop-down to save only the selected slices rather than all slices.

Summary

Wow, what a rush! I covered many topics in this chapter relevant to designers using Drupal. I started by discussing the differences between print and the Web as a design canvas; printers use dots per inch, while monitors display one dot per pixel. The result not only is a difference in the way images are displayed but also means you need to make some minor configuration adjustments to Photoshop and Illustrator to get pixel-perfect images.

I also discussed how to lay out your design files using RocBoxing.com as an example. Each content type, block, and menu lives in its own layer, along with the front page and background. Layers are used to separate content from images so that you can easily slice and save images for your theme.

Chapter 10

Going Live

In this chapter, I review the process of preparing your Drupal site for production and the necessary steps you'll need to take to move it. I start by discussing the need for two versions of a site, one for development purposes and one for production. I cover many useful modules for each version, including a few development tools and some nifty production tools. Next I segue into a step-by-step tutorial to copy a Drupal site using cPanel and SSH, creating a test site available at `http://test.example.com`. I close the chapter by showing how to configure and move this test site to production.

Getting prepared to move a site to production

I've learned there are a number of things to consider when moving a site from your development environment, which I'll call **dev** from here on out, to production, called **prod**. For instance, where did you develop the site? Was it developed locally on your own machine, on a web host at a subdomain such as `http://dev.example.com`, or at the actual prod location (`http://example.com`)? If you set up the site at any other location than prod (which I recommend, because you should *never* develop or configure a site when it's live), you will need to move both the site files and the database from one location to the other. This means minimally you will have two versions of the same site, one for dev and one for prod, and each will have its own set of files and database (I'll discuss how to set up a staging environment in cPanel later in the chapter). This is the best method to use when building Drupal sites for a number of reasons:

- Your prod database is separate from your dev database, which means if anything breaks while you're developing, it won't bring down the production site.
- After the site is live, you can test modules and code changes before committing to production.
- This protects you against breaking your prod site when upgrading Drupal core from 7.1 to 7.*x* (discussed in the next chapter).

Having two versions of the same site presents both some opportunities and some challenges. Because you have two separate databases, it is possible to enable development tools on dev that are disabled on prod. For example, when developing, you may have the following modules enabled:

- Coder (http://drupal.org/project/coder) to assist with code review
- Devel (http://drupal.org/project/devel) to help with items such as clearing the cache, switching users, and more
- Drupal for Firebug (http://drupal.org/project/drupalforfirebug) to display debugging and SQL query information in the Firefox Firebug plug-in
- Testing (core module) to assess the functionality of a site
- Theme developer (http://drupal.org/project/devel_themer) to help during theming

One consideration when moving a site to production is determining which development modules to keep enabled and which to disable. My recommendation is to disable everything that end users of the production site will not use. Some people may opt to set permissions on prod so end users can't access certain modules, which are still enabled. I don't recommend this, simply because I tend to err on the side of caution; why would I want to leave a development tool enabled on a production site that allows users unfettered system access? Although Drupal is a relatively secure system, there may be undiscovered security flaws in a module that a malicious user could exploit to take down your site, and no one wants to own the first site that is taken down by this flaw.

Another consideration when moving a site to production is user permissions. If you are a single site builder and build the entire site logged in as user #1 (not recommended) or as a user with the role **administrator** (recommended), you have full access to all enabled modules. This means the functionality that you see and interact with will not be available to an anonymous or authenticated user. I can't tell you how many times I've pushed a site to production and then received a call from a worried client, "XYZ functionality is not working"! Navigate to **People**, and click the **PERMISSIONS** tab to update permissions.

Change the password for user #1 and any other user accounts used during development. When developing a site, I tend to use a generic one-size-fits-all password for my account. Although people may call this a bad security practice, I've found that it tends to work well with my development practices. This means I absolutely must change the password when the site goes to production; there are many popular tools to generate passwords, such as FreeRandom Password Generator (www.freerandompasswordgenerator.com). Some people advocate using OpenID to log in to a site and may use it for the superadmin account. I don't recommend this, simply because (once again) I err on the side of caution; if someone hacks this OpenID account, that person will be able to access any of sites associated with the account. If you are absolutely paranoid about security, one further action to take is to block user #1 from logging in to the site; navigate to **People** to block and unblock accounts. If you choose to do this, make sure you have a second user account on the site with permission to administer users (**People ➤ PERMISSIONS**); otherwise, you will not be able to unblock the superuser.

Finally, consider which modules and configuration changes you will enable on prod that are not enabled on dev. Some examples include performance caching (**Configuration ➤ Performance**), the Google Analytics module (http://drupal.org/project/google_analytics), and the Boost module (http://drupal.org/project/boost). You may also want to enable the Backup and Migrate module (http://drupal.org/project/backup_migrate), which allows you to configure automatic database dumps based on a configurable schedule.

We will go step-by-step through the process of moving a site to production later in the chapter. To recap, there are a number of issues to consider and actions to take when moving a site to production:

- Disabling all nonessential modules, especially development tools
- Configuring site permissions
- Changing the password of user #1 and any developer accounts
- Enabling and configuring the site for production

Understanding the process

Before we start any step-by-step tutorials, I will spend a few paragraphs discussing the actual process. You have a site that you have been developing called dev. Once the site is ready to be moved to production, you are going to move it first to a test environment to prepare the site for production. This test environment should be an exact replica of your production environment; if you are using cPanel, you want the test environment to be in the same directory that the production site will be located. When the site is moved to test, you are making a copy of the database and files of your dev site, placing them in a new directory and database, and pointing a subdomain to that test site. After you have moved the site to your test environment, you then prepare the site for production, doing all the things discussed in the previous section. This test site will become your production site; when the site is ready for production, you will point `http://example.com` to this installation. In a nutshell, the dev ➤ test ➤ prod process looks like this:

1. Copy the files and database of the dev site to a test environment, which should be an exact replica of your production environment.

2. Configure the test site for production.

3. When the test site is ready, repoint `http://example.com` to the test installation.

I also need to emphasize the conceptual nature of this process and that the process I'm outlining may differ according to your setup. Some people advocate a preproduction environment so that sites go from dev ➤ test ➤ preproduction ➤ production. Other people (myself included) have multiple servers, one for development and testing and one for production. The main point to understand is that regardless of your server setup, you should never, ever make configuration changes to a production site.

I also want to point out that using cPanel to manage your staging environments is compatible with file versioning software such as Subversion or Git. I use cPanel because it's a relatively easy way to manage server configuration, plus it allows me to provide my clients with an easy-to-use interface for their server. I have used cPanel hand in hand with Subversion for many years and am very satisfied with the results. I still follow the process outlined earlier, but I use Subversion to check out files to the different staging environments. To learn more about Subversion, I highly recommend the book *Practical Subversion, Second Edition*, by Daniel Berlin and Garrett Rooney. There is also a good question posted to Slashdot, with insight from many users, on how to configure a dev/test/prod environment: `http://ask.slashdot.org/story/09/10/20/1733228`.

Setting up a staging site in cPanel

Earlier I mentioned you minimally need two versions of a site (dev and prod) when developing; many development shops use more, including a version for each developer and possibly a testing site used before pushing code and/or database changes to production. In this section, I will discuss how to set up and configure cPanel so you can have multiple instances of a site and easily push your development site from dev to prod. Here is a quick snapshot of how the process of setting up a staging site works:

1. Create a copy of the entire Drupal codebase, and rename it.

2. Create a new database, and dump data from the source database into it.

3. Point a subdomain, such as test.example.com, to the new Drupal codebase.

4. Make a few configuration changes to Drupal.

At this point, you will have two instances of the same site. Let's go!

Step-by-step cPanel tutorial

These instructions assume you have been developing the site http://example.com at a location other than http://example.com, such as on your local machine or on a web host at http://exampledev.com. You will need to follow the instructions from Chapter 2 to create a cPanel account for http://example.com. In this tutorial, I will show how to create a copy of http://exampledev.com that can be accessed at http://test.example.com.

1. In cPanel, the ~/public_html folder contains all the files available on the Internet. You need to copy the codebase from http://exampledev.com to a folder *other* than public_html (see Figure 10-1).

Figure 10-1. Copy all files and folders from your development site to the production server; if using cPanel, do not copy everything into the public_html directory.

2. Next, log in to cPanel to create a new database, discussed in length in Chapter 2 (see Figure 10-2). Make sure to save the database name and password; you'll use that in step 6. You can use any database name and password.

Figure 10-2. Create a new database on your production server for the test database.

3. While you're logged in, point a subdomain to the new installation created in step 1 (see Figure 10-3). In cPanel, navigate to **Home ➤ Subdomains**.

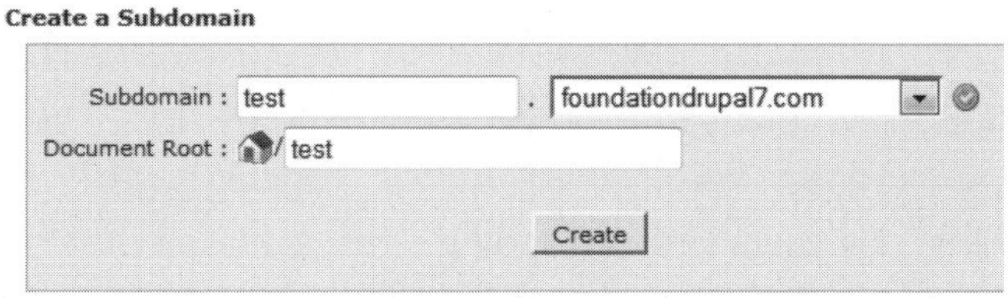

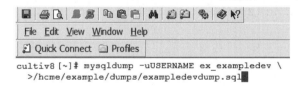

Figure 10-3. Point a new subdomain at the directory created in step 1.

4. Now you're going to dump all the data from the `exampledev.com` database (`ex_exampledev`) into `exampledevdump.sql`; notice I save the file in a folder called `dumps` that is not accessible from the public Internet. You can also use the backup_migrate module to do this through the admin interface (see Figure 10-4).

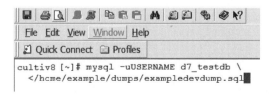

```
cultiv8 [~]# mysqldump -uUSERNAME ex_exampledev \
   >/hcme/example/dumps/exampledevdump.sql
```

Figure 10-4. Create a MySQL dump of the development database.

5. Next, load `exampledevdump.sql` into the database created earlier (`d7_testdb`); notice the direction of > has changed to < (see Figure 10-5). This can also be done through backup_migrate.

```
cultiv8 [~]# mysql -uUSERNAME d7_testdb \
   </hcme/example/dumps/exampledevdump.sql
```

Figure 10-5. Load the database dump from your development site into your test database.

6. Change `~/test/sites/example.com/settings.php` to point to `d7_testdb` (see Figure 10-6).

```
$databases = array (
  'default' =>
  array (
    'default' =>
    array (
      'driver' => 'mysql',
      'database' => 'd7_testdb',
      'username' => 'USERNAME',
      'password' => 'PASSWORD',
      'host' => 'localhost',
      'port' => '',
    ),
  ),
);
$db_prefix = '';
```

Figure 10-6. Point the test site to the correct database.

7. There is a file called `default.sites.php` located in the `~/test/sites` directory; this file controls which URLs can be used to access the site (see Figure 10-7). If the file hasn't been created, you need to rename the file to `sites.php` and save it in the same directory.

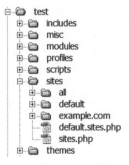

Figure 10-7. Create the `sites.php` file.

8. Update `sites.php` to include the domain `test.example.com` (see Figure 10-8).

```
/**
 * Multi-site directory aliasing:
 *
 * Edit the lines below to define directo
 * signs to enable.
 */
$sites = array(
  'exampledev.com' => 'example.com',
  'test.example.com' => 'example.com',
);
```

Figure 10-8. Update `sites.php` to include the subdomain created earlier.

9. You will need to change the permissions of the `/files` folder to allow uploads by Apache. In cPanel, Apache's user name is **nobody**, so start by changing all files in `/files` to the group `nobody` (see Figure 10-9).

Figure 10-9. Change the permissions of the /files folder to allow uploads by Apache.

    10. Next, change all folders within /files to **775** (see Figure 10-10).

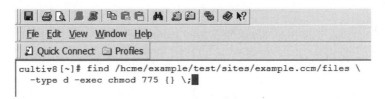

Figure 10-10. Change all folders within the /files directory to 775.

    11. Finally, change all files within /files to **664** (see Figure 10-11).

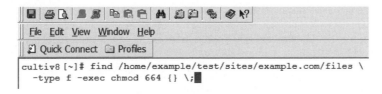

Figure 10-11. Change all files within the /files directory to 664.

    12. Navigate to http://test.example.com, and check the status report for any error messages.

Troubleshooting your staging site

It happens to us all: you spend 30 minutes creating a staging site just to sit and stare at a blank screen. I've found it usually happens when a deadline is looming or when a client is looking over my shoulder. Table 10-1 describes common problems and possible cause(s) and solutions. Sometimes you'll find that a problem is caused by a number of factors; I always recommend retracing your steps and ensuring that each step outlined earlier was successfully completed. I've also found that having a good web host with excellent technical support can be a great reference.

Table 10-1. Typical problems and possible cause(s) when moving and creating staging sites

Problem	Possible Cause(s) and Solutions
Apache default web page: Great Success! Apache is working on your cPanel and WHM Server.	Check with your web host to ensure the domain is properly parked. Note that this problem may persist in some browsers even after the issue is fixed, so plan to test in multiple browsers.
404 Not Found: The requested URL / was not found on this server	Is the domain or subdomain pointing to the correct directory? Check **subdomains** and **parked domains** in cPanel. Is the `sites.php` file properly configured?
White screen with a number of error messages	Was the database imported? Navigate to `http://example.com/install.php` to see whether Drupal will try to install. If it does, it's usually a good sign that data does not exist in the database (however, see the `install.php` problem later in this table). You can also log in to cPanel and navigate to the **MySQL Databases** page to see the size of the database. Sometimes a database will not fully import and will give similar messages. Log in to phpMyAdmin, and ensure the number of tables in your staging site matches the number of tables in your source site.
Access denied for user 'DB_NAME'@'localhost'	Check `settings.php` to ensure the database, user name, password, and host are properly configured.
Site redirects to install.php, tries to re-install Drupal.	Is the domain or subdomain pointing to the correct directory? Is the `sites.php` file properly configured? Was the database properly imported? Check `settings.php` to ensure the database, user name, password, and host are properly configured. When you proceed to install, does it proceed to **verify requirements** and give the messages that **sites/default/files does not exist** and that **the settings file does not exist**? If yes, then the `sites` directory is not properly configured; see Chapter 2 for details.
Changes made to a staging site are also made to the source site.	Check `settings.php` to ensure the site is pointing to the correct database.

Turning on your production site

We discussed how to create a staging site in the previous section so you can have two copies of the same site—one for dev (http://exampledev.com) and one for prod (http://test.example.com). In this section, I discuss changes you'll need to make to http://test.example.com before going live and then how to move http://test.example.com to http://example.com.

Preparing the test site for production

All data for enabling and configuring modules is saved in the database, meaning any changes made to test will not be reflected in dev. The first few steps to prepare your site were discussed in detail earlier.

1. Go to the **Modules** page, and disable all the nonessential modules, including developer tools and any other unused modules (see Figure 10-12). Enable any modules required for production, such as Google Analytics.

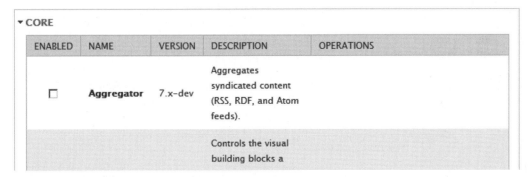

Figure 10-12. Disable all nonessential modules and enable modules required for production.

2. Navigate to **People** and change the password for user #1 and any other developer accounts (see Figure 10-13).

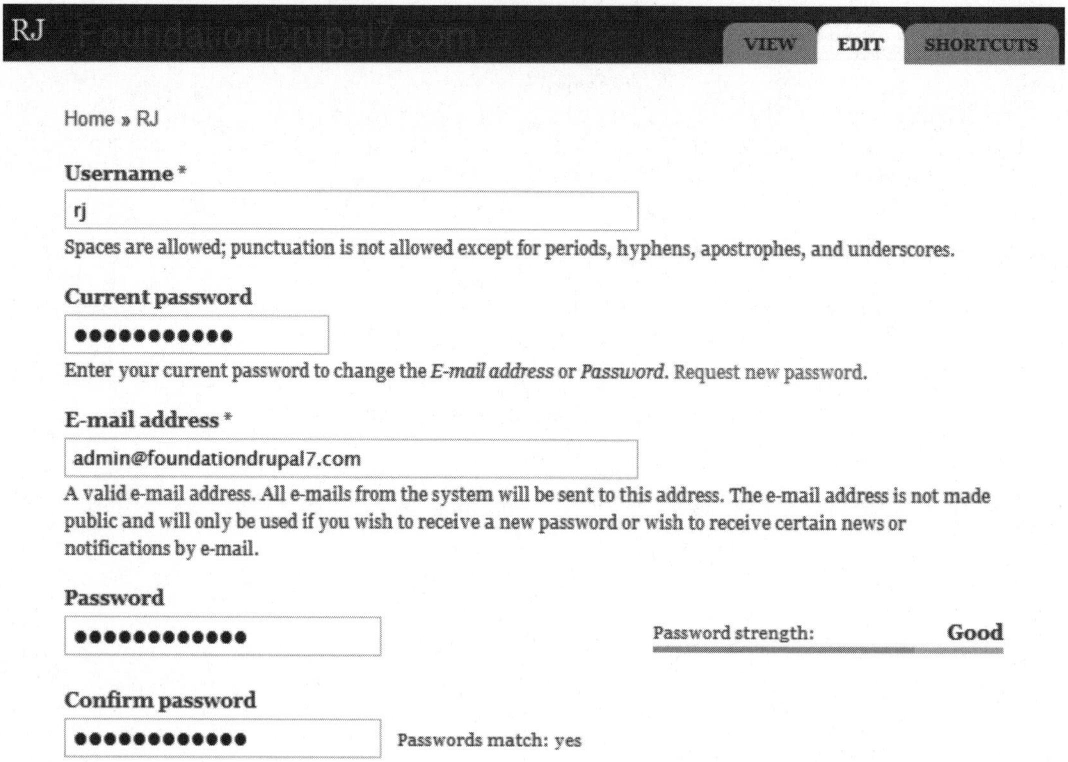

RJ FoundationDrupal7.com   VIEW   **EDIT**   SHORTCUTS

Home » RJ

Username *

rj

Spaces are allowed; punctuation is not allowed except for periods, hyphens, apostrophes, and underscores.

Current password

●●●●●●●●●●

Enter your current password to change the *E-mail address* or *Password*. Request new password.

E-mail address *

admin@foundationdrupal7.com

A valid e-mail address. All e-mails from the system will be sent to this address. The e-mail address is not made public and will only be used if you wish to receive a new password or wish to receive certain news or notifications by e-mail.

Password

●●●●●●●●●●●●   Password strength: **Good**

Confirm password

●●●●●●●●●●●●   Passwords match: yes

Figure 10-13. Change the password for user #1 and any other developer accounts.

3. Enable performance caching at **Configuration ➤ Performance** (see Figure 10-14). Note that if this breaks the test site, you should go back to the dev site and fix it.

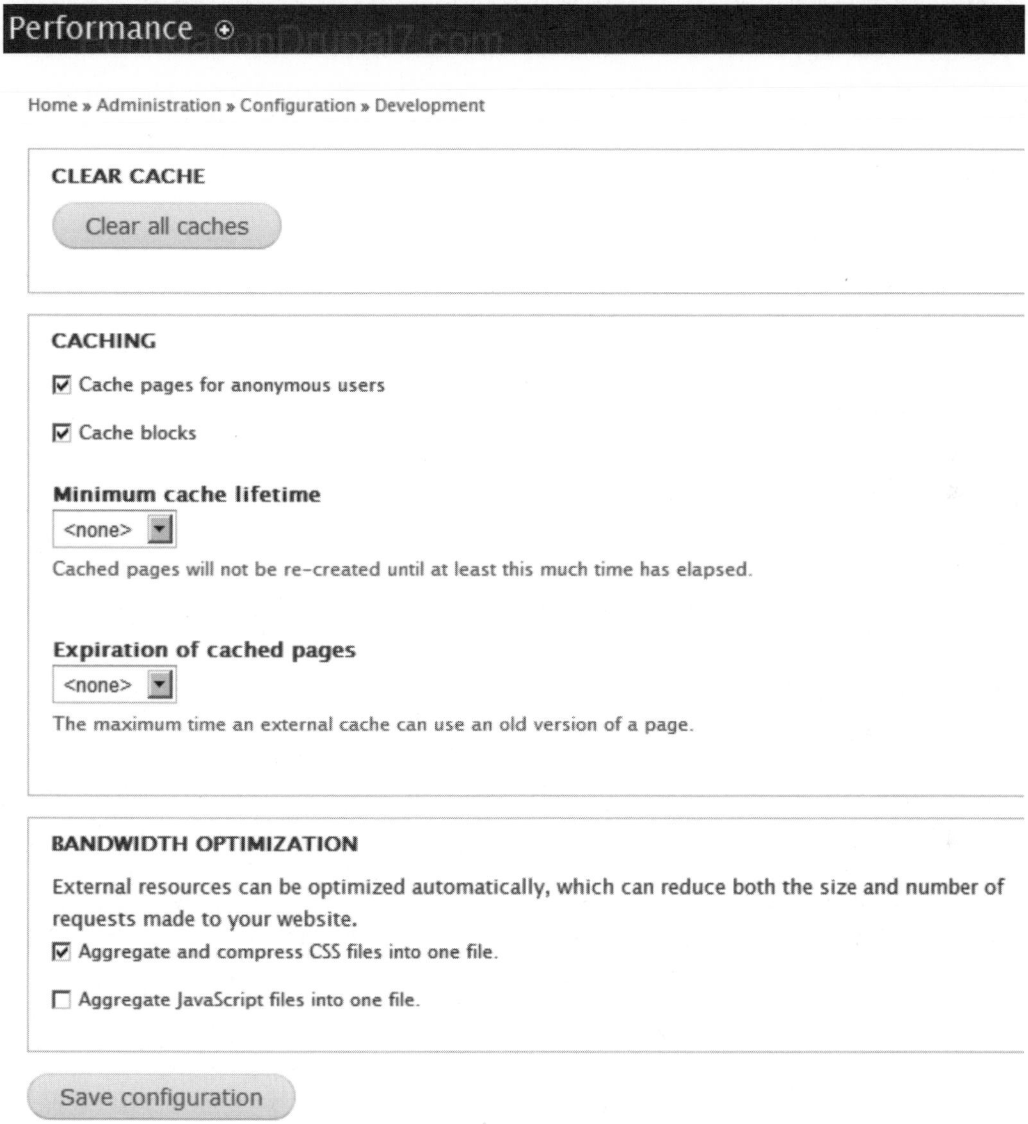

Performance ⊕

Home » Administration » Configuration » Development

CLEAR CACHE

[Clear all caches]

CACHING

☑ Cache pages for anonymous users

☑ Cache blocks

Minimum cache lifetime

[<none> ▾]

Cached pages will not be re-created until at least this much time has elapsed.

Expiration of cached pages

[<none> ▾]

The maximum time an external cache can use an old version of a page.

BANDWIDTH OPTIMIZATION

External resources can be optimized automatically, which can reduce both the size and number of requests made to your website.

☑ Aggregate and compress CSS files into one file.

☐ Aggregate JavaScript files into one file.

[Save configuration]

Figure 10-14. Navigate to **Configuration ➤ Performance**, and enable performance caching.

4. Navigate to **Configuration ➤ Logging and Errors**, and configure error message to not display (see Figure 10-15).

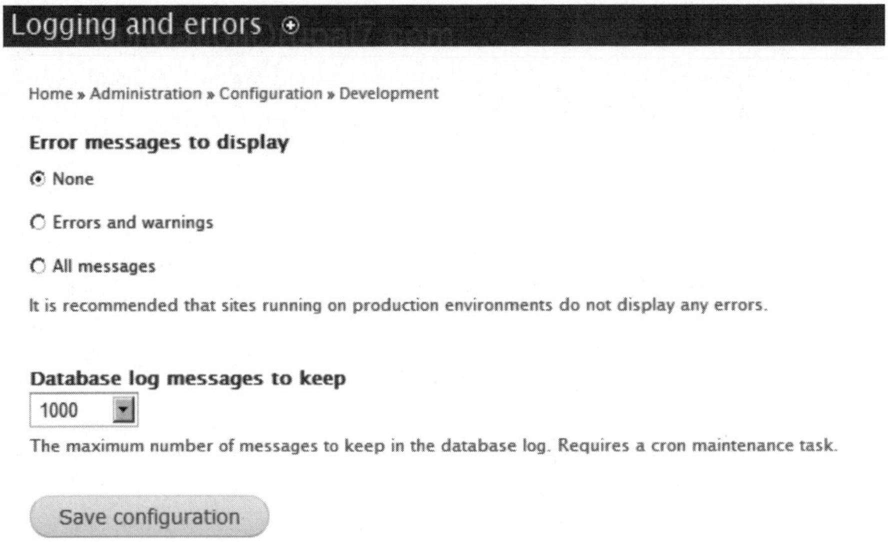

Logging and errors ⊕

Home » Administration » Configuration » Development

Error messages to display

⊙ None

○ Errors and warnings

○ All messages

It is recommended that sites running on production environments do not display any errors.

Database log messages to keep

| 1000 ▾ |

The maximum number of messages to keep in the database log. Requires a cron maintenance task.

(Save configuration)

Figure 10-15. Configure error messages to not print to the screen.

Moving the test site to production

By this point, http://test.example.com should be ready for production. In cPanel, the public_html folder is usually reserved for files available on the Internet (aka web sites). The easiest way to move the test site to production is to delete or rename the public_html folder and create a symlink that points to ~/test.

1. Rename the public_html folder (see Figure 10-16).

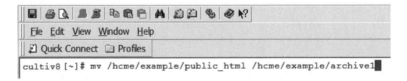

Figure 10-16. Rename the public_html folder.

2. Create a symlink that creates a public_html folder pointing to ~/test (see Figure 10-17).

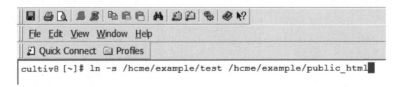

Figure 10-17. Create a symlink pointing to ~/test.

3. Log in to cPanel, and delete the subdomain `http://test.example.com`.

Using steps 1 and 2, you can easily point `public_html` to any folder in your home directory.

Summary

In this chapter, I reviewed the process of preparing a Drupal site for production. I discussed building a staging environment and the need for multiple versions of a site, minimally dev and prod, allowing you to have one version with a set of developer tools enabled and another version for production. I walked you through a step-by-step tutorial to copy a Drupal site using cPanel and SSH and created a test site available at `http://test.example.com`. I closed the chapter with a few simple steps required to move the test site to production.

Chapter 11

Maintaining and Updating a Drupal Site

In this chapter, I show how to lay a basic foundation for maintaining and updating a Drupal site. I start by discussing e-mail alerts, server logs, and site reports—everything you need to ensure your Drupal site is updated and haxxor free. I then delve into the science of updating your site and how Drupal is becoming extremely easy to update compared to previous versions. I close with a number of modules to help with managing multiple Drupal sites.

Maintaining a production site

In my humble opinion, one of the most important aspects of maintaining a production site is ensuring it's up-to-date and haxxor-proof. Provided a site is well-built, the only real tasks you'll be responsible for are checking server logs, creating site reports, and updating Drupal core or contributed modules.

Make sure the Update Manager is enabled! The Update Manager sends you e-mails whenever there's an update available on a site you've built. It's normally enabled when a site is installed using the **standard** install profile (see Chapter 2), but simply navigate to **Reports ➤ Status report** and check the status of **Update notifications** to ensure it's enabled; Drupal will give a warning if it isn't, as shown in Figure 11-1. To enable it, navigate to the **Modules** section, scroll to **Update Manager**, select the **enable** check box, and save.

PHP register globals	Disabled
Unicode library	PHP Mbstring Extension
Update notifications	Enabled

Figure 11-1. Navigate to **Reports ➤ Status report**, and check the status of **Update notifications** to ensure you receive e-mails when a module has an available update.

Once the module is enabled, you can navigate to **Reports ➤ Available update** and click the **SETTINGS** tab, as shown in Figure 11-2. I recommend checking for updates daily, mostly to help with planning purposes; although it's always nice to update a site immediately, sometimes it may take a day or three before there's time. I usually reserve **Check for update of disabled modules and themes** for testing when I'm working on a site. You can also choose to receive updates when a newer version of a module is available or when the version available is a security update. I always check for all newer versions; sometimes a version update includes new features and bug fixes I might be interested in for a future site.

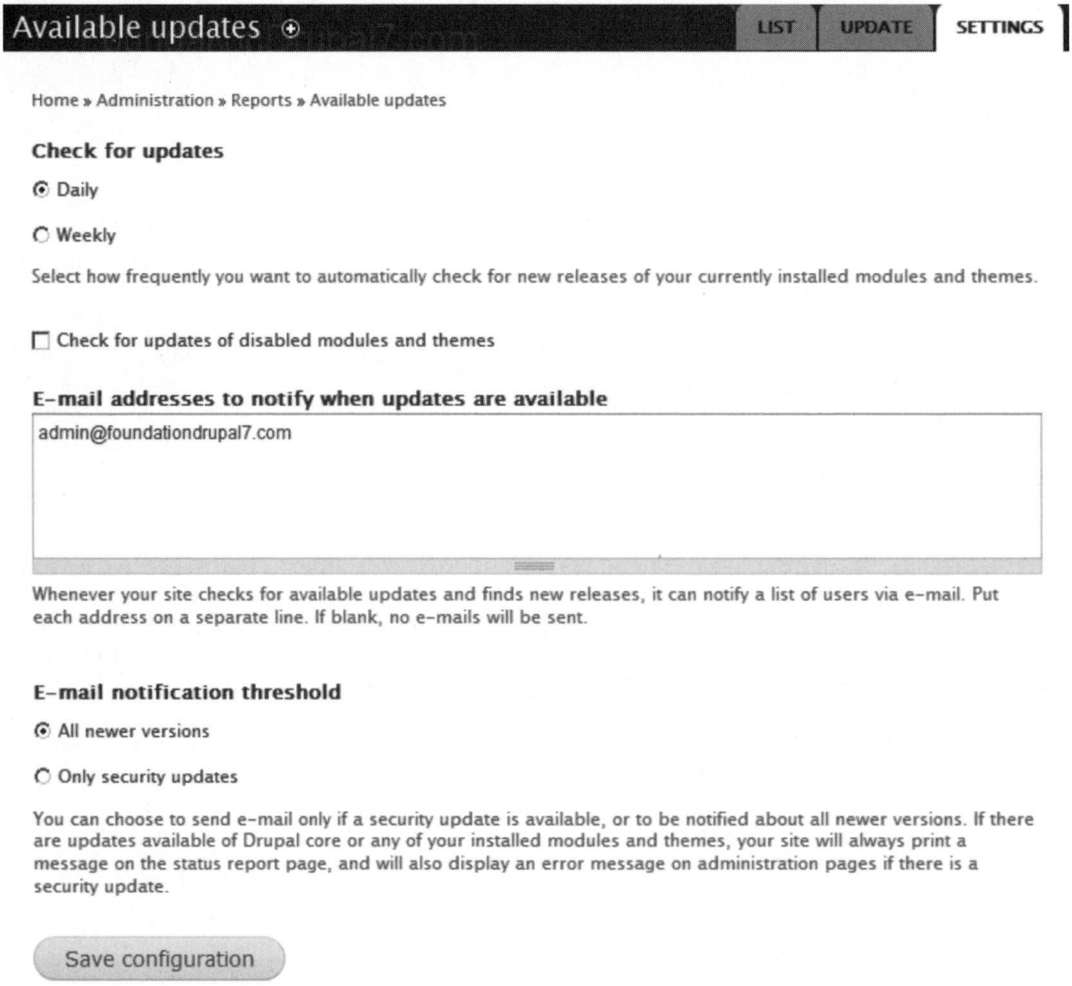

Figure 11-2. Navigate to **Reports ➤ Available updates**, and click the **SETTINGS** tab to configure update notifications.

Signing up for and checking security alerts

Drupal has a low-volume e-mail list dedicated to announcing security issues affecting Drupal core and contributed modules. It's also good to sign up for the Drupal newsletter if you want to hear about Drupal-related conferences and other happenings (see Figure 11-3). Signing up is relatively easy:

1. Create an account at `http://drupal.org`; if you already have one, sign in.

2. Navigate to the **Your Dashboard** page or alternately to `http://drupal.org/user`.

3. Click the **Edit** link, and then click the **My newsletters** tab.

4. Select the **security announcements** check box, and click **save**.

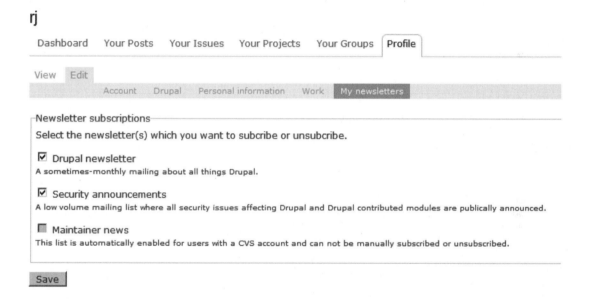

Figure 11-3. Sign up to receive security announcements from Drupal.org.

There are also a few pages on `http://drupal.org` you can visit to see previous security announcements containing a description of found security bugs:

- `http://drupal.org/security` for a list of all security announcements relating to core Drupal
- `http://drupal.org/security/contrib` for all contrib-related security announcements
- `http://drupal.org/security/psa` for all security-related announcements
- `http://drupal.org/taxonomy/term/100` for a list of all core and contrib modules that have updates, in chronological order

Checking the reports section weekly

You can access site reports by clicking the **Reports** link in the administration toolbar, as shown in Figure 11-4. This page contains a number of reports to help you understand site health and usage trends. I recommend you frequently check the reports on this page; I check reports at least once a week for some of my busier sites. The default installation enables several modules that contribute reports to this page, including search, field UI, status updates, and database logging. I also recommend enabling the statistics module, which provides several reports on how users interact with your site.

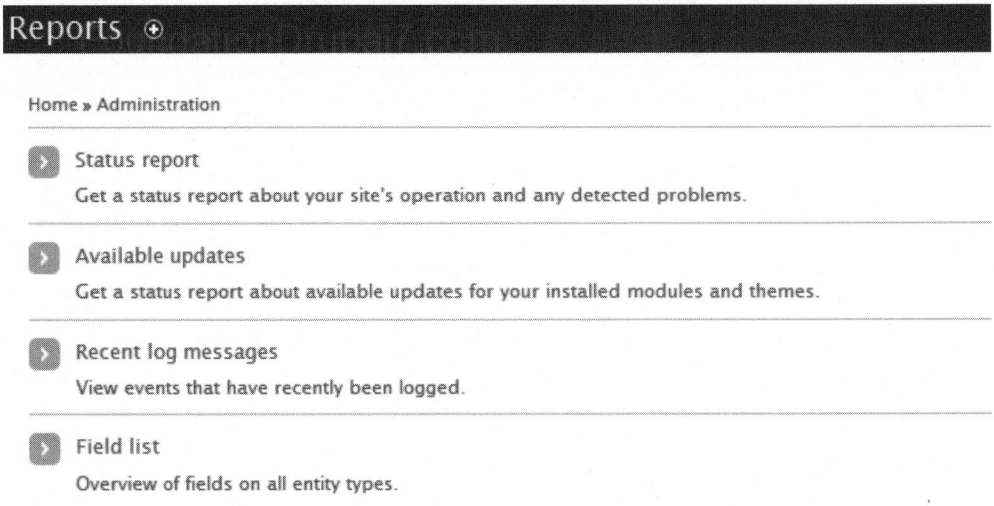

Reports

Home » Administration

> **Status report**
> Get a status report about your site's operation and any detected problems.

> **Available updates**
> Get a status report about available updates for your installed modules and themes.

> **Recent log messages**
> View events that have recently been logged.

> **Field list**
> Overview of fields on all entity types.

Figure 11-4. Full list of all available reports, accessed by clicking the **Reports** link in the administration toolbar.

Enable the statistics module

The statistics module provides you with a number of reports about the usage patterns of users, including **Recent hits**, **Top referrers**, **Top pages**, and **Top visitors**. The **Recent hits** report contains all access logs recorded by the module, such as page, user, and time. The remaining three reports provide you with an overview of the access logs. The search module provides you with a report of top search phrases. If you are serious about viewing and understanding usage trends, I recommend using the Google Analytics module, available at `http://drupal.org/project/google_analytics`. Google Analytics gives you a number of advanced analytical and reporting options not available with Drupal.

You enable the statistics module at the **Modules** page, and you configure it at **Configuration ➤ Statistics**, as shown in Figure 11-5. You will need to select **Enable access log** from the configuration form for the module to work. I recommend adjusting the field **discard access logs older than**, depending on the amount of traffic to your site. On a heavily visited site, the access log will grow quickly; the statistics module adds one entry to the log every time a user visits a page. If your site has 100 visitors a day viewing an average of 10 pages per visitor, this adds 1,000 entries to the log every day; setting **Discard access logs older than** to the maximum setting (three months and three weeks) could easily result in a log with more than 100,000 entries. If this is a concern, I recommend speaking with your web host to find out whether it has a limit on the number of rows in a database table.

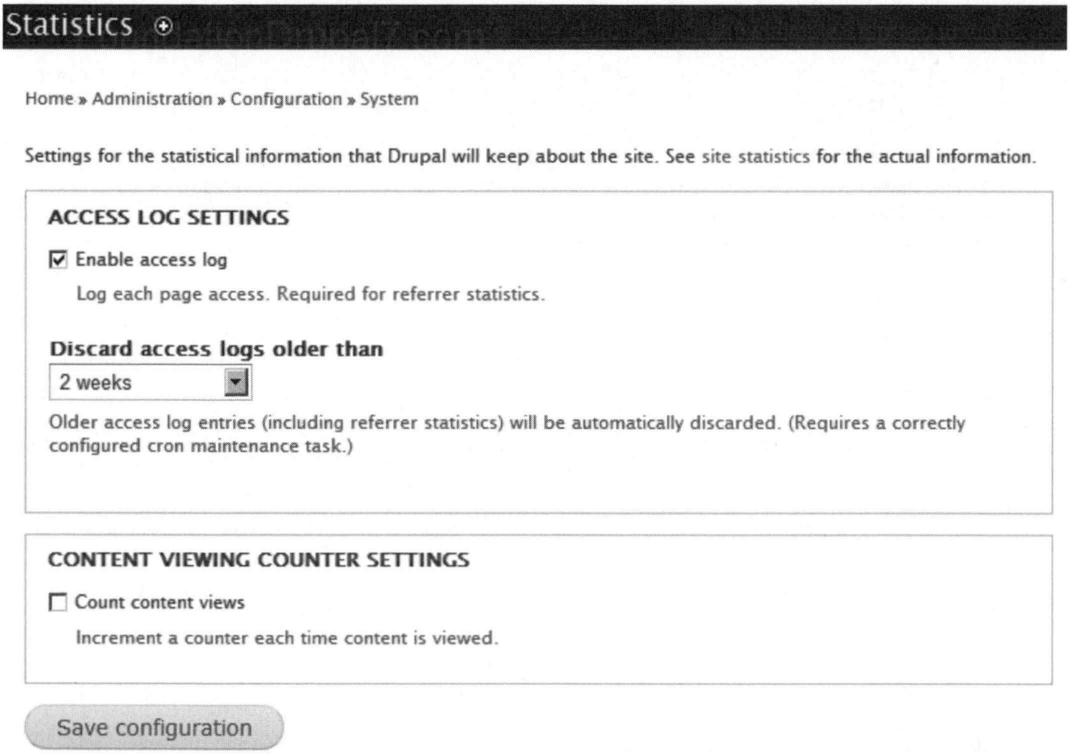

Figure 11-5. Statistics module configuration options, accessed at **Configuration ➤ Statistics**

Selecting **Count content views** enables a counter on every piece of content that displays the number of times a node has been viewed. Permission must be given to users to view the counter.

Note that the statistics module adds one additional database call per page displayed, resulting in an increased load on the server. Disabling this module may help increase the performance of your site for users.

Site health

Site health refers to a number of factors, including error messages, access denied messages, and page not found messages. The **Recent log entries** report contains a list of all system messages added to the log, including access denied messages, content creation messages, PHP error messages, and more (see Figure 11-6). Additionally, the list of entries can be filtered by both message type and severity. Two reports, **top 'access denied' errors** and **top 'page not found' errors**, provide you with a quick report of the most common errors. You will want to frequently check these reports. The **top 'access denied'** report may tell you whether someone is trying to hack into your web site, while the **top 'page not found' errors** report will tell you whether a link is broken or an image is missing.

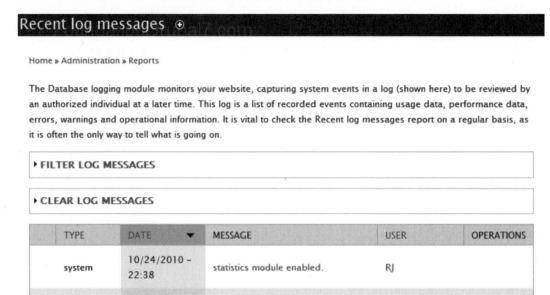

Figure 11-6. Recent log entries, sometimes referred to by early Drupalers as the *watchdog table*

The **Status report** is a special report included with the core system, as shown in Figure 11-7. It tells you whether the server and your Drupal system are configured properly. You should check and fix the issues in this report immediately after installing Drupal.

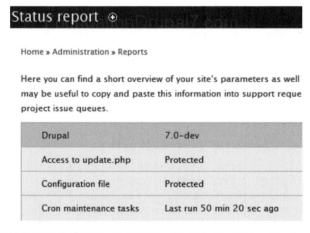

Figure 11-7. Navigate to **Reports ➤ Status report** to view the site status report.

Understanding the update process

Updating a site in Drupal has always been a notoriously time-consuming process, especially for people new to Drupal. Readers familiar with Joomla or WordPress are probably familiar with the one-click update process that does everything for you. Until Drupal 7, Drupal has never had a front-end UI to help with updates; the process has always involved manually moving files and database dumps. Starting with Drupal 7, the Update Manager module is Drupal's core UI for allowing users with the **Run software updates** setting enabled to manage updates through the admin interface. Currently, the module is limited in functionality but will someday have the ability to update core and contributed modules by simply clicking a button.

The goal of this section is to talk through the process of updating a site, whether through the UI or via SSH, so you can understand what happens (and needs to happen!) during an update. The process itself is rather simple:

1. Create a test site, which is basically a clone of your production site, as covered in Chapter 10.

2. On this test site, delete outdated modules, and replace them with the most current version. Drupal allows you do to this through the UI.

Updates are an important reason why you should never haxxor a module: it makes it difficult to update. If you hack a module, make sure to create a patch so that when you upgrade, you can apply the patch to the module to "restore" your previous hacks. The patch may not always apply, because code in the module may have changed, but having the patch around will help you understand the reason for the change in the first place.

3. Run the `update.php` script by navigating to `http://example.com/update.php`.

4. If the update was successful, put your production site in maintenance mode, and follow the same process.

Using the Update Manager module

Click **Modules** in the administration toolbar, and then click the **UPDATE** tab to view the Update Manager, as shown in Figure 11-8. If the update status module is enabled and cron configured, this list will fill with a list of modules with available updates, allowing you to update contributed modules and, eventually, Drupal core through the UI.

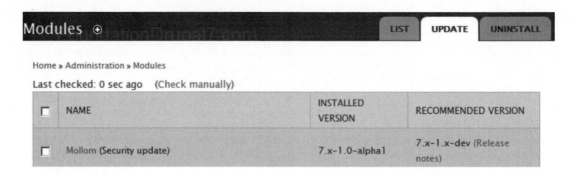

	NAME	INSTALLED VERSION	RECOMMENDED VERSION
☐	Mollom (Security update)	7.x-1.0-alpha1	7.x-1.x-dev (Release notes)

Figure 11-8. Click **Modules** in the administration toolbar, and then click the **UPDATE** tab to view the Update Manager.

How to update a contributed module via Drupal UI

The process is rather simple, although I do cover the technical process in depth in the following section just to give you an idea of what is happening.

1. First, navigate to the **Modules** page, and click the **UPDATE** tab, as shown in Figure 11-8.

2. Click the check box for each module requiring an update, or alternately select the check box that selects all check boxes, and select the **Download these updates** button.

3. Modules will automatically download into your /tmp folder, in directories called update-cache and update-extraction. Click the **Continue** button, and make sure the **Perform updates with site...** check box is selected, as shown in Figure 11-9.

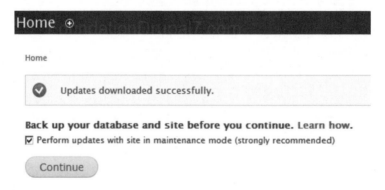

Figure 11-9. Make sure the **Perform updates with site...** check box is selected when updating a site.

4. Make sure you're using an encrypted connection (for example, https://example.com...) before proceeding, because this next step will send FTP data through your HTTP connection. Enter all required fields and press the **Continue** button, as shown in Figure 11-10.

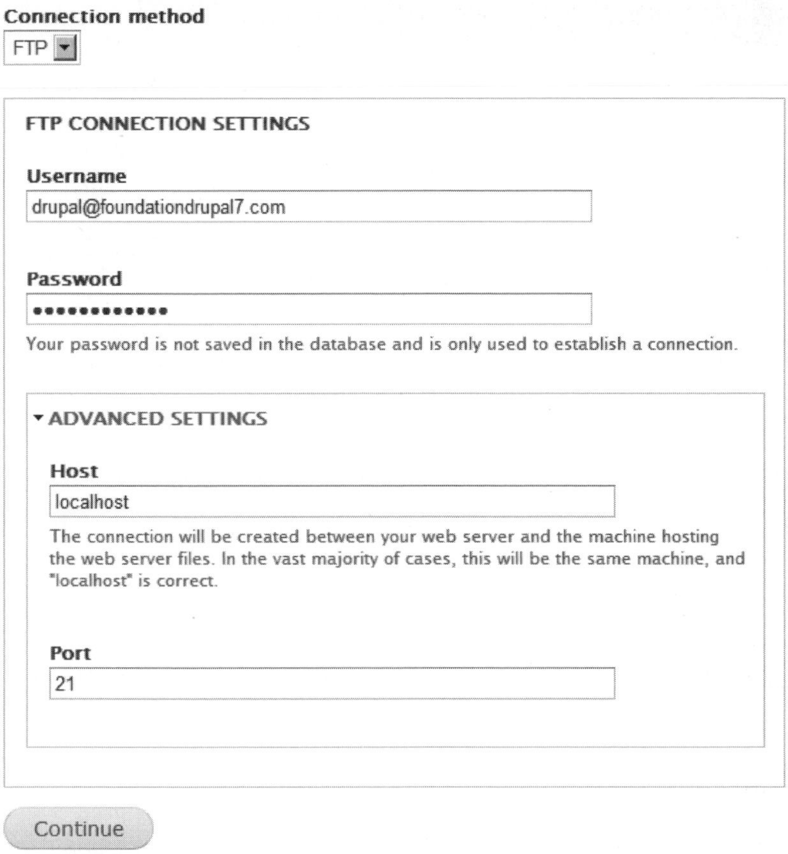

Connection method

FTP ▾

FTP CONNECTION SETTINGS

Username

drupal@foundationdrupal7.com

Password

●●●●●●●●●●●●

Your password is not saved in the database and is only used to establish a connection.

▾ ADVANCED SETTINGS

Host

localhost

The connection will be created between your web server and the machine hosting
the web server files. In the vast majority of cases, this will be the same machine, and
"localhost" is correct.

Port

21

Continue

Figure 11-10. Enter FTP information to complete the module update.

How to update a contributed module via SSH

I described the process earlier, but just to recap, all you're doing is creating a test site, applying updates, and, when ready, applying the same updates to production. To the bat mobile, let's go!

1. Create a test site, which is basically a clone of your production site, as covered in Chapter 10.

2. Make sure you have a backup of your database in case the update fails and you need to try again.

> The backup and migrate module (http://drupal.org/project/backup_migrate) is a good module to quickly back up your MySQL database to either the server or your hard drive.

3. On this test site, delete all outdated modules that need to be updated and replace with the most current version.

4. Navigate to `http://example.com/update.php` to run the update script; make sure you're logged in as an administrator or user 1; otherwise, there are some settings you'll need to change in the `settings.php` file. See Figure 11-11.

---

*If you need to update your site and you are not logged in with **Run software updates permissions**, go to `settings.php` and change $update_free_access to TRUE.*

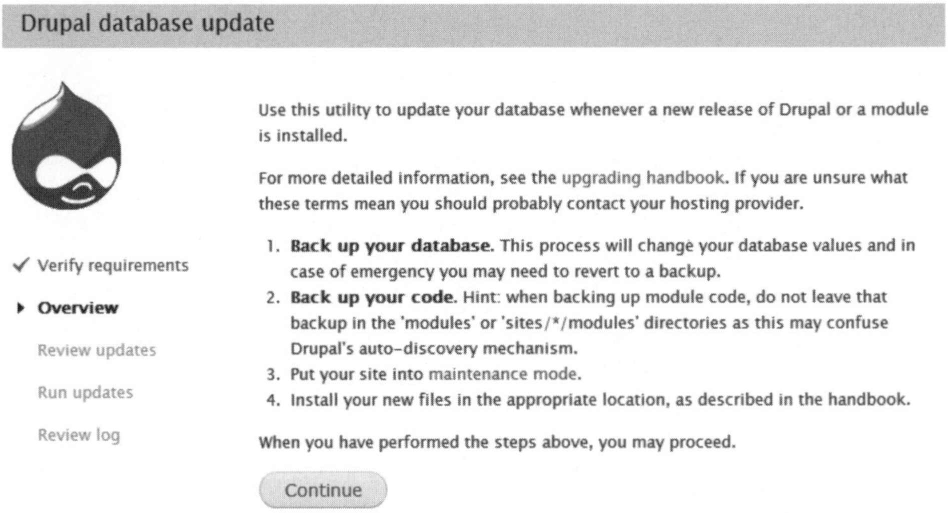

Drupal database update

✓ Verify requirements

▶ **Overview**

Review updates

Run updates

Review log

Use this utility to update your database whenever a new release of Drupal or a module is installed.

For more detailed information, see the upgrading handbook. If you are unsure what these terms mean you should probably contact your hosting provider.

1. **Back up your database.** This process will change your database values and in case of emergency you may need to revert to a backup.
2. **Back up your code.** Hint: when backing up module code, do not leave that backup in the 'modules' or 'sites/*/modules' directories as this may confuse Drupal's auto-discovery mechanism.
3. Put your site into maintenance mode.
4. Install your new files in the appropriate location, as described in the handbook.

When you have performed the steps above, you may proceed.

(Continue)

Figure 11-11. Click **Modules** in the administration toolbar, and then click the **UPDATE** tab to view the Update Manager.

5. If it works, success! It is now time to follow the same process on your production site.

Drupal will alert you if the update fails and provide you with a list of what failed. I have found that if an update fails for you, it probably failed for someone else. I recommend searching the Drupal forums and issue queue for the specific modules that fail.

---

6. Log in to your production site, and navigate to **Configuration ➤ Maintenance mode** to put the site in maintenance mode, as shown in Figure 11-12.

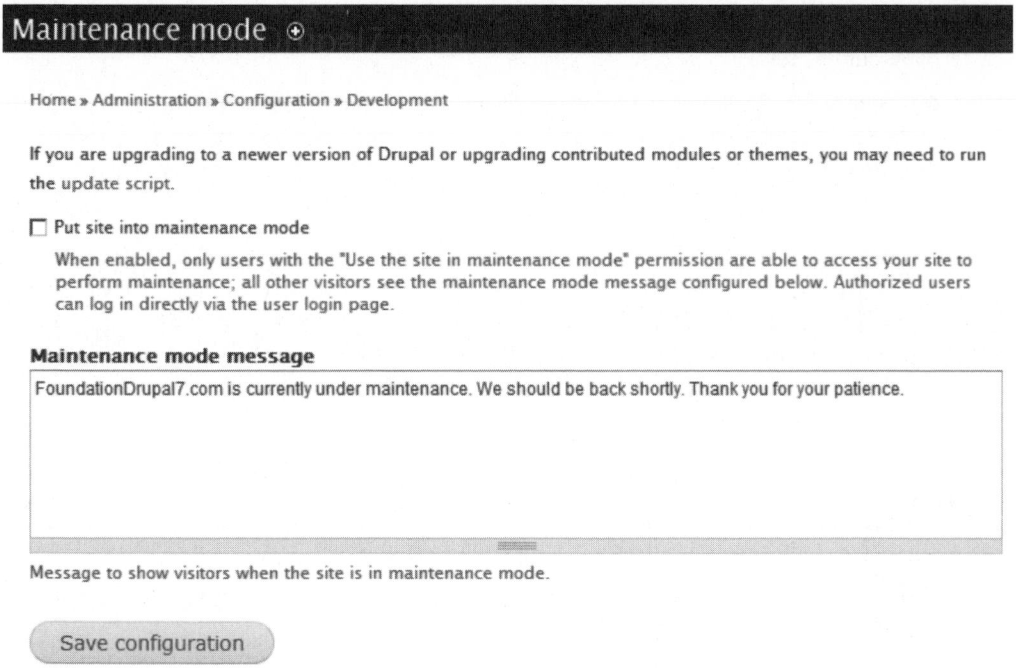

Maintenance mode ⊕

Home » Administration » Configuration » Development

If you are upgrading to a newer version of Drupal or upgrading contributed modules or themes, you may need to run the update script.

☐ Put site into maintenance mode

When enabled, only users with the "Use the site in maintenance mode" permission are able to access your site to perform maintenance; all other visitors see the maintenance mode message configured below. Authorized users can log in directly via the user login page.

Maintenance mode message

FoundationDrupal7.com is currently under maintenance. We should be back shortly. Thank you for your patience.

Message to show visitors when the site is in maintenance mode.

(Save configuration)

Figure 11-12. Click **Modules** in the administration toolbar, and then click the **UPDATE** tab to view the Update Manager.

7. Repeat steps 3 and 4 on the production site.

Instead of redoing steps 3 and 4, you can simply change the live web folder from the outdated version to the most current version. If you do this, my recommendation is to keep the site offline while you're updating the site and turn it back on after you repoint the web folder. This way, you don't lose any data during the transition (new nodes, user account changes, log records, and so on).

8. Take your site out of maintenance mode.

Updating Drupal core via SSH

Updating Drupal core is a similar process to updating a contributed module, except with a few more steps. Many people like to save snapshots of previous Drupal versions at a certain point in time for historical reasons, and a core update is a good time to create this snapshot. Note that your main concern is making sure that everything in the /sites folder is preserved; this is where all your modules, themes, and site-specific files live, so you don't want to lose this.

1. Create a test site, which is basically a clone of your production site, as covered in Chapter 10.

2. Make sure you have a backup of your database in case the update fails and you need to try again.

3. On the test site, copy the `/sites` directory to a directory outside the live web directory (outside of `public_html` in cPanel).

4. Delete the entire directory, and replace it with the most current version of Drupal.

> *Depending on the modules enabled and other custom settings, there may be other changes you'll need to save. Some examples include custom `.htaccess` settings, patches to core, and a custom directory for another web app or script.*

5. Delete the `/sites` directory, and replace with the directory from step 3. This is also a good time to update contributed modules.

6. If it works, success! I recommend repointing the domain to the just-updated version so that you have a historical "this-used-to-be-Drupal-7.x" copy.

7. If using cPanel, follow the steps in Chapter 10 to repoint the domain to the newest version of Drupal.

Useful modules

I discuss several modules in this section that help speed the process of updating and staging sites. I cover modules to help you back up databases and sync nodes and users between sites. Advanced users of Drupal will find this section especially relevant.

How do I back up content?

Drupal can be thought of as two entities, database data and files. Content is usually saved in the database, while code is usually saved in the files (note that this is frequently abused in Drupal and other CMSs). Backing up content is *usually* means backing up the database, but this is frequently abused as well. The best way to easily back up a database is through the backup_migrate module (`http://drupal.org/project/backup_migrate`). This module allows you to save a MySQL dump either to a preconfigured directory on the server or to your local machine. If you are a command prompt guru, you will also appreciate that this module integrates with Drush. Simply point and click to download a database backup and load to another site!

How do I stage content?

When you're doing updates, and especially when you're adding additional functionality (in other words, a blog, forum, or other type of feature), you will frequently need to add content to a test site before adding it to a production site. Sometimes you may have uploaded various types of content, such as image or text fields, as well. The question that naturally comes up is, how to I quickly move content from test to prod? In

Drupal 6, the easiest way to do this is using the node_export module; it is yet to be seen what will emerge in Drupal 7.

How do I stage sites?

When you start dealing with a large number of Drupal sites, the question inevitably follows: how do I have multiple people work on local sites and have each apply local changes to the production site? Unfortunately, this question has yet to be answered in Drupal, and Dries Buytaert (founder of Drupal) has hinted that it may be until Drupal 8 that this question is answered.

In the meantime, the most promising modules are features (http://drupal.org/project/features) and deployment (http://drupal.org/project/deploy). The features module allows you to package exportables (views, content types, fields, and so on) as modules so you can easily sync modules between test and production sites. Many modules integrate with Features, including context (http://drupal.org/project/context), strongarm (http://drupal.org/project/strongarm), and spaces (http://drupal.org/project/spaces), making it easier to separate content from code and move sections from one site to another.

You may also want to check out the Aegir system if you plan to manage a large number of Drupal sites (see http://groups.drupal.org/aegir-hosting-system). Aegir allows you to manage sites as if you were managing nodes, such as automated updates, site creation, and more. With Aegir, creating a site is done through the admin interface, as well as managing core and contributed module updates. All this is possible using a handy helper module called Drush (http://drupal.org/project/drush), a command-line shell and scripting interface for Drupal.

Summary

I cover two very important topics in this chapter: how to manage a production site and how to update a site. I start by discussing everything you need to ensure your Drupal site is updated and safe from hackers, including e-mail alerts, server logs, and site reports. I then delve into the art and science of updating your site and how Drupal is becoming extremely easy to update compared to previous versions. I closed by discussing a number of modules to help with staging and managing multiple Drupal sites.

Chapter 12

Translating Business Requirements to Drupal Functionality

Determining which modules and configuration settings to use when building a site can be a daunting task. Clients want the world: integration with Facebook, user account pages, product reviews, buy-it-now links, and little sparkles that follow the mouse pointer. If there was a module for it, clients would have their web site to bake them a pizza, all for the cost of a cup of coffee!

In this chapter, I discuss several tips, tricks, and tools I use to help understand clients' requirements and "connect" them with Drupal functionality. I talk about documents like a module reference sheet and a time-estimation spreadsheet that can help set expectations around time and cost for both you and the client. I give insights I've gained about what to look for when studying other people's work so you can understand not only how another Drupal site works but also how you can replicate it yourself. Throughout the chapter, I include many URLs that will help you grow in your knowledge of Drupal.

My goal in this chapter is to help you develop the tools and processes to succeed in long-term Drupal site building. It's not a hands-on technical chapter by any means but assumes you're familiar with many of the Drupal concepts covered in this book. Successfully translating business requirements to Drupal functionality is a creative process that requires a mix of planning and foresight. Use this chapter as a springboard to think through and develop your own tools that work best for you!

Increase your knowledge of Drupal

When I first started using Drupal and would ask other developers for advice, I would sometimes hear, "Yeah, that'll work, but it's not very Drupalish." The phrase baffled me for the longest time; if I'm creating a site using Drupal, doesn't that mean it's "Drupalish"? The more I've used Drupal and worked with core and contrib modules, however, the more I've come to understand the term *Drupalish* as a set of development practices driven by knowledge of how Drupal works.

This section discusses many paths to help increase your knowledge of Drupal. I strongly recommend studying other developers' work, and I provide several URLs and questions to ask while doing so. I discuss the benefits of creating and using a module reference document and make suggestions on what should be included in one. I close the section by discussing Drupal best practices I've learned through my own research, experimentation, and errors.

Study other people's work

Sir Isaac Newton was reported to have said, "If I have been able to see further than others, it is because I have stood on the shoulders of giants." In his day, Newton was referring to the amount of research and work that had been done by other people. Building upon their foundation of knowledge, Newton was able to describe universal gravitation, build the first practical reflecting telescope, and develop a theory of color, and he is credited for developing differential and integral calculus. Through his comment, Newton acknowledged the importance and contributions of other people's work to his own accomplishments.

I have learned quite a bit by studying other people's work. There are thousands of active Drupal sites, each created for a unique purpose, with a wealth of information from which I've learned. The first place to look when searching for other sites powered by Drupal is Drupal.org, which has a number of pages for users to show off and discuss their site. Some places to start include the following:

- `Drupal.org/cases` is a list of high-profile companies using Drupal with links to live web sites. Many include a **case study** link to the developer's write-up of the various core, contributed, and custom written modules used on the site.
- `Drupal.org/forum/25` is a forum for users to show off and discuss their site.
- Dries Buyteart, the creator and leader of Drupal, has a list of Drupal-powered sites on his personal blog at `http://buytaert.net/tag/drupal-sites`.
- `Groups.drupal.org/seo-showcase-and-promotion-drupal-sites` has many links to user-submitted Drupal web sites and Drupal showcase directories.

There are also many online directories with listings of Drupal sites, such as `DrupalSites.net`; a search for *best Drupal web sites* or *Drupal showcase* will return a number of sites to get started. When I'm doing research, I usually start at Drupal.org for a similar type of web site or functionality I'm seeking. For example, I may search for *best Drupal e-commerce sites* or *Ubercart showcase* (Ubercart is a popular e-commerce module for Drupal). Once I have a list of five or ten sites, I'm ready to begin researching them.

The easiest type of research is when a developer has described in detail the modules, content types, fields, and other code snippets used to create a site. However, and more often than not, all you will have is a live URL with accompanying HTML and CSS files. Don't fret! There is more than enough information available to infer the modules and methods used to build the site.

The Firebug plug-in for the Mozilla browser is ideal for viewing HTML and CSS files (see Figure 12-1). Although more of a development and theming tool, this plug-in allows you to view the layout of HTML documents, the IDs and classes assigned to tags, and the JavaScript and CSS files. Here are some questions to ask when studying another site:

- What IDs and classes are assigned to the HTML tags around a block? This can give you an idea of the module used to create it.
- What directory are CSS image files located in? The name of the theme may be in the source.
- What directory are HTML images located in? HTML images (those embedded in the HTML files) are usually uploaded by Drupal and can give you an idea of the structure of the **files** directory.
- What JavaScript and CSS files are loaded, and what directory are they located in? This can give you an idea of the modules loaded for a specific page, as shown in Figure 12-1.
- Are any JavaScript files being pulled from another URL? This may suggest one or more features are provided by a third party.

```
⊞ <div id="sidebar-right">
⊟ <div id="sidebar-far-right">
    ⊟ <div id="sidebar-far-right-inner">
        ⊞ <a href="/user/register">
        ⊟ <div id="block-ad-0" class="block block-ad re
            ⊞ <div class="block-inner">
        </div>
    </div>
</div>
⊞ <div id="header-image-left">
```

Figure 12-1. The Firebug plug-in for the Mozilla browser can help you understand how a site was developed. In this example, you can infer the highlighted block was created by the ad module.

Beyond looking at HTML, CSS, and JavaScript files, you can also ask broad "Drupalish" questions about the site, such as the following:

- Is the current page a full-page node view or created by the views or panels module?
- Is a block created by a user, created by the views module, or created by a core/contrib module?
- What field types does a content type require for the full-page node view and any other related blocks or views?
- How many page, node, and block template files (*.tpl.php) appear to be used across the site?

Create a module reference document

I have a document that lists all the modules I use on a regular basis. Let me back up a little and tell you how the document was created and why. I first started surfing the contributed modules section on Drupal.org (http://drupal.org/project/modules) looking for modules to spice up my sites. I bookmarked quite a few and began adding several modules to every site that I built. Eventually, I racked up a huge collection of bookmarks and have more than 100 modules living in the sites/all/modules contrib directory in my multisite setup. This became borderline ridiculous (and obsessive compulsive) to manage, so I created a spreadsheet with a list of all modules and some relevant facts about each:

- Module name
- Located in sites/all/modules: Yes, No
- Have I used before: Yes, No
- Stability: Alpha, Beta, Release Candidate, or Production Ready
- Two to three sentence description of module, usually from project page on Drupal.org
- Link to module on Drupal.org
- Links to setup instructions and common issues

This document helped me reduce the number of modules in `sites/all/modules` to less than 50, a still high but manageable number. I also use this document when deciding which modules to place in the `sites/EXAMPLE.COM/modules` directory (that is, modules for a specific site). I rarely use this document when meeting with clients, except if I open it on a laptop to help remember the name of a module I've used before. Rather, this document is strictly for writing a statement of work (SOW), with modules listed as project deliverables.

If you plan to create more than one Drupal web site, I strongly recommend creating a document that lists the different modules you have used with a brief description of each. Although it doesn't need to be in the same format as the document I use, it can help you evaluate whether a module is a good fit with your project and whether it should be used on another site.

Network with Drupal developers

When you design and build a Drupal-powered web site, you become the Drupal expert. This means if someone has a question about Drupal, you are the person to whom they will go. I recommend surrounding yourself with fellow Drupalers who can help answer questions, point you to the right module/theme/code snippet, or even write a module or code snippet for you. Drupal.org has a number of forums, groups, and IRC channels to help you network with people with varying levels of Drupal expertise. There are Meetup.com groups, student organizations, conferences, and more—all focused on using and building sites with Drupal. I also recommend finding a local web development shop that specializes in Drupal development. They can be an excellent (but sometimes costly) resource to help you in your time of need.

Learn Drupal best practices

Building a Drupal web site is much like building a castle using Lego products. There is a foundation on which to build, a general idea or picture of what the final product looks like, and many pieces that must be assembled from the ground up. Although there isn't a right way or a wrong way to build a Drupal web site (or a Lego castle), there are several best practices you should follow:

- Never ever, ever edit or delete core files. This will create a nightmare of problems when you need to update your site.
- Avoid editing contributed modules, and if you do, place the module in the site-specific `modules` directory (see Chapter 2).
- All content should be saved as a node or block; avoid placing content in the theme.
- Create new content types for major sections of your site, such as latest news, blogs, and store products, even if the content is displayed only through a block.

- Use a test server to develop your site and back up both the database and files. Use a versioning system such as SVN, CVS, or git.
- Avoid using the first user (UID=1) to create content but rather create a different account for this purpose.

Understanding best practices can help you when evaluating modules, creating wireframe outlines, and determining the length of time required to build a site.

Useful communication tools

The decision to build a web site can come from a number of people, such as a client, a manager, or a business partner. Successfully building a web site depends on understanding and meeting their expectations. Clients, for example, may have the expectation they can upload images into an online gallery. When working with these clients, your job is to understand their requirements: How many images? Are images displayed in a slideshow, a grid, a pop-up, or another format? Does Drupal allow this functionality? Not meeting expectations can result in a dissatisfied client and a frustrating and often time-consuming experience for you. In the following section, I discuss several tools so you can understand and meet expectations.

Requirements gathering

Requirements gathering is the process of speaking with key stakeholders to understand and define business requirements. It is often conducted in an interview or focus group setting using open-ended questions designed to elicit nontechnical responses. The goal is to create a list containing several one-to-two sentence descriptions describing in common language (that is, nontechnical) what they want the web site to do. Table 12-1 shows some example questions and answers from a typical interview.

Table 12-1. Example question and answers from a requirements-gathering Interview

Open-ended question	Example response
What is the purpose of the web site?	Inform customers about our product lines and get new customers to our store.
What information would you like to share about your product lines?	One image, price, product number, and product description.
What web site features do you think will get new customers to your store?	A Google map and top search engine rankings.
What other features do you want for your web site?	The ability for visitors to sign up for an e-mail newsletter.
If you could have one feature that dazzled visitors, what would it be?	A homepage slideshow that scrolls through images of our products.

You can then use the responses to the questions to evaluate and select modules. This brings up an important point: responses should be framed such that one or more Drupal modules can be the proposed solution. This requires the ability to guide the conversation using your knowledge of Drupal. Using Table 12-1 as an example; there are several modules and methods to allow users to sign up for an e-mail newsletter depending on their requirements. Does the client want to integrate with a third-party mass mailer? The MailChimp module would be a good solution. Does the client want to use their server to send e-mails (which is less expensive but presents its own set of problems)? The Simplenews module would be a good fit. Does the client just want a form that dumps e-mail addresses into a database with the ability to export to a spreadsheet? The Webform module would be a good fit. As you can see, it is your knowledge of Drupal that guides the interviewee's responses. I have found that creating and using a module reference document, such as the one described in earlier in the chapter, can help guide the conversation.

Using wireframes

A web site **wireframe** is a basic outline of a web site, usually created after gathering requirements but before any artwork has been designed, that displays the basic structure of a single page of a web site. It contains a number of elements, such as menu links, search boxes, module blocks, informational fields, and more. Wireframes are typically used as a working document to communicate expectations between the client, the graphic designer (if it's not you), and the developer (see Figure 12-2). Wireframes help you understand the following:

- The number of blocks on a page and the best method to create each
- How to configure path aliases, view arguments, and block visibility settings
- The number of content types, fields, and views
- Unknown functionality
- The number of templates a theme will require

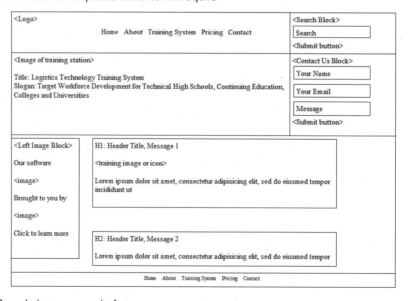

Figure 12-2. Sample homepage wireframe

Creating a wireframe is a relatively straightforward process if you understand requirements and have a general idea of how the client wants their site laid out. I always ask clients for links to at least six web sites they like, three from competitors and three from noncompetitors. I also follow a number of best practices when creating wireframes:

- Start by creating your highest-level <div>s, such as the header, footer, and sidebars.
- Try to keep blocks in consistent locations across wireframes; the more variation between wireframes, the longer it will take to theme and/or build.
- Always keep the header and footer the same.
- Use a 14-point font size and an 18-point line height for all main text, and adjust all other font sizes accordingly.
- Specify all menu links and fields values. Use *lorem ipsum* text for the main content.
- If a module creates a block, include all possible fields the module may output. It is easier to remove a field than add one.
- If you are creating a wireframe for a page view that links to a node, create wireframes for both the page view and the node.
- Create a wireframe for each content type. Include all fields.
- Create a wireframe for the homepage and one for the page content type.

Create an estimated-time spreadsheet

The question that always comes up when meeting with a client is, how much will it cost? In an ideal world, you quote the number of hours it will take, which is more or less accurate, and the client is happy to pay for time that exceeds the original quote. However, in the real world, clients want an exact number with a not-to-exceed-total-number-of-hours clause. This means it's up to you to quote the exact amount of time. If you quote too many hours, then your price will be higher than your competitors, and you'll lose the client. If you quote too few hours, then you'll get the project, but your hourly pay will suffer.

I use an estimated-time spreadsheet to help understand the amount of time it takes to configure certain aspects of a Drupal site (see Figure 12-3). It is a simple document that contains task descriptions of the most common tasks I perform when building a web site (such as configuring the blog module) and the amount of time necessary to configure each. For example, I know that creating a content type, adding fields, and configuring a simple block view takes an hour and a half. Discovering the amount of time of each is the tricky part, and the only advice I can offer is "measure, measure, measure." If you're starting on a new site, take a look at the clock, and time how long it takes to configure a module. After you're done, add 25 percent to both the amount of time it took you and to your hourly rate. This is usually a good indicator of the price you should quote your client.

	A	B	C	D	E
1	Feature	Technical	Hours	Hourly Rate	Total Cost
2	Banner Advertising Blocks	Configure Ad Module	3.25	$85	$276
3	Blog	Add content type, fields, view	2.00	$85	$170
4	Calendar and Mini Calendar	Add content type, fields, date/time, view	3.00	$85	$255
5	Commenting	Enable commenting, theme	1.00	$85	$85
6	Contact Us Form	Webform module	1.00	$85	$85
7	Donations through PayPal	lm_paypal module	3.00	$85	$255
8	Email Newsletter	Constant Contact or Mail Chimp	1.50	$85	$128
9	Employee Directory	Core contact module	1.50	$85	$128
10	Event Registration / RSVP / Signup	Signup module; requires calendar/mini	1.75	$85	$149
11	FAQ Section	FAQ module	1.25	$85	$106

Figure 12-3. Sample estimated time spreadsheet used to calculated the estimated cost of features added to a web site.

This is a useful decision-making tool when you are trying to decide which modules to add or remove from a site and when development time (or cost of implementation) is a critical factor. I also post a client-friendly version of this document on my business's web site so that people have a general idea of price before they call.

Leverage the Drupal community

Drupal is more than just a killer content management platform; it is also a flourishing community of people from around the globe who contribute and make Drupal what it is today. There are conferences, discussion groups, IRC channels, forums, e-mail newsletters, and more. Drupal.org is the primary location for Drupalers to gather and talk about all things Drupal. The site contains a wealth of information (currently more than 500,000 posts), including user-contributed modules, themes, advice, code snippets, instructions, documentation, and more. It is where most development efforts are coordinated and should be your first destination when you're looking for a module, feature, or solution to a problem.

Navigating Drupal.org

Navigating the Drupal web site can be an overwhelming experience. First things first: create an account and join the community. When you log in, click the **my newsletters** tab, and sign up to receive **security announcements**. Although Drupal is one of the safest open source content management systems available, there are sometimes bugs and security issues discovered in core and contributed modules. Signing up for this newsletter informs you of recently discovered security issues, including updates to Drupal core. I have also found this list to be a good source of information to learn about modules I have never used.

There are a number of useful destinations at Drupal.org, many of which are listed in Table 12-2.

Table 12-2. Important destinations in the Drupal.org web site

URL	Description
http://api.drupal.org	Reference guide for Drupal's many APIs; used primarily by module developers.
http://drupal.org/contributors-guide	User-contributed documentation on developing a web site.
http://drupal.org/download	The official download page for Drupal core.
http://drupal.org/forum	Discussion forums. Support forums are a good place to ask questions about Drupal core.
http://drupal.org/handbooks	Official documentation submitted and supported by users; will be moved to http://docs.drupal.org at some point.
http://drupal.org/mailing-lists	Several e-mail lists with archives to which you can sign up.
http://drupal.org/project	Links to lists of user-contributed projects such as modules, themes, and translations.
http://drupal.org/security	Security announcements archive.
http://drupal.org/services	People and organizations offering Drupal-related services.
http://drupal.org/support	Links to many support-related pages.
http://drupal.org/theme-guide	User-contributed documentation on theming a web site.
http://groups.drupal.org	A web site for Drupal users to plan, organize, and work on projects.
http://localize.drupal.org	A web site for Drupal users to help translate Drupal projects into multiple languages.

Posting Guidelines

Many times you will visit Drupal.org with a specific question or a problem that needs to be solved. There are some general posting guidelines that will increase the chance someone will respond:

- Search both the forums (http://drupal.org/search) and the project issues (http://drupal.org/search/issues) for an answer before you post a question.
- Post Drupal-related questions in the support section of the forums.

- Post questions about contributed modules in the module's issue queue (for example, `http://drupal.org/project/issues/INSERTMODULENAMEHERE`).
- Many modules contain a README file that may answer your question; read this before posting.
- Groups are not a good place to post support questions unless the module maintainer has specifically requested you post there.
- If your question regards content in the handbook, post a comment on that specific page.
- Take time writing your question, and be very specific.
- Never post an off-topic question (for example, "I see you're discussing this topic. My problem is similar. Can you help me?").
- If you post a question and figure out the answer, post a follow-up comment and explain the solution.

Finding the perfect functionality

Drupal has thousands of contributed modules, and finding the specific module or code snippet that does exactly what you require can be frustrating and time-consuming. The following are some basic suggestions that will help you during this process.

Searching using the right keywords

Searching using the right keywords is a suggestion that seems like a no-brainer, but there are some caveats. Drupal is very specific in its naming conventions, which you should use during your search. Is the feature for which you're searching a module or a theme? Include that term in the search. Are you trying to enhance the functionality of a module you're currently using? Include the name of the module in the search. Do you know the name of the technology you want to integrate, such as JavaScript or Ajax? Searching for *Drupal module that animates content* is too vague. What type of content do you want to animate? What technology do you want to use? For example, you may want display content in a block that users can update, yet you don't want to give users permission to use the block management form. Your search terms would be *node* (content is too generic), *block*, and *permissions*, and a search would find the NodeAsBlock module, a perfect solution.

Evaluating a module

Oftentimes, you find one or more modules that contain the functionality you require. However, just because a module has the feature you're looking for doesn't mean it should be used on your site. A module should be maintained, well-documented, and tested by a number of users before it's ready for production. A module should always be evaluated based on a number of factors:

- Is there an official production-ready release? If the module version number contains beta or dev, it is probably not ready for production.
- Who is the module maintainer? How many commits has he or she made? When was the last one? More active maintainers are more likely to respond to questions and fix bugs.

- What is the percentage of open issues to total issues? A high percentage suggests the module is no longer maintained.
- Click **view usage statistics** at the bottom of the page; a higher number of users means there's a better chance people are actively maintaining the module.
- What is the date of the last official release?
- How thoroughly documented is the module?

Summary

Successfully translating business requirements to Drupal functionality is a creative process that requires a mix of planning and foresight. In this chapter, I discussed several tips, tricks, and tools I use to help translate clients' requirements into Drupal functionality. I began by discussing steps to take to grow in Drupal knowledge, including studying other Drupal-powered web sites and creating reference sheets. I included links to many popular and informative destinations on Drupal.org. I closed the chapter with a discussion on how to evaluate whether a module is a good fit for a site.

Appendix A

Drupal and Search Engine Optimization

Search engine optimization (SEO) is one of those nebulous terms that means many things to many people. In this appendix, I take a technical approach to Drupal and SEO and show how Drupal can be configured to follow many of the common SEO practices. I review several modules, including Pathauto, Path Redirect, and Global Redirect, and I discuss how they can be used to increase search ranking and how search engines "understand" your web site. I also talk about the importance of theming, header tags, and other settings configurable through Drupal. This appendix will help you leverage Drupal and achieve high search visibility.

What is SEO?

SEO is the process of developing, configuring, and theming a site so that search engines recognize important key words and phrases, resulting in higher search rankings when a user searches for those key words and phrases. To this end, SEO is *not* any of the following:

- A one-time "to-do" item to check off your list
- An exact science with guaranteed results
- Difficult to do in Drupal

As a Drupal developer and themer, I tend to categorize SEO into two aspects, technical and implementation. Technically, SEO involves configuring a site so that key words and phrases are placed in strategic locations, such as in the URL, header tags, meta tags, page titles, and more. Some of this is performed when theming the site (such as when placing node titles in <h1> tags), while other aspects are performed by modules (for example, placing node titles in URLs). I'll expand upon this later in the chapter.

Implementation is both an art and a science. It involves selecting key words and phrases, generating content, building link campaigns, submitting your site to online directories, and more. Most of this happens after a site is built, and as such, I only lightly touch upon this. Note that I say "most of this happens after a site is built" because it's only when a site is live and has been indexed by a search engine that you really know where it's going to land in search results. Achieving first-page results can be challenging for competitive search terms and is often a mixture of trial and error and constantly tweaking a site. When building a site, my initial goal is to provide the client with a foundation to start this process. I never guarantee first-page results—no one can—but I can promise to provide the tools to get their site there.

The goal of this chapter is to discuss the technical aspects of SEO, and as such, I discuss implementation only as it pertains to configuring a site.

Important configuration changes

In this section, I discuss several changes that you can make to core Drupal to help improve your SEO ranking. Changes to the .htaccess and robots.txt files are discussed, as well as enabling title and alt fields for images. This section focuses on core Drupal; contributed modules are discussed in the next section.

Update the .htaccess file

It is a good SEO practice to set a single point of origin for all content; search engines tend to penalize web pages that have duplicate content. For example, search engines will lower search rank if http://example-a.com, http://example-b.com, and http://example-b.com/foo all have the same content. There are a number of workarounds, such as using 301 "permanent" redirects or setting creation dates on meta tags, discussed in the next section.

There is some speculation that search engines may differentiate between domains with and without the www (for example http://www.example.com and http://example.com). Although both are usually the same site, some search engines may penalize you simply because there are two sources. The best practice is to configure the .htaccess file so that the web site always resolves to either http://www.example.com or http://example.com, not both. Making the changes in Figure A-1 changes Apache to redirect all traffic to www.

```
84   # To redirect all users to access the site WITH the 'www.' prefix,
85   # (http://example.com/... will be redirected to http://www.example.com/...)
86   # uncomment the following:
87   RewriteCond %{HTTP_HOST} !^www\. [NC]
88   RewriteRule ^ http://www.%{HTTP_HOST}%{REQUEST_URI} [L,R=301]
89   #
90   # To redirect all users to access the site WITHOUT the 'www.' prefix,
91   # (http://www.example.com/... will be redirected to http://example.com/...)
92   # uncomment the following:
93   # RewriteCond %{HTTP_HOST} ^www\.(.+)$ [NC]
94   # RewriteRule ^ http://%1%{REQUEST_URI} [L,R=301]
```

Figure A-1. Uncomment lines 87–88 to direct all site traffic to http://www.example.com.

Note: Keep in that if you make this change, you will need to update .htaccess again when you update core.

Enable title and alt fields for images

When an image is displayed on a site, it has both a title, displayed on mouse hover, and alternate text, displayed when the image is unavailable or for users with screen readers. Search engines use this text to associate pages with key terms. My recommendation is to write a thorough and relevant `alt` term that describes the picture. For the title, I usually write what I think the end user will find relevant, trying to "salt" the sentence with key terms and words.

If the image is uploaded through a file upload field, not through the WYSIWYG editor, then you will need to enable `alt` and `title` fields on the image field configuration page. To enable, navigate to **Structure ➤ Content types**, and select **manage fields** next to the appropriate content type. Select the image field and scroll halfway down the page, as shown in Figure A-2.

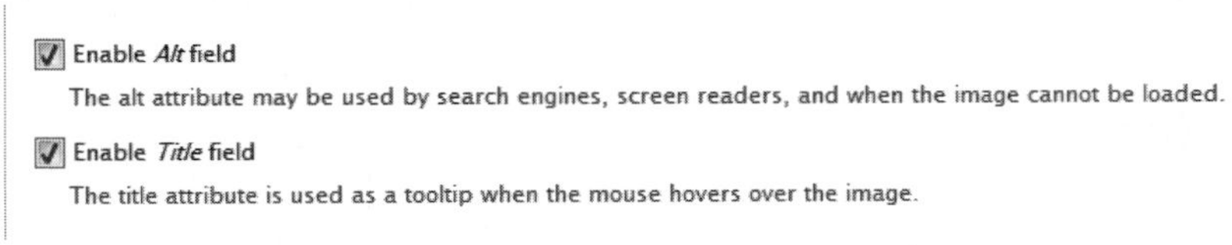

☑ Enable *Alt* field
The alt attribute may be used by search engines, screen readers, and when the image cannot be loaded.

☑ Enable *Title* field
The title attribute is used as a tooltip when the mouse hovers over the image.

Figure A-2. `alt` and `title` fields are enabled for each image field in each content type.

Revise robots.txt

Sometimes there is content you do not want indexed in a search engine but yet the content is accessible to anonymous users and search engines. Other times, content is available on multiple pages, and you want to remove pages that may appear as duplicate content. For example, I frequently have content types I do not want to appear in search indexes. One such example is the FAQ module (`http://drupal.org/project/faq`). This module creates a content type allowing you to create a node with a question and a corresponding answer. Drupal displays this as a full-page node, while the FAQ module also displays all questions and answers on a single page. Some search engines may penalize you because it appears you have duplicate content appearing on multiple site page. To work around this, I configure the Pathauto module (discussed in Chapter 7) with a base URL that I tell search engines not to index.

The `robots.txt` file must be updated to work around this. It tells search engines which directories (that is, paths) should be included in search indexes (see Figure A-3). To ensure paths from specific content types are not indexed, you will need to set the base of the path to `[content-type-name]` and then add `Disallow: /content-type-name/` to robots.txt.

```
41  # Paths (clean URLs)
42  Disallow: /admin/
43  Disallow: /comment/reply/
44  Disallow: /contact/
45  Disallow: /content-type-name/
46  Disallow: /node/add/
47  Disallow: /search/
48  Disallow: /user/register/
49  Disallow: /user/password/
50  Disallow: /user/login/
```

Figure A-3. The robots.txt file is configured to tell search engines not to index pages of a specific content type.

SEO-friendly modules

A number of contributed modules are available to help increase your search engine rank. Some modules allow you to customize HTML output on both a global and a per-page basis, such as meta tags, page titles, and menu attributes. Other modules, such as Path Redirect and Global Redirect, help reduce the chance for duplicate content. Finally, the SEO Checklist module provides you with a list of "SEO to-do items" for you to check off.

SEO Checklist

The SEO Checklist module (`http://drupal.org/project/seo_checklist`) provides a checklist of SEO best practices to help you keep track of what needs to be done on your site. It checks to see all modules installed on your site and gives you a list of to-do items. It also provides you with a date stamp next to each item after it's marked as completed. This is a great module to keep track of all SEO-related tasks that need to be performed on a site, especially if multiple people are working on a site. Follow the conversation at `http://drupal.org/node/610934` to learn when this module will be ported to Drupal 7.

Pathauto

Pathauto, discussed in Chapter 7, allows you to format URL paths for each node. This allows you to customize each URL so that a node can be accessed from both `http://example.com/foo-bar` and `http://example.com/node/1`. It is good practice to configure Pathauto so that URLs contain descriptive words that search engines will find useful. One practice I typically use is setting the URL to contain the node title and noting during site training that node titles should contain search-friendly terms. If the node title is not an option, you can always create a required field specifically for the URL.

Path Redirect and Global Redirect

In the previous section, we discussed how search engines may penalize sites with duplicate content. If you are using Pathauto, then a node can be accessed from two locations, `http://example.com/foo-bar` and `http://example.com/node/1`. Depending on your configuration, your front page may also be accessed from multiple locations. The Global Redirect module (`http://drupal.org/project/globalredirect`) allows you to set a single location for all your pages, using permanent (301) redirects to the "source" page.

Global Redirect gives you a number of configuration changes, accessed at **Configuration ➤ Global redirect**. My recommendation is to use the default configuration settings during development and to enable all options during testing.

The Path Redirect module provides you with an interface to create and manage custom redirects, as well as the ability to create redirects when updating a node. This can be useful when you need to create a short URL that redirects to a long URL, such as in media promotions and advertisements. It also helps if you use Pathauto to customize the URL; if the node title is used in the URL and the node title is changed at some point, resulting in a new URL, Path Redirect automatically creates a redirect from the old URL to the new.

Meta tags

Meta tags were first used, and then abused, by web sites to increase search rank. Although they don't have as much influence on search rank as they once had, meta tags provide basic information to search engines, such as keywords and physical location, that may or may not be used by search engines. The Meta tags module (`http://drupal.org/project/metatags`) allows you to enter meta tags on both a sitewide and an individual-node level. A number of configuration options are available, including which meta tags to use and if users and taxonomy terms should have meta tags. Make sure to enable the **Description** meta tag, because this determines the text displayed when your site shows in search results. You should also set the **Location** meta tag if the business has a storefront or physical location. You will need to set the location using latitude and longitude; I use Google Earth for this.

> *Note: In the early days of search engine ranking, it was common practice to abuse meta tags to increase search rank, and search engines now tend to **penalize you if meta tags are abused. My recommendation is to keep meta tags** short and simple and to have a fresh set of eyes review how your site appears in search engine results.*

Page Titles

Page titles are displayed in the title bar of the browser; by default, Drupal displays your site name and slogan on the front page. Search engines use this content for both search rank and when displaying search results, typically as a header that links to your site. The Page Title module (`http://drupal.org/project/page_title`) gives you precise control over what is displayed in the page title for all areas of your site, including the front page, comments, users, content types, and vocabulary. You can also use tokens to insert field values or other variables. The Page Title module is configured by navigating to content and selecting the **PAGE TITLES** tab, as shown in Figure A-4.

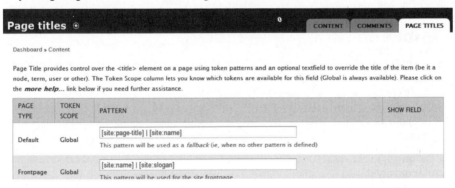

Figure A-4. The Page Title module is configured by navigating to the **Content** section and selecting the **PAGE TITLES** tab.

Menu Attributes

The Menu Attributes module (`http://drupal.org/project/menu_attributes`) allows you to add additional attributes to menu items, such as an ID, name, and class. Important to SEO, it allows you to specify `rel="nofollow"` on certain menu items, telling the search engine not to use the link in determining search rank. For example, you may write a blog post about a specific product, but you don't want to give the site an "endorsement." Some sites may use the `nofollow` attribute to sculpt page rank; see `http://mattcutts.com/blog/pagerank-sculpting` for details.

> Note: Page rank sculpting is not generally used on most sites but should be reserved for content-intensive sites with deep links or when a particular word or phrase is extremely competitive.

XML sitemap

Site maps list all pages available on a web site and are used to make sure all pages are found by a search engine. The XML sitemap module (`http://drupal.org/project/xmlsitemap`) automatically creates and updates a site map, including automatic submission to several major search engines, as shown in Figure A-5. The module has a number of submodules, including those to create custom links, menu links, internalization, user links, and more; navigate to the **Modules** page to see all available submodules.

Navigate to **Configuration ➤ XML sitemap** to set up and configure the module. A large number of configuration options are available, and although most default settings will work, I recommend the Drupal handbook for additional information: `http://drupal.org/handbook/modules/xmlsitemap`.

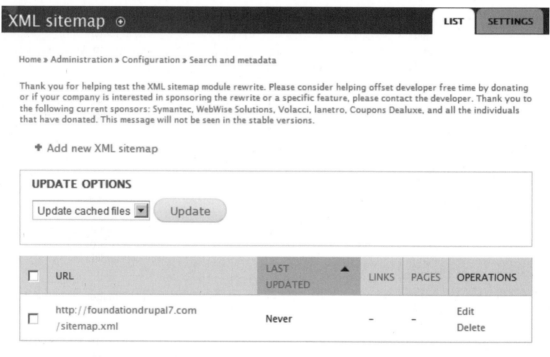

Figure A-5. Navigate to **configuration ➤ XML sitemap** to set up and configure the module.

Boost

Google announced in April 2010 that it uses site download speed as a "new signal in our search ranking algorithms" (`http://googlewebmastercentral.blogspot.com/2010/04/using-site-speed-in-web-search-ranking.html`). The Boost module (`http://drupal.org/project/boost`) significantly decreases the amount of time it takes for your site to load by caching HTML pages and completely removing all database queries. The module works hand in hand with Drupal's JavaScript and CSS caching, providing GZIP compression as well as a number of configuration options to improve download speed. See `http://drupal.org/node/545908` to learn more about installing and configuring Boost.

> *Note: The Boost module works only for anonymous users; you will need to use an alternate caching method for authenticated users, such as memcache (http://drupal.org/project/memcache). Note that as of publication, Google will never be an authenticated user, so memcache will never help search engine results.*

Please note that, as of publication, Boost is not stable for Drupal 7; follow the conversation at `http://drupal.org/node/325813`.

Structure your theme

`<h1>` tags are heavily weighted by search engines, and a best practice is to ensure each page has only one `<h1>` tag that contains key search terms. By default, Drupal uses the node title within the `<h1>` tag and for blocks uses the block title within an `<h2>` tag. You'll need to make changes to the theme if you want, for example, a block header to use an `<h1>` tag.

Placing important and keyword-intense content earlier in the HTML file may influence search engine rankings. Simply stated, you want to output the node's body as early in the template as possible. The Zen theme is ideal for this; it prints out the content region first and uses CSS to position sidebars and primary navigation afterward.

Page Optimization

As mentioned earlier, site speed influences site rank, and as such, a theme should be maximized for download speed. An easy way to optimize download speed is to reduce the number of HTTP `GET` requests. Every time a browser requests an image, it makes two `GET` requests, which dramatically increases download time when 30 or more images are required. The yslow module for Firefox provided by Yahoo! does a great job of helping you optimize your site, as well as providing you with additional optimization techniques not covered in this appendix.

To reduce the number of required images, you can start by limiting the number of images called from the CSS file; when a browser opens a web page, it downloads all CSS images, regardless of whether the image is used on the page. This means if you have 20 images embedded in your CSS file, the browser is going to make 20 separate image requests. A CSS sprite allows you to combine many of these images into a single image, significantly reducing the number of required image files. A program to help create CSS sprites is available at `http://spriteme.org`.

Furthermore, you can embed images using the `src` tag so that an image will be downloaded only when a user visits that specific page. For example, you may have an image that appears in the header of a blog section but not on the homepage. My recommendation is to create a block specifically for the blog section and add your `src` tag directly into the block body. Using this approach, the block will appear only in the blog section, at which point the image will be downloaded.

How to emphasize content in a WYSIWYG editor

Entering SEO-friendly content in a WYSIWYG editor is largely a process of emphasizing specific key words and phrases. Search engines weigh words that are in bold or italics. For this reason, you will want to "salt" your content with key words and phrases that are then emphasized through the editor.

It's also good practice to make sure all links have a title, as shown in Figure A-6. Most editors have the ability to add this, including advanced configuration options to add `rel` tags as well.

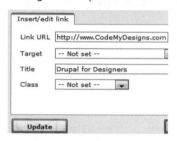

Figure A-6. Adding a title to a link using the TinyMCE editor

Appendix B

Drush, the Command-Line Shell for Drupal

Drush is a command-line shell for Drupal. If you use the command prompt with any frequency or you're just looking to speed up the amount of time it takes to create and build a Drupal site, this is the module for you. Drush allows you to manage sites from the command prompt, including enabling modules, running cron, syncing Drupal sites and databases, and more.

What is Drush?

Drush, which is a portmanteau of the words *Drupal* and *shell*, is a command-line shell with a number of built-in commands designed specifically for managing Drupal and multiple Drupal sites. Drush will save you a significant amount of time if you work with Drupal on any type of regular or semiregular basis. It allows you to download and enable modules, run cron, rsync Drupal site files, sync databases, and more, all using commands structured in the familiar **drush download backup_migrate** style.

Drush commands are run from the command prompt, like Putty or Secure Shell Client. While you can run these commands by simply typing them in, you can also include them in command-line scripts to further customize your development environment. As an example, the Aegir hosting system (`http://groups.drupal.org/hostmaster2`), which is a front-end Drupal system to manage multiple Drupal sites, uses the power of Drush through custom scripting.

Drush can be used with cPanel or most other server administration software, as long as you have the required permissions to install and configure Drush (installation is discussed later in the chapter). I use Drush with cPanel on an almost-daily basis to automate a number of functions, such as creating sites, moving sites through the staging process, updating modules, and more. I hope after reading this chapter you have a love (or at least an appreciation) for Drush and the amount of time it can save if you plan to regularly build Drupal sites.

Expanding Drush functionality through contributed modules

Many modules provide Drush commands; a complete list of modules is available at `http://drupal.org/taxonomy/term/4654`. I have found a number of Drush modules I use on a frequent basis, discussed in the following sections.

Backup and Migrate

The Backup and Migrate module (`http://drupal.org/project/backup_migrate`) allows you to back up the database, the `files` directory, or both through the Drupal admin section. It also supplies several Drush commands that allow you to back up or restore databases through Drush.

Drush Cleanup

Drush Cleanup allows you to quickly and easily delete all text files not needed with Drupal, such as `INSTALL.txt`, `UPGRADE.txt`, and more. To run it, simply navigate to the directory of the Drupal site in question, and enter **drush cleanup**.

See `http://drupal.org/project/drush_cleanup` for details.

Drush EM

If you manage the Drupal web site staging process or a number of Drupal sites, you will eventually encounter the issue of pushing site changes from one site to another. That is, say you have three versions of a single site, all belong to different developers, and a developer makes a change to a view. How do you push the change to this view to all developers without requiring a sync of the databases?

Generally speaking, Drupal is moving in the direction of creating "exportables" to solve this problem, in which data files are used to save database changes (views, content types, field changes, and so on). The eventual result is that you can make changes to one site and "push" changes to another site.

Drush EM (`http://drupal.org/project/drush_em`) helps you in this process. Technically it dumps and updates exportables from modules such as CTools and Views. This allows you to use a versioning system (or rsync) to sync exportables between sites, from which Drush EM can update the database. The process looks like this:

1. Developer A makes changes to a view.

2. Developer A runs the command `drush em-dump`, dumping the exportable into a module.

3. Developer A commits the module to the repository.

4. Developer B updates their local copy.

5. Developer B runs the command `drush em-update`, updating the local database to the current view.

See `http://github.com/xendk/em` for details.

Drush Make

Drush Make is one of the most useful modules you will ever encounter. Drush Make allows you to create a single file that is used to download Drupal core and contributed modules into a single directory. That is, you can create a file that lists all required modules, run the Drush Make command, and the site is automatically built. See Figure B-1 for a sample Drush Make file.

```
1   core = 7.x
2
3   projects[drupal][version] = "7.1"
4   projects[] = ad
5   projects[] = addthis
6   projects[] = admin_menu
7   projects[] = advanced_forum
8   projects[] = advanced_help
9   projects[] = ajax
10  projects[] = author_pane
11  projects[] = autologout
12  projects[] = autosave
13  projects[] = backup_migrate
14  projects[] = blocks404
```

Figure B-1. Sample make file for Drush Make

Drush Make files are saved with a .make extension and have a number of capabilities:

- Download core and contributed modules
- Check out code from the git, SVN, CVS, and bzr repositories
- Create a .tar, .gz, or .zip file of all modules defined in the makefile
- Fetch and apply patches

See the Drush Make project homepage (http://drupal.org/project/drush_make) for syntax, example usage, and more.

How to install Drush on cPanel

Drush is installed on cPanel on an account-by-account basis; that is, each user (for example, /home/fd7) has its own Drush installation and configuration. Installing Drush is a matter of downloading files, configuring .bashrc, and (optionally) creating a symlink.

You have a few options to think through for your first step: should cPanel users have their own version of Drush, or should users link to a single, master version? Depending on the number of developers on a team or how you configure your development environment, you may want all developers to have access to a shared version of Drush. The benefit of this is that you can create an "admin" account that has source versions of all software and scripts, which can help when troubleshooting software-based bugs.

First, download Drush into a directory on your server; you'll need to create a new user if you're using shared software, as explained earlier. I usually create a folder named drush with two folders, drush and drush_mods, located within; if I'm sharing scripts, I include them in the primary drush folder (see Figure B-2).

Figure B-2. The drush folder contains Drush, additional Drush commands (modules), and other shared scripts

Next, you need to configure .bashrc so that Drush is recognized as an executable script (see Figure B-3). **.bashrc** is modified on an account-by-account basis, so make sure to modify the correct user's file. Users will need to log on and log in before updates are enabled.

```
1   # .bashrc
2
3   # User specific aliases and functions
4
5   # Source global definitions
6   if [ -f /etc/bashrc ]; then
7       . /etc/bashrc
8   fi
9
10  PATH=$PATH:/home/cultiv8/drush/drush
11
```

Figure B-3. ~/.bashrc is modified so that Drush is recognized as an executable script.

Finally, you need to enable Drush modules if you are using any. This is simply a matter of downloading all Drush modules to a single directory (see Figure B-4). Depending on how you share software, you may want to symlink to a single version or download all modules into **~/.drush**.

```
⊞─📁  drush
⊟─📁  drush_mods
    ⊞─📁  drush_cleanup
    ⊞─📁  drush_em
    ⊞─📁  drush_make
    ⊞─📁  gittyup
    ─📄  enable-modules      1KB
    ─📄  makesite.sh         3KB
    ─📄  stageburner.make    3KB
```

Figure B-4. To enable Drush modules, add the modules into a drush_mods folder and symlink the folder .drush in the user's home directory.

After enabling Drush, type drush help at the command prompt for a list of available commands.

Popular Drush commands

Table B-1 explains the Drush commands that I use on a frequent basis. Navigate to http://drupal.org/node/477684 to see the full list of Drush commands.

Table B-1. Popular and commonly used Drush commands

Command	Details
cache clear (`cc`)	Clear all Drupal caches or a specific cache.
`cron`	Run all cron hooks.
`disable (dis)`	Disable one or more modules or themes.
`download (dl)`	Download core and contributed modules and themes; this is great when used in parallel with Drush Make.
`enable (en)`	Enable one or more modules or themes; this is great when used in parallel with Drush Make.
`statusmodules (sm)`	Print a list of all available modules and themes.
`status`	Prints status information about the Drupal site, such as Drupal version, site path, database username/password, and so on.
`sql cli (sqlc)`	Open a SQL command-line interface using the site's database user name and password.
`sql dump`	Export the Drupal database using `mysqldump`.
`sql sync`	Copy a source database to a target database using rsync; this is great when used to push staging sites from one location to another.
`uninstall`	Uninstall one or more modules.
`update (up)`	Update contributed modules and apply database updates (that is, run `update.php`); this works with many file versioning systems.
`updatecode (upc)`	Update project code without applying database updates.
`updatedb (updb)`	Run the `update.php` script from the command line; note that you may need to use the batch-process command to make this work (see `http://drupal.org/node/873132`).
`variable delete (vdel)`	Delete a variable.
`variable get (vget)`	List all or some site variables.
`variables set (vset)`	Set a variable.

Command	Details
`watchdog delete (wd-del)`	Delete watchdog messages, also known as status messages.
`watchdog list (wdlist)`	Show all available status messages.
`bam backup`	This requires the backup_migrate module; it backs up the site's database.
`bam restore`	Requires the backup_migrate module; it restores the site's database.
`bam backups`	Print a list of previously created backup files.

Appendix C

50+ Contributed Modules to Spice Up Any Site

Core Drupal is great; it provides the basic framework for creating some pretty cool web applications. However, the true greatness of Drupal comes with its modular framework and the thousands of contributed modules available to spice up and improve your site. When building a site, the common saying is "there's a module for that."

In this appendix, I point out some of the more popular contributed modules, divided into a number of categories such as development tools, site-building tools, field types, site administration tools, theming tools, and more. Although this is not an exhaustive list by any means, these are some of the modules I install on most sites I build.

Development tools

I begin the appendix by discussing several modules that help during the development process. Many of these modules are for advanced users of Drupal who have a solid understanding of PHP.

Chaos tool suite

The Chaos tool suite, more commonly called CTools, is a set of APIs and tools that help when developing modules or creating forms, among other things. The module currently has the following tools:

- Ajax responder, making it easier for modules to handle Ajax requests
- Content, to create content types used in panels and other modules
- Contexts, providing an API to create and accept objects as input
- CSS tools to help sanitize user-inputted CSS

- Dependent, a widget to make form items appear and disappear depending upon other form items, which is much easier than using JavaScript to do the same
- Exportables, allowing modules to have objects that live in database or code, such as module configuration settings or user-entered data
- Form tools to help forms interact with Ajax.
- Form wizard to help make multistep forms
- Modal dialog to place forms in a modal dialog
- Object caching to edit and cache an object across multiple page requests, for example when adding a multipage form
- Plug-ins, so modules can let other modules implement plug-ins from include files

CTools is available at `http://drupal.org/project/ctools`; download the module and read documentation in the help directory. Currently, the module is not completely ported to Drupal 7. Follow the conversation at `http://drupal.org/node/589636` to learn more about porting the module to Drupal 7.

Devel

Devel is a suite of modules that anyone who builds a Drupal site, regardless of experience, will find useful. It contains a number of helper functions for developing, building, and troubleshooting a site. It can print a summary of all database queries for a page, print well-organized `dprint_r($array)` and `ddebug_backtrace()` functions, generate dummy content, display node access entries for a node, switch between users, quickly empty all caches, view and log performance statistics, and more. It provides its own block with menu links but, more conveniently, integrates with the administrative menu (discussed later in the appendix). Devel is available at `http://drupal.org/project/devel`.

Drupal For Firebug

Firebug is a plug-in and web development tool for the Mozilla Firefox browser, available at `http://getfirebug.com`. Drupal For Firebug (`http://drupal.org/project/drupalforfirebug`) displays Drupal debugging and SQL query information in the Firebug window (Devel must be enabled to view SQL query information). Drupal For Firebug also works with the Google Chrome browser.

Features

The Features module, discussed in Chapter 11, allows you to package exportables into a module to be easily moved and implemented on other sites. Examples of features might include a blog, a media gallery, or a collection of views. I have found that Features can help sync changes made to multiple sites, such as if a view or content type is changed by one developer and the changes need to be pushed to other developers' sites. Features is available at `http://drupal.org/project/features`.

Context

The Context module (`http://drupal.org/project/context`) allows you to manage conditions and reactions for different sections (aka contexts) of your site. For each context, you can choose the conditions that trigger the context and how Drupal should react. For example, you may want to create a blog context that displays certain blocks when a user is logged in. I find this module most beneficial to control the layout of blocks and then, through the Features module, sync changes made to the layout of blocks between staging sites.

Spaces

The Spaces module is an API that allows you to create a "space" that overrides the default values of Drupal configuration settings. In the same way that the Context module is ideal for laying out the blocks on a section of your site, Spaces is ideal for creating "sections" of Drupal configuration settings. See http://drupal.org/project/spaces to download the module, and see the readme for details on how to use and implement it.

Strongarm

The Strongarm module (http://drupal.org/project/strongarm) allows you to override the default variable values provided by Drupal core and contributed modules. Although these variables can be changed through the Drupal UI, you may want to programmatically change values. For example, if you create an installation profile, you can use Strongarm to change default variable values when the install profile is run. Strongarm also uses CTools to provide exportables, meaning you can also use Strongarm to sync changes made to Drupal variables between multiple staging sites.

Site-building tools

Site building refers to creating a site through the Drupal UI, which is fundamentally different from developing a module; site building is more a matter of pointing and clicking to configure Drupal, while module development involves writing code to add Drupal functionality. In this section, I cover a number of modules that help make the site-building process flow as smoothly and quickly as possible without requiring the time-consuming task of writing a module.

Automatic Nodetitles

Every node created in Drupal requires a title. In some instances, you may not want the user to enter a title but rather have the title created automatically. Enter Automatic Nodetitles (http://drupal.org/project/auto_nodetitle); this module allows you to automatically generate a node title based on token values. You can set the node title as optional, meaning it will be automatically generated if the field is left blank, or you can hide the node title entirely. Automatic Nodetitles is configured on the content type configuration page for each content type.

Custom Breadcrumbs

The Custom Breadcrumbs module (http://drupal.org/project/custom_breadcrumbs) allows you to fine-tune the display of breadcrumbs for content types in version 7.*x*-1.*x* and views, panels, taxonomy terms, paths, and more, in version 7.*x*-.2.*x*. For example, you can easily style the breadcrumbs on a blog content type to read "Home // All Blogs // User Blog // 2010 // September // Blog Title."

Custom Search

Custom Search (http://drupal.org/project/custom_search) allows you to change both the appearance of the search block and how content is searched. Some of the options I use this module for on almost every site I build include the following:

- Specifying which content type(s) to search, for example if I want to restrict search to one or two content types
- Changing or removing the default search label (appears to the left of the search box)
- Adding default text within the search box (which disappears when the search box becomes active via JavaScript)
- Changing the default submit button image
- Changing the default submit button text

The module also includes several submodules:

- Custom Search Blocks, providing multiple numbers of search blocks, each with different settings
- Custom Search Taxonomy, providing options to search taxonomy terms
- Custom Search Internationalization, providing locale settings

This module provides a number of settings not discussed; visit the project page for a full list of available configuration changes.

Flag

The Flag module (http://drupal.org/project/flag) is a bookmarking system in that it allows you to create an unlimited number of flags to flag content such as nodes, comments, users, or other items. This module is perfect for marking content as important, creating bookmarks, flagging content as inappropriate, and more. It integrates with the views, rules, and actions modules, allowing you to build out complex systems to display flagged content and create rules and actions when content is tagged. There are a number of flag-related modules:

- Flag Weights (http://drupal.org/project/flag_weights), used to add weights to flags to make items orderable (such as when displaying flagged content in a view)
- Flag Terms (http://drupal.org/project/flag_terms), used to flag taxonomy terms

Menu attributes

Menu attributes (http://drupal.org/project/menu_attributes) allows you to specify additional attributes for menu items, such as id, name, class, style, and rel. This module is perfect in a number of situations:

- When theming and you want to apply a CSS style to a specific menu link
- When you want to add a `nofollow` to certain menu items
- When you want to easily select a menu items using jQuery or JavaScript

Menu block

Menu block (`http://drupal.org/project/menu_block`) allows you to create a block containing a menu tree starting at any arbitrary level of any menu. I find there are two circumstances where I most frequently use this module. First, let's say I'm displaying primary menu items horizontally in the site header and using a module like nice_menus or superfish to display secondary menu items as drop-down menu items. However, I don't want tertiary (or deeper) menu items to display in the site header; I want them to display only in a sidebar (or other area) when I'm on a secondary menu page. The Menu block module allows me to configure a menu block that displays only these menu links.

I also use this when it is better to group multiple menus into a single menu. For example, one common trend in web design is to place four or five columns of menu links into the footer of a site. It is easy to create four or five different menus and place each menu into the footer, but this can clutter the menu administration page and make it difficult to add menu links when creating nodes. Alternatively, I create a single menu and then create four or five menu blocks based on this menu, each starting at the secondary level. This results in multiple menu blocks managed through a single menu.

Nice Menus

Nice Menus (`http://drupal.org/project/nice_menus`) provides both horizontal and vertical expandable menus. It uses the Superfish jQuery plug-in for all browsers and falls back to CSS only if JavaScript is disabled on the browser; you can also disable Superfish to provide a CSS-only expandable menu. Navigate to the project page for a full description of this module, including documentation, troubleshooting tips, and more.

Nodequeue

Nodequeue (`http://drupal.org/project/nodequeue`) is similar to the Flag and Flag Weights modules in that it allows site administrators to place nodes in an arbitrarily ordered group. The main difference, aside from a few configuration options, is that Nodequeue automatically creates a "nodequeue" administration page accessed on every node page through a menu tab. I use this module when a site requires one or more blocks to which nodes are promoted. For example, the homepage of a site might have a block that rotates images using the views slideshow module, and the client may want to promote only four images to that block at a time. Using Nodequeue, I can add a "front-page slideshow" nodequeue that allows up to four nodes to be added at a time, to which the client can add, remove, and order nodes. The nodequeue is then added as a filter to the view so that only nodes added to the nodequeue are displayed.

Panels

The Panels module (`http://rupal.org/project/panels`) allows site builders to create customized page layouts using a simple drag-and-drop interface. One of the advantages of Panels is that it allows content placed on the page to be aware of what else is being displayed. For example, a block in the sidebar region can be aware of content displayed in blocks in the footer region, something not possible in existing Drupal core. You can also create mini-panels, which makes it very easy to display content and blocks without needing to create custom regions or write a lot of CSS.

Panels is a powerful module with a vast number of options and configuration settings. Navigate to http://drupal.org/node/496278 for documentation and to learn more.

Rules

The Rules modules (http://drupal.org/project/rules) allows you to create actions that occur based on defined events. For example, you may want to create customized e-mails that are sent to users when a user account is created or create a custom redirection or system message after a user creates an account. Rules is a powerful and flexible module; navigate to http://drupal.org/node/298476 to learn more.

Site map

Not to be confused with XML sitemap, the Site map module (http://drupal.org/project/site_map) provides a one-page overview of your site, including nodes, taxonomy terms, RSS feeds, and more. This is an ideal module if you're looking for an easy, low-maintenance way to give users an overview of your site.

String Overrides

String Overrides (http://drupal.org/project/stringoverrides) provides a quick and easy way to replace any text on the site. It is so simple to use that it is easy to go overboard and use this module in ways that it should not be used. My recommendation is to use this module when another module provides default text and does not provide a way to change default text through the UI. For example, the core Blog module provides a page that displays all blog posts from all users, available at http://example.com/blogs, with the title "Blogs" displayed at the top of the page. Rather than hacking the Blog module (bad practice) or creating a custom theme template (time-consuming) to change the title, simply create a string override that replaces all occurrences of "Blogs" with the new page title. A word of caution: the module evaluates all strings passed through the t() function, which means all other occurrences of the string "Blogs" will be replaced.

> Note: If you only need to make one or two strong overrides, see the "String overrides" section in settings.php. If you need a lot of changes and would prefer to keep all overrides in code (rather than saving them in the database), consider using a full-blown language translation, as discussed in Chapter 6.

Workflow

The Workflow module (http://drupal.org/project/workflow) is a great solution for creating content publishing workflows. It allows you to create and assign workflows and workflow states to node types. For example, you can assign a workflow with the states Draft, Review, Revise, and Publish to a blog node type. Furthermore, actions can be assigned to changes between workflow states so that an e-mail is sent to users when a blog is moved from Draft to Review or a node is published when a blog is moved from Review to Publish. You have fine-tuned control over which user roles have permission to move a node between states; this means you can create two user groups, such as editor and publisher, and give permissions only to publishers to move a node from Review to Publish.

The Workflow module is currently being ported to Drupal 7; navigate to http://drupal.org/node/732578 to track its current status.

Modules that add additional field types

Fields, which are added to content types, user profiles, and comments, are rather simple in their current form; you can add text or file uploads. A number of modules are available that expand upon this functionality, giving you the ability to control how users enter and format field data, including date fields, phone fields, and more.

Content Construction Kit (CCK)

Prior to Drupal 7, the core fields module was part of the CCK module (http://drupal.org/project/cck). Although much of the functionality of CCK was moved to core, there are still a few important modules within the CCK module that are useful. The nodereference module allows you to create a customized field to reference nodes. For example, you can create a field populated with all nodes from the Article content type. The userreference module works in the same way; it allows you to associate a user with a node.

Date

The date module (http://drupal.org/project/date) creates a date field type with an optional JavaScript calendar pop-up used to select dates. There are a number of options to configure how date data is saved and displayed, each on a node type by node type basis. It integrates with the Calendar module (discussed later in the appendix), creating the perfect solution for creating calendars in Drupal. Navigate to http://drupal.org/node/262062 to learn more about this awesome module.

Email

The Email module (http://drupal.org/project/email) provides a field type for collecting and storing e-mail addresses. It includes many features, such as validation of e-mails and encryption of e-mail addresses, and integrates with both views and rules modules. Furthermore, you can change the display settings of the field so that instead of displaying the e-mail address, it displays a contact form to send e-mail to the e-mail address.

Embedded Media Field

Embedded Media Field (http://drupal.org/project/emfield) allows you to embed video, image, and audio files from various third-party providers such as YouTube and Flickr. It also includes an Embedded Media Thumbnail module, allowing you to override the default thumbnail provided by providers with your own.

Field Permissions

The Field Permissions module (http://drupal.org/project/field_permissions) allows you to set permissions to view and edit fields. For example, you may want to create a content type with three fields, and one of these fields should be viewed and edited only by users of the "administrator" role. This module is currently being ported to Drupal 7; see http://drupal.org/node/598924 for details.

Link

The Link module (http://drupal.org/project/link) allows you to add a field type specifically for links, including the URL, title, target attribute, and rel=nofollow attribute.

Name

The Name module (http://drupal.org/project/name) provides several components used to enter a person's name:

- Title, such as Mr., Mrs., Dr., and so on
- Given name, or first name
- Middle name
- Family name, or last name
- Generational suffix, such as II, III, Jr., and so on
- Credentials, such as CPA, and so on

All components are available to Views, meaning you can sort by last name while displaying the full name, making this a good alternative to using regular text fields when entering people's names.

Phone

The Phone module (http://drupal.org/project/phone) provides a field for users to enter phone numbers. The module includes validation of phone numbers for a number of countries, support of international phone numbers, formatting of phone numbers, and more.

> Note: As of publication, the Phone module implements each country as its own field, which means that each field can validate for only one country. This means, for example, a Phone field configured for U.S. validation will not accept Swiss phone numbers, and vice versa.

Site administration tools

In this section, I cover a number of modules to help with site administration and make your (or your clients') job easy!

Administration menu

The Administration menu (`http://drupal.org/project/admin_menu`) improves upon the core Drupal admin menu by rendering all administration menu items through a CSS-based menu. It also contains local tasks, giving you the ability to customize the menu, and integrates with Devel, providing you with fast access to any administrative links and functions available in your Drupal site. This module is a must-have for all Drupal developers and site builders.

Advanced help

The Advanced help module (`http://drupal.org/project/advanced_help`) allows modules to store and display help documentation as `.html` files. Many popular modules include advanced help files, including Views, which can be displayed as a pop-up or inline.

Content Management Filter

The Content Management Filter (`http://drupal.org/project/cmf`) is an alternative to the content display page, giving administrators additional options for searching and filtering content. Furthermore, it gives you the ability to allow users to use the filter content page without needing to give users the "administer nodes" permission.

Feedback

Feedback (`http://drupal.org/project/feedback`) provides a fixed-position form for users to quickly send feedback messages about the currently displayed page to site administrators. The form is submitted via Ajax and collects a number of data points, including date submitted, page submitted from, and message. I typically use this module during user acceptance testing when the client is evaluating the site, giving them a mechanism to submit feedback and "wouldn't it be awesome if" recommendations for site changes. I rarely use this when a site is in production.

LoginToboggan

LoginToboggan (`http://drupal.org/project/logintoboggan`) provides many modifications to the user login and registration system:

- Users can log in with either user name or e-mail address.
- Users can register and log in immediately, rather than logging in through the login link provided during e-mail registration, and redirect to a specific page.
- Users must provide two e-mail fields during registration.
- It displays a customized message after login.
- It displays a JavaScript login block so users don't leave the page if they log in from a block.

Transliteration

The Transliteration module (`http://drupal.org/project/transliteration`) takes Unicode text and translates it to US-ASCII characters for file uploads, URL paths, and other Drupal modules. Generally speaking, this module is a must-have if you allow users to upload files and then do some type of PHP processing on the files, such as resizing images. I have also found this module useful for ensuring user-submitted files can be imported into a versioning system such as Subversion, because the module removes many of the characters not supported by Subversion.

User Protect

User Protect (`http://drupal.org/project/userprotect`) allows you to prohibit either specific users or users of a certain role from editing user fields such as the user name, e-mail address, or password.

Theming tools

These are a few modules that I find indispensible when theming a site.

Content Template (Contemplate)

When working with content types and fields, one of the issues with Drupal is that it does not output fields (that is, everything within the `$content` variable) in a CSS-friendly manner. The solution is the Content Template module (`http://drupal.org/project/contemplate`), which allows you to modify output on a per-content-type basis. It allows you to rearrange fields, remove fields, add HTML such as `<div>` tags, and more. In addition to modifying full-page output, it also allows you to modify RSS feeds, search index results, and search summary (aka teaser) results.

Theme developer

The Theme developer module (`http://drupal.org/project/devel_themer`) gives you the ability to click any part of the page and view which theme functions and templates are used (and can be used) to output the HTML. Navigate to `http://drupal.org/node/209561` for a great tutorial on how this module works.

ThemeKey

ThemeKey (`http://drupal.org/project/themekey`) allows you to define rules for when a theme should be used. For example, you may have a site that requires three different themes—one for the blog content type, one for user pages, and one for everything else.

It's very easy to get carried away with this module, especially for new themers; how do you know when to use a new theme and when to add more changes to your current theme? My general recommendation is to take a few things into consideration:

- Do you need to add two or more regions that will be unused in all other areas of the site?

- If you use the current theme, will it result in a doubling in length of the current CSS file? Are more than 50KB of image files required by CSS?
- Will it require a major reworking of the layout of blocks?

If you answered yes to any of these questions, chances are that your site requires more than two themes and may benefit from ThemeKey.

Zenophile

The Zenophile module (http://drupal.org/project/zenophile) automates the process of creating Zen subthemes, removing all manual tasks required when creating subthemes. It includes two submodules:

- Zenophile Midnight, which adds CSS and graphics for creating a light-on-dark subtheme
- Zenophile Sidebars, which allows you to adjust the width and placement of sidebars without manually changing code

JavaScript, jQuery, and Drupal

JavaScript is used by browsers to provide dynamic web sites and user interfaces; jQuery is a JavaScript library that handles animation, Ajax interactions, event handling, and more. If you want your web site to look like it belongs in the 2010s, then JavaScript and jQuery will be part of it. There are a number of modules that use JavaScript and integrate many popular jQuery libraries into your site, discussed in this section.

Colorbox

Colorbox is a customizable lightbox plug-in for jQuery 1.3 and 1.4, allowing for image pop-ups commonly seen on many sites where the web site is grayed out and the image is emphasized. There are many modules and jQuery plug-ins that achieve this effect; see http://drupal.org/node/266126 for details.

External Links

External Links (http://drupal.org/project/extlink) uses jQuery to find all external links on a page, optionally adding an icon for either external links or mailto: links. Additional configuration options include opening external links in a new window and providing a confirmation message when leaving the site.

jQuery UI

jQuery UI (http://drupal.org/project/jquery_ui) is a wrapper module around the jQuery UI effect library (http://jqueryui.com), which provides advanced animation and effects for web sites. This module does not do anything on its own but rather is required by modules.

jQuery plugins

The jQuery plugins module (`http://drupal.org/project/jquery_plugin`) provides many jQuery plugins that can be called from any module or theme. GPL-licensed bundled plug-ins include the following:

- Cycle (`http://plugins.jquery.com/project/cycle`)
- Date input (`http://plugins.jquery.com/project/dateinput`)
- Expose (`http://plugins.jquery.com/project/expose`)
- Flash embed (`http://plugins.jquery.com/project/flashembed`)
- History (`http://plugins.jquery.com/project/tabs`)
- Metadata (`http://plugins.jquery.com/project/metadata`)
- Mousewheel (`http://plugins.jquery.com/project/scrollable`)
- Overlay (`http://plugins.jquery.com/project/overlay`)
- Range input (`http://plugins.jquery.com/project/rangeinput`)
- Scrollable (`http://plugins.jquery.com/project/scrollable`)
- Tabs (`http://plugins.jquery.com/project/tabs`)
- Tooltip (`http://plugins.jquery.com/project/tooltips`)
- Validate (`http://plugins.jquery.com/project/validate`)
- Validator (`http://plugins.jquery.com/project/html5validator`)

jQuery Update

The jQuery Update module (`http://drupal.org/project/jquery_update`) updates jQuery in Drupal core for any modules that require a newer jQuery version. There is no need to use this module unless it's required.

Superfish

Superfish (`http://drupal.org/project/superfish`) integrates the jQuery Superfish plug-in (`http://plugins.jquery.com/project/Superfish`) with Drupal menus, creating a configurable number of Superfish menu blocks for each site. Although the Nice Menus module achieves the same thing, the benefit of this module is that it is purely Superfish, meaning that it does not have any of the additional functions provided by Nice Menus.

Quick Tabs

The Quick Tabs module (`http://drupal.org/project/quicktabs`) allows you to create blocks of tabbed content using jQuery and Ajax so that content in a block is available without requiring a page refresh. Content can be nodes, blocks, views, or other quick tabs, with the option to determine whether the quick tab should be displayed using Ajax. See `http://drupal.org/node/507894` for the current port to Drupal 7 status.

Mass e-mail

A number of modules for Drupal integrate with third-party e-mail providers, allowing users (anonymous or authenticated) to register for e-mail when registering for your site. That is, users have a Drupal account on your site with the option of creating an account on your e-mail provider as well. Two of the most popular include MailChimp (http://drupal.org/project/mailchimp) and Constant Contact (http://drupal.org/project/contstant_contact). If you or your client is committed to a specific e-mail provider other than these two, my recommendation is to search Drupal.org or Google.com to see whether someone else has developed a module.

Simplenews (http://drupal.org/project/simplenews) is a good solution if you are considering running a mass e-mail server from Drupal. Simplenews is a Drupal-based mass e-mailer with a number of related modules; see the project page for details.

E-commerce for Drupal

Currently, Ubercart (http://drupal.org/project/ubercart) is the most commonly used module that allows e-commerce integration. The module includes a number of payment gateways, including Authorize.net and PayPal. It also includes a number of modules yet-to-be-ported to Drupal 7, including Affiliate (http://drupal.org/project/uc_affiliate2), Discount Coupons (http://drupal.org/project/uc_coupon), Recurring Payments (http://drupal.org/project/recurring), and Wishlist (http://durpal.org/project/uc_wishlist). You will also want to keep your eye on the commerce module (http://drupal.org/project/commerce), because this is more of a "Drupalish" approach to e-commerce.

Social networking

A number of modules are available to create a Facebook or MySpace-like site using Drupal, allowing users to form relationships between one another. Although this is a short overview of some of the most common, a Google or Drupal.org search of the specific functionality you require will help you find the functionality you require.

Drupal for Facebook

The Drupal for Facebook module (http://drupal.org/project/fb) allows you to embed site content and features within Facebook or, alternatively, allow users to log in to your site via Facebook Connect. This is a powerful module with a number of options; see http://drupal.org/node/195035 for a full list of available functionality.

Facebook-style Statuses (Microblog)

Facebook-style Statuses (http://drupal.org/project/facebook_status) allows you to imitate Twitter or Facebook's "wall" feature where each user gets a "status" or microblog where they can share messages with the entire community. Users can post on other users' profiles or make references to other users.

Organic groups

The Organic groups module (`http://drupal.org/project/og`) allows users to create and manage their own groups, with each group having subscribed users and communication among themselves. There are a number of options and configuration settings; see the project page for details. Note that this module will be renamed to Groups (`http://drupal.org/project/groups`) at a future point.

Privatemsg

Privatemsg (`http://drupal.org/project/privatemsg`) allows site users to send private messages to each other, including between multiple users, threaded conversation, and more.

Twitter

The Twitter module provides API integration with Twitter, allowing you to associate one or more Twitter accounts with Drupal users. This means you can give permission to users to post messages to Twitter and, more commonly, use the Views module to display users' Twitter messages. You can also use the 3.x version of the module to allow users to log in using Twitter credentials; see `http://drupal.org/node/649714`. This is a relatively straightforward module to configure; see the project page for details (`http://drupal.org/project/twitter`).

User Relationships

The User Relationships module (`http://drupal.org/project/user_relationships`) allows user to create relationships between each other, such as friends, co-workers, neighbors, and more. There are a number of included modules; see the project page for details.

User Points

The User Points module (`http://drupal.org/project/userpoints`) allows users to gain points for doing things such as posting nodes, commenting, moderating modules, making purchases, and more. See `http://drupal.org/project/userpoints_contrib` for the full list of contributed modules.

Appendix D

Views Recipes

Views is a flexible query builder that can be used to format and display data in powerful ways. If you come from a background of hand-coding MySQL queries, you will absolutely love the point-and-click nature of building queries and the ability to override every step of the process. In this appendix, I show the flexibility of views by stepping through the process of creating a number of views I typically use when creating a site. My recommendation is to use this chapter as a starting point when creating views and then search Drupal.org for follow-up questions. Before reading this chapter, read the section on the Views module in Chapter 7.

Please note that I will frequently add to and update this chapter, which is available for download on the Apress web site (www.apress.com).

Article listing

A content-type listing is a simple list of nodes belonging to a single content type (see Figure D-1). In this example, a content type called Events has been created with a number of fields, including an event title, event description, event type (provided by a core taxonomy module), and event date (provided by the Date module). A second content type called Sponsor has been created with several fields, including the sponsor name, homepage link (provided by the Link module), logo, and sponsor description. In this setup, one or more sponsors are associated with a single event. When creating an event, site admins can select a "node reference" field (provided by the CCK module) to associate an unlimited number of sponsors with an event, assuming sponsor nodes have already been created. The site requires a mini-calendar block view, a full-page calendar view of all job listings, a block listing the next two events, and a full-page view of each event. Full-page views and block views should display event information plus sponsorship information. Note that this view works pretty nicely with the sign-up module, which allows users to sign in for a node; refer to http://drupal.org/node/808310 for updates on a Drupal 7 port.

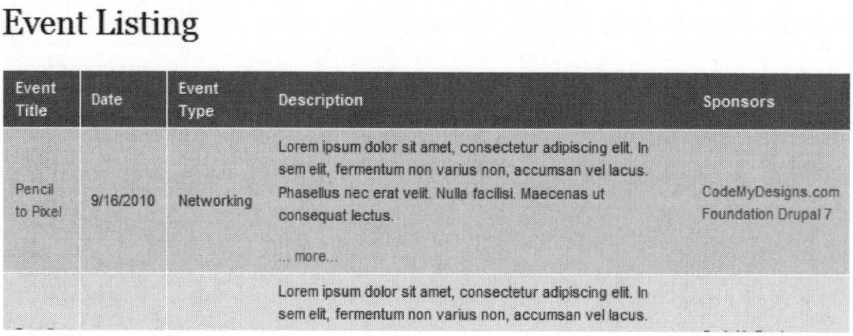

Event Listing

Event Title	Date	Event Type	Description	Sponsors
Pencil to Pixel	9/16/2010	Networking	Lorem ipsum dolor sit amet, consectetur adipiscing elit. In sem elit, fermentum non varius non, accumsan vel lacus. Phasellus nec erat velit. Nulla facilisi. Maecenas ut consequat lectus. ... more...	CodeMyDesigns.com Foundation Drupal 7
			Lorem ipsum dolor sit amet, consectetur adipiscing elit. In sem elit, fermentum non varius non, accumsan vel lacus.	

Figure D-1. A full-page listing of upcoming event posts

I always start with the full-page display and build out from there (see Figure D-2). Starting under **Style settings**, you'll notice I set the style to **Table**; a number of styles are available, including ordered lists, unordered lists, grid view, and more, to style your list page as required. Selecting the gear icon next to the table style allows me to configure the table to sort rows if a user clicks a table header item.

Note: Items with italic text are shared across all subviews, while regular text is specific to a subview.

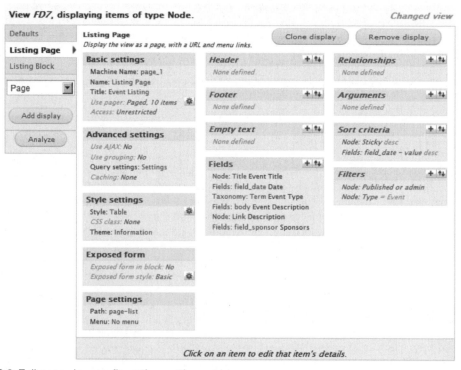

Figure D-2. Full-page view configuration settings

I also set **Use pager** to **Paged, 10 items**, which places a pager at the bottom of the full-page view if there are more than ten items per page. The Use AJAX selector controls how content is queried—through Ajax, meaning the page does not refresh when paging, or via page refresh, which is better suited for search engine optimization (SEO). If entered, the title is displayed at the top of the view.

Next, I filled in **Page settings**, including the **Path** and, optionally, **Menu** links. A quick note about the **Menu** link: I recommend setting this through the view rather than adding a menu item through the menu configuration screen, because I have found this helps with configuring active menu trails.

I did a few interesting things with the fields to get them to display as I wanted. I wanted two of the fields, **Fields: body** and **Node: Link**, to appear in a single column so that **Fields: body** displays only 200 characters with a **more** link displaying immediately afterward. First I configured **Fields: body** to be excluded from the display, and then I rewrote the output of the **Node: Link** field to include the previously excluded field (see Figure D-3).

Label

    Description

The label for this field that will be displayed to end users if the style requires it.

☐ **Exclude from display**

    Check this box to not display this field, but still load it in the view. Use this option to not show a grouping field in each record, or when doing advanced theming.

☑ **Rewrite the output of this field**

    If checked, you can alter the output of this field by specifying a string of text with replacement tokens that can use any existing field output.

Text

    [entity_id_1][view_node]

The text to display for this field. You may include HTML. You may enter data from this view as per the "Replacement patterns" below.

☐ **Output this field as a link**

    If checked, this field will be made into a link. The destination must be given below.

Replacement patterns

The following tokens are available for this field. Note that due to rendering order, you cannot use fields that come after this field; if you need a field not listed here, rearrange your fields.

[title] == Node: Title
[entity_id] == Fields: field_date
[name] == Taxonomy: Term
[entity_id_1] == Fields: body
[view_node] == Node: Link

Figure D-3. Field output can be modified to include previous fields, HTML, and more.

Sort criteria sorts the results by two fields, including **Node: Sticky** and **Fields: field_date - value**. The first field uses the **Promote node to top of list** check box when creating or editing a node, allowing users to promote one or more nodes to the top of the list. You can use a number of fields to sort a view; **field date**

is simply one of them. You can also use **Global: Random** to sort the list randomly (as long as **Caching** under **Advanced Settings** is set to **None**), **Node: Title** to sort by title, or even **Node: Updated date** to sort by the last time the node was updated.

Filters are used to filter nodes from the view. In this example, I wanted only nodes that were **Published** or **admin** (meaning unpublished nodes will display to site administrators) and nodes that were of the type **Node: Type = Event** to appear.

After creating the full-page block view, it's relatively easy to create the block view (see Figure D-4). You'll notice there are a lot of shared field values between the full-page view and homepage block view. Most importantly, you'll notice that I added a "yes" to the **More link** option, enabling a **More** link on the block that links to the full-page list view. I also set **Use pager** to display **2 items**.

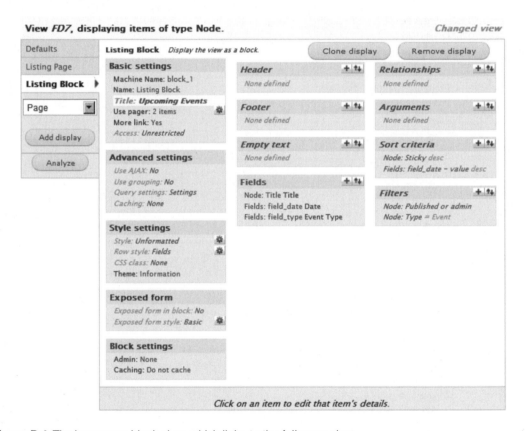

Figure D-4. The homepage block view, which links to the full-page view

Archive

An archive is a block that displays monthly or yearly links to a full-page view containing all nodes within the selected week, month, or year (see Figure D-5). While this view groups by year, it is just as easy to group by month or week.

Figure D-5. A yearly archive block; each year links to a full-page view listing all events during that specific year.

Views includes an archive with a block view, a full-page view, and an argument. I begin first by enabling the **archive** view. After I have configured basic settings, page settings, fields, sorting, and filters, I configure the argument for the date (see Figure D-6). In our case, an argument is a variable in the URL, **year**, which will be appended to the end of the URL (for example, **events/2010**). Following Figure D-6, I have configured the full-page view to do the following:

- Display the year, if available, before the phrase "Events Archive" in the title and breadcrumb
- Display all values if the year is not included in the URL
- Set the granularity to year

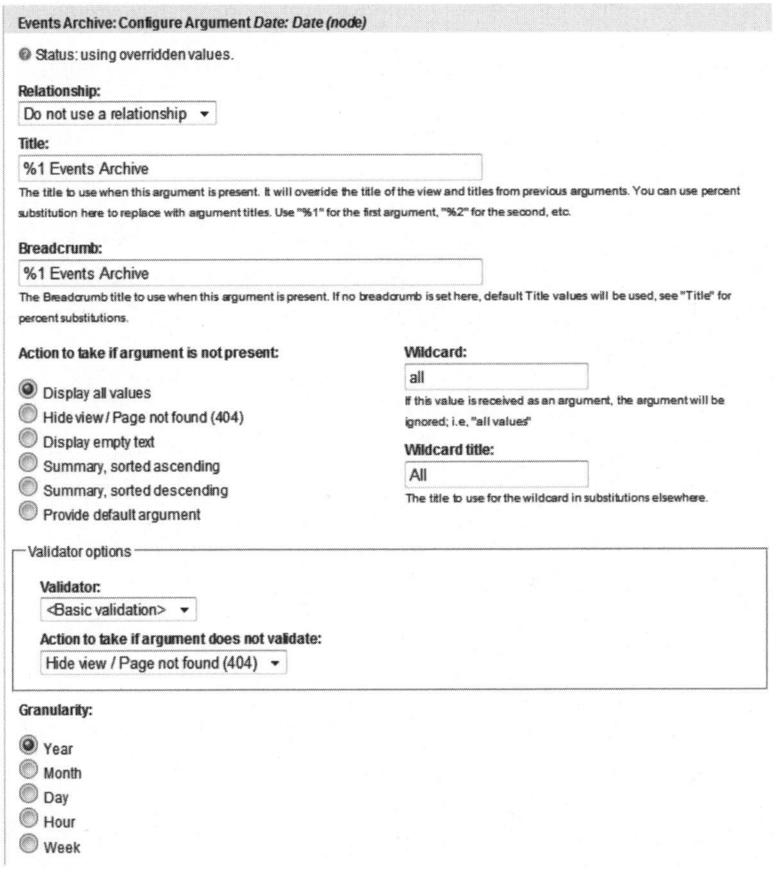

Figure D-6. Adding an argument to a full-page view to filter by year, if year is included in the URL

Next I create the block as discussed earlier in the appendix. However, instead of selecting to display all values as the action to take if an argument is not present, I select a summary, sorted in descending order. This tells Drupal that it should display a summary of results and gives you the option to select whether the summary should be presented as a jump menu, a list, or unformatted (see Figure D-7). After selecting the summary style, a gear icon will appear under the argument, allowing you to configure different options for the summary view, such as displaying the number of nodes in each month/year.

Figure D-7. When a summary is selected, views provides options to format the output.

Calendar

The Calendar module (http://drupal.org/project/calendar) creates a view containing a number of displays to display a full-size and mini-calendar on your site. It is disabled by default, so you will need to go to the list of all views, scroll to the bottom of the page, and click **enable** next to the calendar view. By default, a view is enabled that displays a full-page calendar, available at http://example.com/calendar (see Figure D-8).

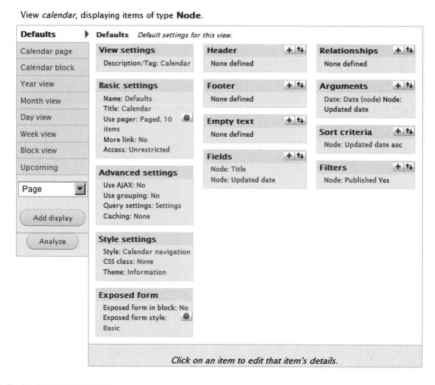

Figure D-8. Default calendar view

You will immediately notice a number of included displays and default settings in the calendar view, including a calendar page, calendar block (with mini-calendar), year view, month view, block view, feed, and more. My recommendation is to first update the default view and then update other views as required. Using the event example from earlier, I updated the fields, argument, sort criteria, and filters. You will also want to change the corresponding fields in both the iCal feed and the Upcoming block, because these two views have overridden fields and filters and do not use the default settings.

Next I'll go in and make a few updates to views as required. The calendar page, which configures how the full-page calendar displays, has a few interesting settings under **Calendar settings**, including the ability to include CSS classes depending on terms, allowing you to theme certain days depending on the taxonomy term assigned to the event node. There is also an option to display a pop-up **Date changer**. The calendar block is a miniature calendar that can be placed in sidebars or other relatively small areas. When displaying events in a year, month, day, or week view, the corresponding views can be used to change the display, such as outputting different fields.

Image slideshow

A number of views plug-ins are available to create image and node slideshows, the most popular of which is Views Slideshow (http://drupal.org/project/views_slideshow). This module allows you to create a jQuery slideshow that fades node fields from one node to the next. Another popular slideshow plug-in is Views Carousel (http://drupal.org/project/viewscarousel), based on the jCarousel jQuery plug-in, which allows you to move node fields either vertically or horizontally.

A related style appears in the style selection box after enabling the views plug-in; select the appropriate plug-in (Views Slideshow or Views Carousel), and select the default settings. Next, select the fields you want output; more than likely, if you want just a slideshow of images, you will select only one field to display (that is, the image). I recommend creating an image preset that automatically resizes the image for all slideshows simply because this makes sure the slideshow will fit and display properly within its area.

The majority of the work in creating a slideshow is theming. Navigate to http://drupal.org/node/755010 for Views Slideshow documentation and http://drupal.org/node/324777 for Views Carousel documentation.

Image gallery

It is easy when working with Drupal to assume there must be an "image gallery" module responsible for displaying images. There is, and it's called the Views module using the **Style: Grid Style settings**. The grid style allows you to output field data (in other words, images, content fields, and so on) in a grid pattern with a configurable number of columns. For example, you can display 50 images in a 5 column by 10 row full-page view. Combine this with an image-resizing preset that scales and crops images to a preset dimension, and you're ready to rock 'n' roll.

First, create an image gallery content type and add all required fields, including an image upload field. Next, add a view and select the grid style; see Figure D-9 for the available options. You'll want to make sure to use a pager and set the items to display to a number greater than 10, depending on how large your grid and image thumbnails are.

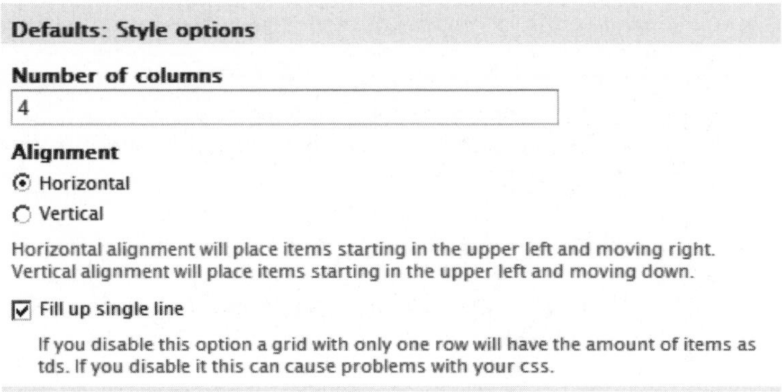

Defaults: Style options

Number of columns

4

Alignment

⦿ Horizontal

◯ Vertical

Horizontal alignment will place items starting in the upper left and moving right.
Vertical alignment will place items starting in the upper left and moving down.

☑ Fill up single line

If you disable this option a grid with only one row will have the amount of items as
tds. If you disable it this can cause problems with your css.

Figure D-9. Available options when configuring the grid style

Promoted block

Frequently on homepages, I like to use views blocks to display node images and/or fields that users have promoted to that specific block. This is simply a matter of configuring and creating a nodequeue (as discussed in Appendix C) and creating a block that filters for nodes in that nodequeue. The benefit of this is that nodequeue adds a tab on the node edit page, which users can select to add or remove the current node. Optionally, it will also add links at the end of the node through the $links template variable.

When creating a view using a nodequeue, you will first need to tell views to associate the node with the nodequeue object. Click the add icon under the relationships category, and select **Nodequeue** (see Figure D-10).

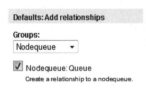

Figure D-10. A nodequeue relationship is first added.

Next, limit the nodequeue relationship to one or more queues; this will be used to filter the results of the block view. See Figure D-11 for an example.

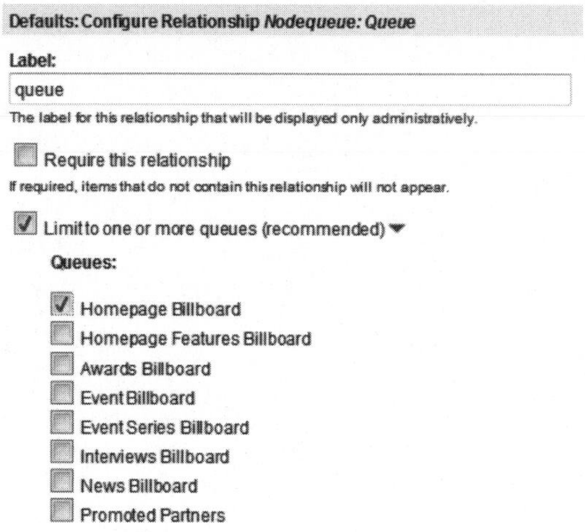

Figure D-11. The nodequeue relationship is limited to one nodequeue.

Finally, add a filter for the specific nodequeue. Click the add icon under the filters category, and select the name of the relationship you just added in the previous step (see Figure D-12).

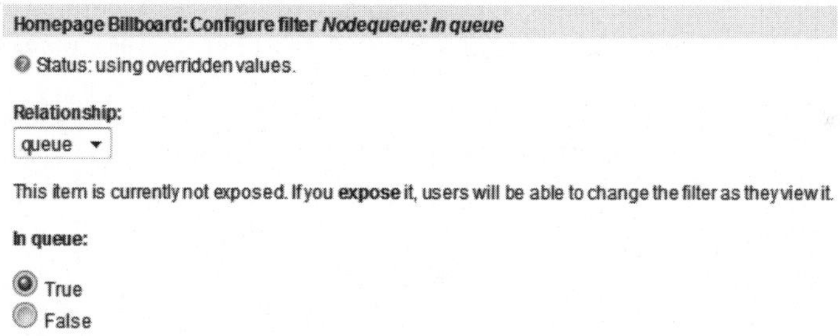

Figure D-12. Add the nodequeue relationship as a filter.

Another option is to use the Flags module, which essentially does the same thing but has a different user interface and a few different options, such as creating a Bookmarks tab with all flagged content.

Index